It

Shocks

The

Conscience

Bobie Kenneth Townsend

Dedicated to my wife, Carolyn

Thanks for not leaving me

I know it takes patience to live with a Bull in a China Shop

CONTENTS

Preface

Ever wonder if you had the ability to be your own lawyer? Do you know what the attorneys go through that makes them qualified, to represent you in a legal matter? They get a high school diploma, just like you. They go to Junior College and take all the classes that will transfer, to a more prestigious College— where they have to get their Bachelor's degree. Then, they have to pass a Law School Admission Test, also known as LSAT, before they can be considered as a candidate for law school. The examinations include five multiple-choice question sections and an unscored writing sample. The LSAT measures candidates' skills in critical areas of future legal work, including reading comprehension, information management, analysis and critical thinking, reasoning, and argumentation. Remember while you go through this book, attorneys are supposed to have obtained "critical thinking". The closed-shop business has the Law School Admission Council control the law-school application process. The goal of all attorneys is to obtain the Juris Doctor degree, to be recognized by the system—to practice law. There is no process available to attorneys, to test to be proficient, in law. They must practice law for the rest of their life, as the rules of procedure are only a guide line—which can be interpreted in a number of ways as the wind blows. The people (Judges & Justices) that bend as the wind blows, are known to their peers as a Master of Law (LLM) and/or a Doctor of Philosophy (PhD)—whether they are or whether they are NOT. The American Bar Association (ABA) is the group of folks that control the system, within that ten (10) square-mile area known as Washington, D.C.. The many State Bar Associations are the minions that do the bidding of the ABA, if these individual State attorneys have a desire to keep their State BAR Card membership, they listen to the Great and Powerful OZ. Me, on the otherhand....

The author is one of the unfortunate ones that had the opportunity to go down the rabbit hole and converse with the Great and Powerful OZ. One such opportunity was in 1989 where a Federal Tax Court Judge in Houston, Texas stated to my wife and I out in the hall of the federal court building: "You see son, I have a right to lie to you because you have the right to appeal." As the judge turned and walked away, my blood drained to my feet and I felt sick. I remember it as well as the day when I heard President Kennedy was shot. It will be burned into my brain until I cannot reason anymore. If this book does NOT **Shock the Conscience**, then you need to try really, really hard to leave Pokémon alone for a spell and pay attention. Experience will always cost you as you journey through the illusion that you think is real, but the cost can be rewarding as well.

As of the publishing of this book, I have initiated an email address for those that would like to see the actual proof alleged in this book. There will be several people that monitor this email address that will have the ability to email you a link to view and download the information referenced in this book. Consider downloading the information first, so that you will have direct access to information referenced in the book as you are reading. The reference material is less than five (5) Gigabytes, but the data may take a while to download.

Simply send an email to { nildebt777@gmail.com }, place in the subject line a reference concerning this book. Examples are: [Send Me the Link to the Shocking Proof]; or [Send Me The Proof]; or [It Shocks The Conscience Proof] or some other reference that the monitor of the email will recognize. The information has been placed in the Cloud for those that hunger for knowledge, but you must ask for its access. Your email address will not be shared with others. But, you may request to be on my info list, if you so desire.

ACKNOWLEDGMENTS

I give thanks to Dr. Norris Austin, my teacher of Constitutions.
Dr. Austin was a gentle man with a strong message, many
thousands of us will share his direction of the pursuit of Happiness.

I give thanks to Mr. Daniel Schinzing by proving to the masses,
"The State of Texas is a Liar."
Many of us miss his research discoveries and friendship.

I give thanks to many hundreds of people that have shared their
support and their research making this book possible.

I especially give thanks to the ex-public servant that has quit their
public job and found rewarding work in the private sector, rather
than feeding at the public trough. Where continued employment
requires quotas, lying, stealing property, incarcerating lives that
never harmed people or property and turning a blind eye to the
actions of other public servants that rape and pillage their fellow
man & woman.

Thank you for quitting.

"These are the times that try men's souls. The summer soldier and the sunshine patriot will, in the crisis, shrink from the service of their country; but he that stands now, deserves the love and thanks of man and woman.

Tyranny, like hell, is not easily conquered; yet we have this consolation with us, that the harder the conflict, the more glorious the triumph. What we obtain too cheap, we esteem too lightly; 'tis dearness only that gives everything it's value. Heaven knows how to put a proper price on it's goods; and it would be strange indeed, if so celestial an article as freedom should not be highly rated."

Thomas Paine

CHAPTER 1
BEING FREE

The hardest thing, about being free, is allowing the other SOB to be free. Most people have been indoctrinated to think, "There ought to be a law," to regulate the activity of their fellow man or woman. Because of that brainwashing in the public fool system, millions of laws are now published and can be found in Law Libraries throughout the world. The systematic creation of all these laws has caused the second hardest thing about being free; that being the struggle to keep your neighbor from trying to regulate every aspect of your life. The result has led to the incarceration of many of our fellow man convicted of an activity that never harmed anyone nor damaged any property. There are many court cases documenting how the freedom to be left alone was slowly converted into a 'directory' to ask for permission to live one's life—or otherwise could, possibly, might, may, or else face certain consequences if you fail to ask, "May I?" from the Great and Powerful OZ. Your grandparents told your parents. Your parents told you. You told your children. Your children told your grandchildren. But, has anyone actually seen the law that supposedly regulates your activity of life? If you will take the time to read some of the opinions of judges commenting on such encroachment, sooner or later you'll run across the phrase, "**It Shocks The Conscience.**"

> *"...conduct that "`**shocked the conscience**' and was so `brutal' and `offensive' that it did not comport with traditional ideas of fair play and decency" would violate substantive due process; So-called `substantive due process' prevents the government from engaging in conduct that `**shocks the conscience**,'. . . or interferes with rights `implicit in the concept of ordered liberty'" (quoting Rochin v. California, supra, at 172, and Palko v. Connecticut, 302 U. S. 319, 325-326 (1937)). County of Sacramento v. Lewis, 523 US 833 - Supreme Court 1998*

*Despite the limited nature of the district court's discretion in granting a new trial because a jury's verdict is against the weight of the evidence, we recognize that considerable deference remains due to that court's determination that a verdict is against the weight of the evidence. The trial judge observes "the witnesses and follow[s] the trial in a way that we cannot replicate by reviewing a cold record." Roebuck, 852 F.2d at 735. Nevertheless, new trials because the verdict is against the weight of the evidence are proper **only** when the record shows that the jury's verdict resulted in a miscarriage of justice **or** where the verdict, on the record, cries out to be overturned or **shocks our conscience**. See Delaware Dep't of Health, 865 F.2d at 1413. Williamson v. Consolidated Rail Corp., 926 F. 2d 1344 - Court of Appeals, 3rd Circuit 1991*

This book will attempt to take the blinder from your eyes, where you can look at the status quo with the right side up, and hopefully give you some tools that can help many of us to challenge—or possibly change—the system for the better. The experience may encourage you to write your own book, about your own adventure in conversing with neighbors that are skilled, in the art of magic. I intend to prove to you that certain activity of public servants canNOT be explained in any other way. Since you are the King or Queen of your domain, why would the King or Queen allow a public servant to make a law, to put the King or Queen in jail—that never physically harmed anyone or anything? When you look and really see what your neighbors are doing, as public servants, **'It Shocks The Conscience.'**

"Occupants of public offices love power and are prone to abuse it."
— *George Washington*, Farewell Address

CHAPTER 2
FEAR

Sadhguru Jaggi Vasudev: When 90% of the steps people take are in search of security, how much effort is left for Joy, Love and Freedom?

Human nature is the urge to control his fellow man. Being in a Gang makes it easier to be on the winning side. Like Joe Cocker said: "Oh, I get by with a little help from my friends." The history of the world has seen many Gangs come and go. Technology has made Gangs less of a threat and has made the power of one a force to be reckoned with. Some wise guy said: "Cut the head off and the body will die." Willie Nelson said, in the movie, "Barbarosa": "O' Sam Colt makes everybody just about the same size." But then, I get ahead of myself.

Many studies have been done showing that if you give someone a little authority over someone else, it leads to behavior that is far from: "Treat your fellow man as you yourself would like to be treated." You need only to Google the "Lucifer Effect," to find out about experiments that have been done, to show what human nature will evolve into when given the ability—or rather the belief—that a particular someone has the authority to control another. Conditioning has a lot to do with the ability/susceptibility to be controlled. Hypnotists have found it easier to condition their fellow man than non-hypnotists have. The Bible shows in Genesis 17, Verse 6: "I will make you exceedingly fruitful; and I will make nations of you, and kings shall come forth from you". So literally, some people believe that the Lord has granted them authority over you. It is more likely that the devil made them do it.

Some will come to realize that it is a form of "brainwashing" that takes effect. But, it really comes down to conditioning. Mandatory attendance of public schools creates a captured audience of future obedient workers. Certain actions will produce a desired reaction when the appropriate stimulus is applied. A little complement here and there may speed things along like sugar attracts the taste buds more than vinegar. I have found that asking the right questions with a smile, instead of a frown, can spread throughout a municipality that you should be treated with caution and respect because the public servants soon experience that you are NOT cost-effective to deal with. They will soon realize that you have the capability and desire to take up vital resources from the system when your rights are in jeopardy.

At this moment, you probably believe that: "You can't fight city hall"; "What comes up must come down"; "You don't spit into the wind"; "You don't pull on Superman's cape"; "If you go faster than that sign, you will get a ticket," etc., etc., etc. If people hear it enough times, people will come to believe it. Fear is the most debilitating emotion that man or woman can have. When you finally come to realize that the wave of fear, that drowns your soul, is being done to you by someone's neighbor; the fear will diminish to a point that it will have no effect on your daily life unless you allow it. With a little soul searching, you will finally come to the understanding that in a hundred years, what was the worry all about? Life is too short to fear the actions of a neighbor, no matter if he/she is wearing a costume. It is Halloween every day to some of these people, but it still is just a costume of a Gang. When you stop feeding the beast, the Gang will reduce in size and have less and less effect on you and your family's daily life. Don't we all just want, "To Be Left Alone, Enjoy the Limited Life We Have, And Pursue Happiness"? The power of knowledge will reduce the fear. Hosea 4, Verse 6: "My people are destroyed for lack of knowledge ..."

A five-year old child will drive you crazy by responding to your instructions and demands with the word "Why?" "The sky is blue." "Why?" "It looks like it might rain." "Why?" "Put your seat belt on." "Why?" "Clean your room." "Why?" But, when you become an adult, it seems that the word "Why?" never crosses your lips. Let's reduce the fear by asking "Why?" instead of automatically acting upon the direction and demands from your neighbors. Pull back the curtain and see who claims to be 'the Great and Powerful OZ'. Their response, or lack thereof, may surprise you.

CHAPTER 3
THERE OUGHT TO BE A LAW

Government is the force of a gang. It has the ability to use force, for protection or for suppression. It is up to each and every one of us, to decide which force will be administered by the gang, and act (or react) accordingly.

Do you think the employees of government have the authority to create a law that would mandate that you and your family get out of your home each morning at 8:00am and do jumping jacks in the middle of your yard? Do you really? What if the Great and Powerful Oz determined that **if** everyone would do the jumping jacks each morning, you and your family would live longer, live healthier, have less medical issues and be more productive citizens and be less burdensome—on the society in which you live? Do you think the thing called government, your neighbors, has that ability (authority) to make people perform for the betterment of society? If you do, then I expect that you also think that people need to have a gun put to their head, and be forced to do many other things, for the betterment of society.

So, there ought to be a law, but don't interrupt my favorite TV program. Human nature is in the DNA. Those with the means will take advantage of the flaw and make money because of it. The system has realized for hundreds, if NOT thousands of years, if it will provide Entertainment to the populace, you will ignore your surroundings and you will ignore what is being done to your fellow man—like the Roman bread & circuses.

Ever been to a Law Library? You really should go. Take a walk through the aisles of book shelves and pull out a book—any book—open it anywhere, and stick your finger on a part of a page; and just read the paragraph your finger landed on. You'll be amazed what you will find. Let me give you an example what you will find.

I walk down the aisle and stop. I reach up to the height of my head, and reach for a book on the fourth shelf. I found the Texas Code of Criminal Procedure. I open the book and it falls open to page 219. I place my finger in the book and it lands on Art. 17A.01. What law have I found?

Texas Code of Criminal Procedure
CHAPTER 17A. CORPORATIONS AND ASSOCIATIONS
*Art. 17A.01. APPLICATION AND DEFINITIONS. (a) This chapter sets out **some** of the procedural rules applicable to the criminal responsibility of corporations and associations. Where not in conflict with this chapter, the other chapters of this code apply to corporations and associations.*
*(b) **In this code, unless the context requires a different definition**:*
*(1) "**Agent**" means a director, officer, employee, or other person authorized to act in behalf of a corporation or association.*
*(2) "**Association**" means a government or governmental subdivision or agency, trust, partnership, or two or more persons having a joint or common economic interest.*
*(3) "**High managerial agent**" means:*
(A) an officer of a corporation or association;
(B) a partner in a partnership; or
(C) an agent of a corporation or association who has duties of such responsibility that his conduct may reasonably be assumed to represent the policy of the corporation or association.
*(4) "**Person**," "he," and "him" **include** corporation and association.*
Added by Acts 1973, 63rd Leg., p. 979, ch. 399, Sec. 2(D), eff. Jan. 1, 1974.

Texas Code of Criminal Procedure
*Art. 17A.02. ALLEGATION OF NAME. (a) In alleging the name of a defendant corporation, it is sufficient to state in the complaint, indictment, or information **the corporate name**, or to state **any** name or designation by which the corporation is known or may be identified. It is **NOT necessary** to allege that the defendant was lawfully incorporated.*
(b) In alleging the name of a defendant association it is

CODE OF CRIMINAL PROCEDURE
*sufficient to state in the complaint, indictment, or information the association's name, or to state any name or designation by which the association is known or may be identified, or to state the name or names of one or more members of the association, referring to the unnamed members as "others." It is **NOT necessary** to allege the legal form of the association.*
Added by Acts 1973, 63rd Leg., p. 979, ch. 399, Sec. 2(D), eff. Jan. 1, 1974.

First, I read above that the chapter is entitled, "Chapter 17A Corporations and Associations". The Chapter must be for entities charged with a criminal offense. But, something does NOT seem right. Under 17A.01(b)(1) it states: "**In this code, unless the context requires a different definition:**". Do you see it? The Texas Legislature specifically states that the following definitions are the same, **throughout** the entire Code of Criminal Procedure, **unless** the term is defined somewhere else in the code. Do you see they defined what the term "Association" is, but **failed** to define the term "Corporation"? But, everybody knows what a corporation is, right? Maybe, you really don't know. Didn't you learn in the government school that you are a "person"? When someone says, "he" did that or it was "him" that did the act, are they talking about you or **something else**, in law? But what If you're NOT really a "person," when it comes to legal matters? Now go back and look, at Art. 17A.01(b)(1), and see that it states: "**In this code,...**", and now look at Art. 17A.01(b)(4). Are you really the "he," "him" or "person" that is referenced in the Texas Code of Criminal Procedure?

Let's open the Texas Code of Criminal Procedure book, up to page 1. There you find Art. 1.03 entitled "**Objects Of This Code.**"

Texas Code of Criminal Procedure
*Art. 1.03. OBJECTS OF THIS CODE. This Code **is intended** to embrace rules applicable to the prevention and prosecution of offenses against the laws of this State, and to make the rules of procedure in respect to the prevention and punishment of offenses intelligible to the officers who are to act under them, **and to all persons** whose rights are to be affected by them. It seeks:*
1. To adopt measures for preventing the commission of crime;
2. To exclude the offender from all hope of escape;
3. To insure a trial with as little delay as is consistent with the ends of justice;
*4. To bring to the investigation of each offense on the trial **all the evidence tending to produce conviction or acquittal**;*
*5. **To insure a fair and impartial trial**; and*
6. The certain execution of the sentence of the law when declared.
Acts 1965, 59th Leg., vol. 2, p. 317, ch. 722.

When you think, 'there ought to be a law,' keep in mind that what is charged by the public servant, and what is the actual intent of the Texas Legislature, maybe entirely different—when the revenue agents drags you in front of a judge. When the judge asks if you understand the charges against you, can you **really understand** what the judge is asking if the judge sees you as something that you are not? Are we NOT all Legally blind if we are denied full disclosure of facts of the matter? Being wrong, when you think you are right, is worse than being wrong, if you do NOT know or understand, what is being said. This is NOT patriot mythology. I am showing you facts that you can verify for yourself. But why should you **really understand**, if you are NOT provided with full disclosure?

Look at your watch. Your favorite TV program is just about to start, and I am about to get into stuff that will alter your brain chemistry. What you thought before, about things in your world, will be altered. Don't be scared. Everything will be all right. You will get through this, OK. I know, because I did, and I actually went through it. Take a break. Before you close this book each time, don't forget to mark the page. You wouldn't want to waste your time and accidentally reading something over again, as it may cause déjà vu. (In 'The Matrix' movie, that dangerously meant the artificial system, in control, had changed something.)

The world is NOT designed to be fair.
Fairness is NOT an objective quality of reality. It's purely subjective.
As soon as you allow yourself to believe in something call 'fairness', you cannot get to a solution, because you will be in this mental frame that is purely imaginary.
Scott Adams – Creator of Dilbert comic strip

"..it does not require a majority to prevail, but rather an irate, tireless minority keen to set brush fires in people's minds."
- Samuel Adams

"There are a thousand hacking at the branches of evil to one who is striking at the root."
Henry David Thoreau

"Most people prefer to believe their leaders are just and fair even in the face of evidence to the contrary, because once a citizen acknowledges that the government under which they live is lying and corrupt, the citizen has to choose what he or she will do about it. To take action in the face of a corrupt government entails risks of harm to life and loved ones. To choose to do nothing is to surrender one's self-image of standing for principles. Most people do not have the courage to face that choice. Hence, most propaganda is not designed to fool the critical thinker but only to give moral cowards an excuse not to think at all."
Michael Rivero

CHAPTER 4
DRIVER LICENSE

Will you admit that a majority of traffic accidents involve people that had or have a Driver License (DL), at the time of the accident? Wouldn't you think that the requirement, of having a Driver License, should have prevented the people, with the DL, of having the accident? But, it didn't. People that have a DL still have accidents on the roadway. So what is the purpose of a DL, if it does NOT prevent accidents on the roadway? It is just another means of control by the system, and a DL is simply used as a get out of jail free card. That is, as long as you pay up, when you are picked for the tax. That's right; the traffic citation is just another form of tax. It can't be a debt. There are no more debtor prisons, right? Don't be found in an automobile, by the road pirates, and you will never be picked for that tax. Today, when a police officer asks to see your DL, have you ever asked yourself, "What is the real purpose of the DL, and why does the police officer need to see it—with the availability of technology today?" The police officer probably does NOT even need to see it, if there is a license plate on your conveyance—as long as there is a VIN number, within view of the public. Let me be the first to tell you that your life is an open book. If you have elected to create a "Facebook" profile, (which I haven't) then your life has been well-read, by the world. What is placed on the Web stays on the Web, forever. Even if you think your information has been deleted, the information is always there, for the whole world to see—if you only know where to look.

Let's run a scenario. The police officer runs the license plate or VIN number found on your conveyance. With that information, the police office knows who the owner claims to be, whether the owner has insurance, the names of the people on the insurance policy, the Driver License Number(s) of the people on the insurance policy, whether if any of the people on the insurance policy has a warrant out for either of them, or whether the warrant was issued by another state that is a member of the Multistate Tax Compact—which was passed in June 13, 1967 (See the Texas Tax Code Chapter 141). The officer sees the pictures of the people on the insurance policy, whether if the conveyance has had a recent inspection, whether it passed inspection, whether the current registration is valid, your medical history, your social security number and among other things—that data mining by government have acquired about you and yours—in the last two minutes. Other than if the conveyance has been stolen, I ask you, for what purpose does the police officer ask for your Driver License? It is just another means of control and another opportunity, for the police officer, to gather additional evidence against you—during the road side interrogation; I'm sorry, I meant 'interview.' Most of the time, the police officer is calling his wife or girl friend—about what they are going to do later that day or that night; instead of contacting the dispatch about the traffic stop. Think about it. Who's being paid during the traffic stop? Does the police office have any incentive to hurry up? You must understand that the police officer is being paid while you sit there, with your hands on the wheel, and it is very likely that you are NOT being paid, to be a captured audience. You never know whether the police officer's wife asked for a divorce that morning, or that the police officer's girl friend told him to move out. You never know. I have found it is always better to say as little as possible and be on your way. (Side Note: Google, "Don't Talk To The Police" to hear an attorney's suggestion.) I always take mental notes of what had occurred at the traffic stop, then make an affidavit within a week of the event and put it away. It may be one of the most important documents I create. We currently live in a police state, but it is up to us to change the state we find ourselves in. It is NOT your representative's fault and it is NOT your senator's fault the way things are, if you fail to instruct them to do what you want them to do. You knew they were a damned old snake when you elected them. What did you expect to happen if you let them play with each other, unsupervised?

Rabbit Trail: You now have two options, of doing the verification of your affidavit. Most people find it more reassuring, to have a Notary witness the signing of their affidavit. A Notary has been determined by the court system to be a credible witness, so the document is usually NOT questioned, except by people like me. I don't trust notaries that work for companies, where the notaries verify documents for other employees, in the same company. I have had notaries decide NOT to renew their Notary stamp, just in hopes that I would NOT sue them, for past actions on their part. But that is another story that I may get to later.

The other form of affidavit recognized by the courts as being valid comes from the Texas Civil Practices and Remedies Code Section 132.001.

Texas Civil Practices and Remedies Code
CHAPTER 132. UNSWORN DECLARATIONS
Sec. 132.001. UNSWORN DECLARATION. (a) Except as provided by [s]ubsection (b), an unsworn declaration may be used in lieu of a written sworn declaration, verification, certification, oath, or affidavit required by statute or required by a rule, order, or requirement adopted as provided by law.
(b) This section does not apply to a lien required to be filed with a county clerk, an instrument concerning real or personal property required to be filed with a county clerk, or an oath of office or an oath required to be taken before a specified official other than a notary public.
*(c) An unsworn declaration made under this section **must be**:*
(1) in writing; and
(2) subscribed by the person making the declaration as true under penalty of perjury.
*(d) Except as provided by Subsections (e) and (f), an unsworn declaration made under this section **must include** a jurat in substantially the following form:*

"My name is _____ _____ _____, my (First)
(Middle) (Last) date of birth is _____, and my address
is _____, _____, _____, _____,
(Street) (City) (State) (Zip Code) and _____. I declare
under penalty of (Country) perjury that the foregoing is true and
correct.
Executed in _____ County, State of _____, on the _____
day of _____, _____. (Month) (Year)

_____
Declarant"
(e) An unsworn declaration made under this section by **an inmate**
must include a jurat in substantially the following form:
"My name is _____ _____ _____, my (First)
(Middle) (Last) date of birth is _____, and my
inmate
identifying number, if any, is _____.
I am presently incarcerated in _____
(Corrections unit name) in _____, _____, _____,
_____. I (City) (County) (State) (Zip Code) declare under
penalty of perjury that the foregoing is true and correct.
Executed on the _____ day of _____, _____. (Month) (Year)

_____
Declarant"
(f) An unsworn declaration made under this section by an employee
of a state agency or a political subdivision in the performance of the
employee's job duties, must include a jurat in
substantially the following form:
"My name is _____ _____ _____, my (First)
(Middle) (Last) and I am an employee of the following governmental
agency: _____. I am executing this declaration as
part of my assigned duties and responsibilities. I declare under
penalty of perjury that the foregoing is true and correct.
Executed in _____ County, State of _____, on the
_____ day of _____, _____. (Month) (Year)

_____
Declarant"

Added by Acts 1987, 70th Leg., ch. 1049, Sec. 60, eff. Sept. 1, 1987.
Amended by:
Acts 2009, 81st Leg., R.S., Ch. 87 (S.B. 1969), Sec. 25.011, eff.

CIVIL PRACTICE AND REMEDIES CODE

Statute text rendered on: 4/4/2014 - 498 -

September 1, 2009.
Acts 2011, 82nd Leg., R.S., Ch. 847 (H.B. 3674), Sec. 1, eff. September 1, 2011.
Acts 2013, 83rd Leg., R.S., Ch. 515 (S.B. 251), Sec. 1, eff. September 1, 2013.
Acts 2013, 83rd Leg., R.S., Ch. 946 (H.B. 1728), Sec. 1, eff. June 14, 2013.
(Jumping off that rabbit trail.)

Remember, the officer may be having a bad day. I say as little as possible, at the traffic stop. I am always courteous, and when I respond to the nice road pirate, I say, "Yes Sir or No Sir." The only things I try to say, to a highway bandit at a traffic stop, is:
A) **"Do you know that I have a right to assemble?"** If the officer says "Yes", just say "Thanks." Any other reply, by the officer, does NOT deserve a response.
B) If the officer asks: "Do you know why I stopped you?" My response: "I was enjoying music while traveling down the road, I expect that you will tell me what the problem is."
C) If the officer asks if he can search the conveyance: "Respectfully Sir, I do NOT consent to any type of invasion of my person or my private property."
D) If the officer is persistent and tells me to get out of the vehicle: I get out and lock the door behind me, and put the keys in my pocket. If the officer gets physical with me, I do NOT resist; and I say "Officer, I know you have the ability to do what you are attempting to do, but I also know you do NOT have the authority to do it."

E) Before signing the citation, I ask: "Officer, what were the circumstances existing that lead you to believe that I was NOT being reasonable and prudent, on the road?"

F) I autograph the citation, and hopefully go on my merry way.

A little further in the book you will learn more about Sec. 545.351(a) in the Texas Transportation Code, referencing, "circumstances existing." On the stand in court, the police officer will get another opportunity, to explain the "circumstances existing" at the time of the traffic stop; and if I am lucky, I will hear a different response, on the video of the stop, than I heard the road pirate say, on the stand.

"The guaranty of trial by jury contained in the Constitution was intended for a state of war, as well as a state of peace, and is equally binding upon rulers and people at all times and under all circumstances."
Ex parte Milligan, 71 U.S. 2, U.S. Supreme Court (1866)

Certainly one of the highest duties of the citizen is a scrupulous obedience to the laws of the nation. But it is not the highest duty.
Thomas Jefferson (1743-1826)
Third president of the United States.

CHAPTER 5
EXAMPLE OF OUR ABILITY TO CHANGE THE CURRENT SYSTEM OF EXTORTION

Ever get a traffic citation? Well, if you have, it is possible that you have been privileged to see the traffic court work its magic. Let's say you got a citation, for allegedly going 75, in a 65 mile per hour zone, and you know you were going the proper speed [A]llowed (*sic*) by law—and you want your day in court. The nice police officer hands you the citation and asks you to sign the document—pointing out that by signing the citation you have promised to appear, on or before a certain date, at the local Justice of the Peace Court, or a city municipal court. The address of the court is circled, on the back of the citation, showing the location of the court. The police officer tells you to have a nice day, as he waddles back to his police cruiser to look for more prey. You show up on the day you promised to appear, at the location circled on the back of the citation, and you notice as you enter the court room that there is standing room only. The court room is packed. You're thinking to yourself that if the Fire Marshal could see this place he would shut it down, for violation of the maximum occupancy limit of the room. You are instructed by the Bailiff or the Judge to answer when your name is called by standing and stating your attorney's name or state that you have no attorney. You notice, as the docket is being called, there are a few names called, where you do NOT hear anyone say anything. These are the poor SOBs that forgot, or their car broke down, or the traffic was so bad they failed to show up on time, or pick some other one of a thousand other excuses that they could claim—that they were unavailable to say "present," on that particular day at the appropriate time. What the rules say, and what the employees of the courts do, usually have nothing to do with each other.

*Art. 22.13. CAUSES WHICH WILL EXONERATE. (a) The following causes, and no other, **will exonerate the defendant and his sureties**, if any, from liability upon the forfeiture taken:*
*3. The sickness of the principal or **some uncontrollable circumstance which prevented his appearance at court, and it must, in every such case, be shown that his <u>failure to appear arose from no fault on his part</u>**. The causes mentioned in this subdivision shall NOT be deemed sufficient to exonerate the principal and his sureties, if any, **unless such principal appear <u>before final judgment on the bond</u> to answer the accusation against him, or show sufficient cause for NOT so appearing.***

Many courts, if NOT all, run on a thing called "custom and policy;" and it is NOT an actual procedure mandated by the Constitution, or even in the written Rules of Procedure. I am very familiar with Texas rules of court and the Texas Constitution, but most other jurisdictions have similar mandates that the courts never follow there, as well.

In Texas, the Code of Criminal Procedure specifically mandates that you have a right to receive a copy of the complaint, twenty-four hours before any proceeding (TCCrP Art. 45.018). The tricky question is: What is a proceeding? Well, it really isn't a trick question at all. A court proceeding is when you are scheduled (mandated) to appear in a court room, where if you didn't show up, a warrant could be issued by the court for your failure to appear. It's pretty straight-forward. A police office has you sign a citation promising to appear, at a certain place on a certain day at a certain time. Next time just ask the police officer, "What if, for some reason that is completely out of my control, I fail to show up at court, what will likely happen?" I guarantee that the police office will inform you that a warrant will be issued for your arrest; and the next time you are pulled over for a traffic stop, your conveyance will be towed—and you will be taken directly to jail, for failing to appear where you promised to do so. If you have talked with friends, or other people, who went through this dog and pony show, before; they will tell you the scenario, for failing to appear at the court proceeding.

Rabbit Trail: Have you ever thought about the term "appear"? Isn't this something a magician does on stage? The magician goes in one box and disappears and the magician "appears" in another location. Could it be that the court does NOT recognize you to have appeared, until you cross the magical area where the judge is located? I have heard many attorneys designate this area, by, "crossing the bar." "Crossing the bar"—is this a magical place, where you can "appear" just like a magician? It appears so.
(Jumping off that rabbit trail.)

So I gather, you understand what a proceeding is, and if you do and read TCCrP Art. 45.018, you would expect to be able to receive a copy of the complaint—the day before you are required to show up for court. Well, don't count on getting a copy. Just because the rules mandate the court personnel give you a copy of the complaint, if requested; does NOT mean that the employees of the court will abide by their required administrative duty—and provide you with a copy of the complaint, for your review, at the time you have the right to view it.

I myself experienced a City of Houston, Texas municipal court judge call down to the court clerk's office and demand that the court clerk generate a copy of the complaint, on the day of the court arraignment proceeding; whereby the court clerk informed the judge that the complaint was NOT generated, until after the accused enters a plea. As I pointed out before, the system runs on "custom and policy," and NOT by the rule of law mandated, by the Texas Legislature or the Texas Supreme Court or the Texas Court of Criminal Appeals. When the municipal court judge informed me of their custom and policy, I said "I thought you were a judge?" The judge said "I thought I was, too." The case was dismissed the following hearing, but that is another story. So, if you are expecting the court system to follow any of the rules, you are likely going to be sadly disappointed.

I am finally getting to the subject of this chapter title "Example of Our Ability To Change The Current System of Extortion." As stated before, in the court room you see that there is standing room only. What if everyone required, to "appear" in the court room that day, told the judge, clerk, prosecutor, that, "I plead NOT Guilty and I want a Trial By Jury"? What would this court do? There are over Three-Hundred people that just asked for a Trial By Jury that same day. Now there are only Three-Hundred and Sixty-Five days in a year, but there are holidays and weekends that must be removed from the trial schedule. What if everyone that went before the court for that entire month said, "I plead NOT Guilty and I want a Trial By Jury"? What would this court do? If the court only scheduled one day a week to hear people's plea to the charges, that could equal up to Twelve-Hundred (1,200) Trials By Juries that need to be scheduled in one month. What if everyone that "appeared" at that court room stated that, "I plead NOT Guilty and I want a Trial By Jury," for the entire year? What would this court do? That could equal up to Sixty-Two Thousand Four-Hundred (62,400) Trials By Juries that need to be scheduled. As stated before, there are only Three-Hundred and Sixty-Five (365) days in a year, but there are holidays and weekends that must be removed from the trial schedule. We all could stop this extortion within thirty (30) days. Think about having some organizations putting ads in the newspapers, web sites, interviews on news organizations, getting the word out in the community. "Everyone Plead NOT Guilty and demand a Trial By Jury. Let's Stop the Extortion Together." It wouldn't help, even if the system found a way to run multiple trials, twenty-four (24) hours a day. If all courts had the same problem, the system would crash in a short period of time.

In Texas, there is another problem the court system has to deal with. Article 5, Section 12 and Article 5, Section 17 of the Texas Constitution mandate a procedure that all Texas Criminal Courts are bound by law to go by.

Texas Constitution, Article 5
*Sec. 12. JUDGES TO BE CONSERVATORS OF THE PEACE; INDICTMENTS AND INFORMATION. (a) **All judges** of courts of this State, by virtue of their office, are conservators of the peace throughout the State.*
*(b) **An indictment** is a written instrument presented to a court by a grand jury charging a person with the commission of an offense. **An information** is a written instrument presented to a court by an attorney for the State charging a person with the commission of an offense. The practice and procedures relating to the use of indictments and informations, including their contents, amendment, sufficiency, and requisites, are as provided by law. **The presentment of an indictment or information to a court invests the court with jurisdiction of the cause**.*
(Amended Aug. 11, 1891, and Nov. 5, 1985.)

Texas Constitution, Article 5
*Sec. 17. TERMS OF COUNTY COURT; PROSECUTIONS; JURIES. The County Court shall hold terms as provided by law. Prosecutions may be commenced in said court **by information** filed **by the county attorney**, or by affidavit, as may be provided by law. **Grand juries empaneled in the District Courts shall inquire into misdemeanors, and all indictments therefor returned into the District Courts shall forthwith be certified to the County Courts or other inferior courts, having jurisdiction to try them for trial**; and if such indictment be quashed in the County, or other inferior court, the person charged, shall NOT be discharged if there is probable cause of guilt, but may be held by such court or magistrate to answer an information or affidavit. A jury in the County Court shall consist of six persons; but no jury shall be empaneled to try a civil case unless demanded by one of the parties, who shall pay such jury fee therefor, in advance, as may be prescribed by law, unless the party makes affidavit that*

the party is unable to pay the jury fee.
(Amended Nov. 5, 1985, and Nov. 6, 2001.) (TEMPORARY
TRANSITION PROVISION for Sec. 17: See Appendix, Note 3.)

THE TEXAS CONSTITUTION
APPENDIX. ***Notes*** *on Temporary Provisions for Adopted*
Amendments
3. *H.J.R. No. 75, Section 9.01, 77th Legislature, Regular Session,*
2001.
Temporary Transition Provision. (a) This section applies to the
amendments to this constitution proposed by H.J.R. No. 75, 77th
Legislature, Regular Session, 2001.
(b) The reenactment of any provision of this constitution for
purposes of amendment does NOT revive a provision that may have
been impliedly repealed by the adoption of a later amendment.
(c) The amendment of any provision of this constitution does NOT
affect vested rights.

The system was NOT was created to come against Texians,
except where injury to people or property had occurred. This is
why the people made it mandatory, that the County and District
Attorneys are required to take a criminal complaint to a Grand
Jury. If there is an indictment, the indictment is returned to a
District Court Judge. The District Court Judge then transfers the
indictment to some inferior court, Justice of the Peace, Municipal
Court, or some County Court. Your case should NOT be placed
with a court that has a conflict of interest. Like the cop and judge
is paid by the same entity. Article 5, Section 17 of the Texas
Constitution shows that an indictment can be quashed, but in that
case, the County or District Attorney can create an information, or
just rely upon the affidavit supporting the complaint, to charge
the accused with a crime; but the relevant issue is, the Grand Jury
has the first say, on charging the accused for a traffic citation—
and NOT any city attorney or assistant district attorney relying
upon a fraudulent complaint, to charge an accused with a crime.
Read it for yourself, above. Article 5, Section 12 of the Texas
Constitution requires an indictment from a Grand Jury, or an

information created by a County or District Attorney, if the indictment is quashed. There is no provision, in the Texas Constitution, that allows the Texas Legislature to create a statute, to amend this Texas Constitution mandate. This is apparent, by the Temporary Provision shown under Article 5, Section 17 found under the Appendix of Note 3, subsection (c), showing that the vested rights of people are NOT affected—by any change, found under Article 5, Section 17 of the Texas Constitution. Don't take my word for it. Read it for yourself.

Many times I have pointed out to the judges, sitting on the bench, that they lack subject matter jurisdiction—since there is no information found in the file. Most, if NOT all, judges claim to have never heard of such a thing. As indicated above, the courts run on a system of "custom and policy," instead of Texas Law and Procedure. Most of the attorneys snap to the facts presented, and find some other excuse to dismiss the case. "The State is NOT Ready." "The Police Officer Failed to Appear." "The Location of the Stop Was NOT Correct." "There Were No Records Found That the Speed indicating Device Had Been Calibrated." "The Video of the Traffic Stop Lacks Audio." "The Video System of the Traffic Stop Was Malfunctioning That Hour", "The Dog Ate My Homework"; or like in one of my recent case, "Dismissed in the interest of justice".

Rabbit Trail: One of the things, for which attorneys get the matter dismissed, is what they call, "the complaint is absent of the "Exception Clause." Most speeding tickets are based upon Section 545.351 of the Texas Transportation Code. A few sections down from that one, you will find Section 545.365.

*Sec. 545.365. SPEED LIMIT EXCEPTION FOR EMERGENCIES; MUNICIPAL REGULATION. (a) The regulation of the speed of a vehicle under this subchapter **does not apply** to:*
(1) an authorized emergency vehicle responding to a call;
(2) a police patrol; or

(3) a physician or ambulance responding to an emergency call.
(b) A municipality by ordinance may regulate the speed of:
(1) an ambulance;
(2) an emergency medical services vehicle; or
(3) an authorized vehicle operated by a blood or tissue
bank.
Acts 1995, 74th Leg., ch. 165, Sec. 1, eff. Sept. 1, 1995.

The attorneys have concluded the elements of the charge need to be extended, where the prosecution is required to prove that you were NOT one of the exceptions, concerning the regulation of your speed. I have seen complaints where it claims you were NOT doing any of the exceptions stated above. This should give you an idea of other exceptions NOT indicated in the complaint. Make them jump through hoops.
(Jumping off that rabbit trail.)

Let's everyone plead, "NOT Guilty, I Demand a Trial By Jury," and reset the system.

"The purpose of a jury is to guard against the exercise of arbitrary power -- to make available the commonsense judgment of the community as a hedge against the over- zealous or mistaken prosecutor and in preference to the professional or perhaps overconditioned or biased response of a judge."
-- Justice Byron White, Taylor v. Louisiana, 419 US 522
U.S. Supreme Court

CHAPTER 6
BY WHAT AUTHORITY

"By What Authority" is a phrase that has the same effect, on a public servant, that it does to a vampire—where you are holding a cross in front of you. Another magical phrase is, "What Is The Known Legal Duty?" If you have a duty to perform, then there must be a "Known Legal Duty" that requires you to perform, or there is no duty; and performing must be voluntary, on your part. Now this alleged mandate, by no means, has anything within the formula, that requires a gun be pointed at your head—for the duty to attach. A gun to the head definitely gives you the "Known Duty" to perform, but the act extracts the term, "Legal," from the phrase. Unless there is a contract, of which you have voluntarily accepted, that creates the "Known Legal Duty;" then you may have misunderstood your alleged obligation was actually voluntary—rather than an actual "Known Legal Duty". A good way, to question whether a mandated obligation exists, is to take the situation; and ask yourself, if your neighbor has the authority, to make you do the alleged duty. An example to question such authority would be an Order from a judge ordering you to jump flat footed over the court building to be released from custody. Judges cannot require an impossibility as a condition of performance. The law of necessity overrules demands from the court. The judge states: "Say one more word and I will hold you in contempt of this court." The supreme courts have mandated that you have the right to be heard in court. The court cannot order an impossibility that you be muted forever. I have see people hold their hands in front of themselves and state: "I am here to purge myself from contempt. You cannot ask me to do an impossibility and I cannot do what you demand. What will you have me do?" The judge the continued as though nothing had occurred concerning the contempt charge.

If you can stand to be shocked and at the same time be amused by the names that some people have called judges, see the case of United States vs. Fylint, 756 F2d 1352 (1985)

CHAPTER 7
YOU CAN'T CLAIM RIGHTS
YOU DO NOT KNOW ABOUT

You have vested rights, just like the SOB that you deal with every day has the same vested rights. "Vested Rights" have been so-named, due to the blood that has been previously spilled—in defending those rights. It is like something that has already been paid for, you have the receipt of the purchase, it's yours and yours alone and is so securely attached; it canNOT ever be removed, except by your own consent—or lack of knowledge, to claim what is rightfully yours. The men that were involved, in the creation of The United States of America, had bold statements—about such rights, in a document that is entitled "The Declaration of Independence." And I Quote: "We hold these truths to be self-evident, that all men are created equal, that they are endowed by their Creator <u>with certain unalienable Rights</u>, that **among these** are Life, Liberty and the pursuit of Happiness. - That to secure **these rights**, Governments are instituted among Men, <u>deriving</u> **their** just powers <u>from the **consent** of the governed</u>,...". Please focus on the term "among these," stated above. "Life, Liberty and the pursuit of Happiness" is NOT all there is, when you speak of vested rights. If you do NOT know what your rights are, they will NOT exist for you, and you and your loved ones will be taken advantage of—by your neighbors.

Now whether you like it or not, you canNOT get around the material fact that "You Were Created." Whether you came into existence by a simple act by your parents, a scientist took materials and made you what you are today or you have been told that you appeared from a beam of light; there is a fox in the chicken house that got things moving, without your help or consent.

If you were lucky enough to be created, in the "land of the almost-free," or found your way to the "land of the almost-free," over time; it is a well-established "custom and policy," in the "land of the almost-free," that all people have rights that the neighbors need to recognize; or such lack of recognition—by the neighbors—could invoke self-preservation of rights, to be activated by the people.

What's my point? The point is: What we have been told all our lives, about "authority," has been misrepresented, drastically; and I hope to put you on the path **to know** what some of your rights are, where you will automatically question any alleged obligation, to perform like a seal that we all have done in the past, without thinking or asking "Why?" If you do NOT know what your rights are, then, you lack the ability, to claim those rights you and your family actually have. Silence equals acquiescence (consent). Rights NOT claimed are considered waived, by our so-called legal system. Understand that, if nothing else. Don't misunderstand your responsibility on this planet. If your actions harms another or their property, you will have the opportunity to explain yourself to your neighbors. You have NO right, to take the right of another. The people to whom I have delegated my authority, to deal with certain situations, will bring you in front of neighbors—to determine if you did what is alleged, beyond a reasonable doubt. I expect them to give you a fair trial and protect your vested rights. If they don't, then they will answer to the over 300,000,000 of us that have the same vested rights.

Shades of grey wherever I go
The more I find out the less that I know
Black and white is how it should be
But shades of grey are the colors I see
  Billy Joel, Shades of Grey, from the *River of Dreams* album (1993)

CHAPTER 8
ARTICLE 1, SECTION 29
OF THE TEXAS CONSTITUTION

In my opinion, this is the **most** important section of the Texas Constitution:

Texas Constitution-Original 1876 & Current, Article 1
Sec. 29. PROVISIONS OF BILL OF RIGHTS EXCEPTED FROM POWERS OF GOVERNMENT; TO FOREVER REMAIN INVIOLATE. *To guard against transgressions of the high powers herein delegated, we declare that **everything** in this "Bill of Rights" **is excepted** out of the **general powers of government**, and **shall forever** remain inviolate, and all laws **contrary** thereto, or to the following provisions, **shall be void**.*

This is a necessity that you get your mind around, what the intent of the people was in Texas—way back in 1876—when they chose those exact words that are stated above. You may want to look up the definition, of the term "inviolate." My definition is as follows: "You can't touch it with a thousand-foot pole." In other words: "Hands Off, You CanNOT Touch This, By Any Means." Now my interpretation goes even further than law dictionaries, as the term "inviolate" means to me, the Texas Legislature has no authority to get around what is stated, in the original Texas Constitution, other than by a constitutional convention—where every sentence is up for grabs. Even then, if you will read, 'The Constitution of No Authority,' written by Lysander Spooner in 1869; this will bring a new light into your mind, concerning the alleged authority, of all so-called constitutions, to obligate you to anything—if you have NOT taken an Oath to it.

What the Texas Legislature has done, after the fact, has manipulated the public to believe they (the public) can just simply vote their rights, away. Well, this is where you must recognize the major differences, in the terms, "republican form of government" and "a democracy." There are many historical documents that spell out the differences, but, to my understanding and belief, a democracy is where Fifty-One (51%) percent of the Gang can vote to kill Forty-Nine (49%) percent of the Gang. There is no better way to explain the term. Majority rules everything, no matter the subject, no matter the right being voted away, no matter the religion being disposed of, no matter the race to be disposed of; no matter what: majority rules. People who vote in a representative republic have restrictions set upon them, where certain things canNOT be voted on and such things, as rights, are considered taboo. Ninety-Nine (99%) percent of the Gang canNOT vote to take a right away from any living breathing person, as the issue canNOT be brought to a vote.

There is a famous quote, by Chief Justice John Marshall of the Supreme Court of the United States of America, in the **Marbury v. Madison,** 5 U.S. 137, 2 L. Ed. 60, 1 Cranch 137 (1803) decision about unconstitutional acts. "...in declaring what shall be the *supreme* law of the land, the *constitution* itself is first mentioned; and not the laws of the United States generally, but those only which shall be made in *pursuance* of the constitution, have that rank. Thus, the particular phraseology of the constitution of the United States confirms and strengthens the principle, supposed to be essential to <u>all written constitutions,</u> that **a law repugnant to the constitution is void**; and that *courts,* as well as other departments, are bound by that instrument." Found also in the same **Marbury v. Madison** case, we find: "The very essence of civil liberty certainly consists in the right of every individual to claim the protection of the laws, whenever he receives an injury. One of the first duties of government is to afford that protection."

Eighty-Three (83) years later, nothing had changed in the minds of the then-sitting justices of the Supreme Court of the

United States of America. We find, in the case of *Norton v. Shelby County*, 118 U.S. 425 (1886), where Mr. Justice Field delivered the opinion of the court, and stated: "An unconstitutional act is not a law; it confers no rights; it imposes no duties; it affords no protection; it creates no office; it is, in legal contemplation, as inoperative as though it had never been passed."

Members of the Texas Legislature have their hands tied behind their backs, by Article 1, Section 29 of the Texas Constitution, but they are slick to make the population believe the people can just simply vote their rights away. Evidence is clearly apparent, of the unconstitutional manipulation of the Texas Constitution, by the past Texas Legislatures.

Some examples of the unconstitutional manipulation are apparent, by reviewing Article 1, Section 3 of the Texas Constitution, then, by reviewing the restriction of the rights of people, by the Texas Legislature—after democracy took over, in November of 1972. Below, you see the original Section 3 of the original Texas Constitution, back in 1876. It is still in the current Texas Constitution, but more subsections were added, unconstitutionally, by the Texas Legislature, providing additions they recommended to the Texas people, to allow the voters to vote their rights away.

Texas Constitution-Original 1876 & Current, Article 1
Sec. 3. ***All free men,*** *when they form a social compact,* ***have equal rights****, and no man, or set of men, is entitled to exclusive separate public emoluments, or privileges, but in consideration of public services.*

Texas Constitution, Article 1- { }Added Restrictions
{Sec. 3a. EQUALITY UNDER THE LAW. ___*Equality*___ *under the law shall not be denied or abridged* ___**because of**___ *sex, race, color, creed, or national origin. This amendment is self-operative.}*
(Added Nov. 7, 1972.)

What other reason could it be than to restrict the rights of individual people, by listing the rights of different Gangs? Doesn't Section 3a, above, really state: "Equality under the law will be withheld from all that fail to claim the injury was due to sex, race, color, creed or national origin"? Was it the intent of the people of Texas to list restrictions in the Texas Bill of Rights? I think, NOT. Section 3a above should never have been set on the voting ballet, where Fifty-One (51) percent of those that bothered to vote could just vote their own rights away, as well others or the one.

Some examples of the unconstitutional manipulation are apparent, by reviewing Section 10, where restrictions of rights of the people were placed on the ballot, by the Texas Legislature—after democracy took over, in November of 1918. Below, you see the original Section 10 of the original 1876 Texas Constitution.

Texas Constitution-Original 1876, Article 1,
*Sec. 10. In all criminal prosecutions the accused shall have a speedy public trial by an impartial jury. He shall have **the right** to demand the nature and cause of the accusation against him, and to have a copy thereof. He shall not be compelled to give evidence against himself. He shall have **the right** of being heard by himself or counsel, or both; shall be confronted by the witnesses against him, and shall have compulsory process for obtaining witnesses in his favor. And no person shall be held to answer for a criminal offense, unless upon an indictment of a grand jury, except in cases in which the punishment is of fine, or imprisonment otherwise than in the penitentiary, in cases of impeachment, and in cases arising in the army or navy, or in the militia, when in actual service in time of war or public danger.*

Texas Constitution, Article 1 {Added Restrictions}
*Sec. 10. RIGHTS OF ACCUSED IN CRIMINAL PROSECUTIONS. In all criminal prosecutions the accused shall have a speedy public trial by an impartial jury. He shall have **the right** to demand the nature and cause of the accusation against him, and to have a copy thereof. He*

*shall not be compelled to give evidence against himself, and shall have **the right** of being heard by himself or counsel, or both, shall be confronted by the witnesses against him and shall have compulsory process for obtaining witnesses in his favor, {**except** **that when the witness resides out of the State and the offense charged is a violation of any of the anti-trust laws of this State, the defendant and the State shall have the right to produce and have the evidence admitted by deposition, under such rules and laws as the Legislature may hereafter provide}**; and no person shall be held to answer for a criminal offense, unless on an indictment of a grand jury, except in cases in which the punishment is by fine or imprisonment, otherwise than in the penitentiary, in cases of impeachment, and in cases arising in the army or navy, or in the militia, when in actual service in time of war or public danger. (Amended Nov. 5, 1918.)*

Above, you can see the changes made, by the Texas Legislature, which allowed the voters to simply vote their rights away. What possibly reason could anti-trust laws need clarification, in the Bill of Rights? Makes you wonder why just putting the provision in rules of procedure, or in the form of statutes, would be unconstitutional, doesn't it?

Some examples of the unconstitutional manipulation are apparent, by reviewing Section 11 in the original 1876 Texas Constitution, and then, reviewing the restriction of the rights of people by the Texas Legislature—after democracy took over, in November of 1956, 2005 and 2007.

Texas Constitution-Original 1876, Article 1
*Sec. 11. BAIL. All prisoners **shall be bailable by sufficient sureties**, unless for capital offenses, when the proof is evident; but this provision shall not be so construed as to prevent bail after indictment found upon examination of the evidence, in such manner as may be prescribed by law.*

Texas Constitution, Article 1 { } Added Restrictions

*{Sec. 11a. MULTIPLE CONVICTIONS; DENIAL OF BAIL. (a) Any person (1) accused of a felony less than capital in this State, who has been theretofore **twice convicted** of a felony, the second conviction being subsequent to the first, both in point of time of commission of the offense and conviction therefor, (2) accused of a felony less than capital in this State, committed while on bail for **a prior felony** for which he has been indicted, (3) accused of a felony less than capital in this State involving the use of a deadly weapon after being convicted of a prior felony, or (4) accused of a violent or sexual offense committed while under the supervision of a criminal justice agency of the State or a political subdivision of the State for a prior felony, after a hearing, and upon evidence substantially showing the guilt of the accused of the offense in (1) or (3) above, of the offense committed **while on bail** in (2) above, or of the offense in (4) above committed while under the supervision of a criminal justice agency of the State or a political subdivision of the State for a prior felony, **may be denied bail** pending trial, by a district judge in this State, if said order denying bail pending trial is issued within seven calendar days subsequent to the time of incarceration of the accused; provided, however, that if the accused is not accorded a trial upon the accusation under (1) or (3) above, the accusation and indictment used under (2) above, or the accusation or indictment used under (4) above within **sixty (60) days** from the time of his incarceration **upon the accusation**, the order denying bail shall be automatically set aside, unless a continuance is obtained upon the motion or request of the accused; provided, further, that **the right** of appeal to the Court of Criminal Appeals of this State is expressly accorded the accused for a review of any judgment or order made hereunder, and said appeal **shall be given preference** by the Court of Criminal Appeals.*

(b) In this section:

(1) "Violent offense" means:

(A) murder;

(B) aggravated assault, if the accused used or exhibited a deadly weapon during the commission of the assault;

(C) aggravated kidnapping; or

(D) aggravated robbery.

(2) "Sexual offense" means:
(A) aggravated sexual assault;
(B) sexual assault; or
(C) indecency with a child.}
(Added Nov. 6, 1956; amended Nov. 8, 1977; Subsec. (a) amended and (b) added Nov. 2, 1993.)

*{Sec. 11b. VIOLATION OF CONDITION OF RELEASE PENDING TRIAL; DENIAL OF BAIL. Any person **who is accused** in this state of a felony or an offense **involving** family violence, who is released on bail pending trial, and whose bail is subsequently revoked or forfeited for a violation of **a condition of release** may be denied bail pending trial if a judge or magistrate in this state determines **by a preponderance of the evidence** at a subsequent hearing that the person violated **a condition of release** related to the safety of a victim of the alleged offense or to the safety of the community.}*
(Added Nov. 8, 2005; amended Nov. 6, 2007.)

*{Sec. 11c. VIOLATION OF AN ORDER FOR EMERGENCY PROTECTION INVOLVING FAMILY VIOLENCE. The legislature **by general law** may provide that any person who violates an order for emergency protection issued by a judge or magistrate **after an arrest for an offense involving** family violence or **who violates** an active protective order rendered by a court in a family violence case, **including** a temporary ex parte order that has been served on the person, or **who engages in conduct** that constitutes an offense involving the violation of an order described by this section may be taken into custody and, pending trial or other court proceedings, **denied release on bail** if following a hearing a judge or magistrate in this state determines by a preponderance of the evidence that the person violated the order or engaged in the conduct constituting the offense.}*
(Added Nov. 6, 2007.)

Section 11 specifically states that people have the right, to be bailed out of jail, while the trial is pending. The Unconstitutional Sections, of 11a, 11b and 11c, are apparent that such right has been restricted by democracy. Sections 11a, 11b and 11c state that Fifty-One (51) percent of the Gang can make it impossible to pay, for certain criminal acts you are convicted of; and you will always be treated as a criminal, even if you completely pay—what the law states how the payment of the crime will be paid. Do you really believe that Sections 11a, 11b and 11c should have been placed in the Bill of **Rights**?

Some examples of the unconstitutional manipulation are apparent, by reviewing Sections 15 & 15a of the Texas Constitution that restrict the rights of the people, by the Texas Legislature—after democracy took over, in August of 1935 and November of 1956.

Texas Constitution-Original 1876, Article 1
Sec. 15. ***The right*** *of trial by jury **shall remain** inviolate. The Legislature shall pass such laws as may be needed to regulate the same, and to maintain its purity and efficiency.*

Texas Constitution, Article 1 { } Added Restrictions
*Sec. 15. RIGHT OF TRIAL BY JURY. **The right** of trial by jury **shall remain** inviolate. The Legislature shall pass such laws as may be needed to regulate the same, and to maintain its purity and efficiency. {**Provided, that the Legislature may provide for the temporary commitment, for observation and/or treatment, of mentally ill persons not charged with a criminal offense, for a period of time not to exceed ninety (90) days, by order of the County Court without the necessity of a trial by jury.**}*
(Amended Aug. 24, 1935.)

*{Sec. 15-a. COMMITMENT OF PERSONS OF UNSOUND MIND. No person shall be committed as a person of unsound mind **except** on competent medical or psychiatric testimony. The Legislature may enact all laws necessary to provide for the trial, adjudication of insanity and commitment of persons of unsound mind and to **provide for a method of appeal** from judgments rendered in such cases. Such laws may provide for **a waiver of trial by jury**, in cases where the person under inquiry **has not been charged with the commission of a criminal offense**, by the concurrence of the person under inquiry, or his next of kin, and an attorney ad litem appointed by a judge of either the County or Probate Court of the county where the trial is being held, and shall provide for a method of service of notice of such trial upon the person under inquiry and of **his right** to demand a trial by jury.}*
(Added Nov. 6, 1956.)

We apparently canNOT afford to give crazy people the same rights that sane people have. But then again, what if there is a way to restrict the sane person's rights, by simply making the allegation, the person is of unsound mind? Sounds like a tool the government may be able to use, to their advantage, and they actually have their tool placed in the Bill of Rights. Don't forget these unsound-mind people need to be given legal notice that they have a right to a trial by jury, even though Section 15 states that the right to a trial by jury canNOT be denied, for lack of notice. By the way, how do you have a trial, when the defendant **has NOT been charged with the commission of a criminal offense**?

Some examples of the unconstitutional manipulation are apparent, by reviewing Section 17 of the Texas Constitution that restricts the rights of the people, by the Texas Legislature—after democracy took over, in November of 2009.

Texas Constitution-Original 1876, Article 1 [ ] Removed
*Sec. 17. No person's property shall be taken, damaged, or destroyed for or applied to public use without adequate compensation being made, unless by the consent of such person, [**and, when taken, except for the use of the State, such compensation being first made, or secured by deposit of money, and no irrevocable or uncontrollable grant of special privileges or immunities shall be made; but all privileges and franchises granted by the Legislature or created under its authority shall be subject to the control thereof.**]*

Texas Constitution, Article 1 { } Added Restrictions
*Sec. 17. TAKING, DAMAGING, OR DESTROYING PROPERTY FOR PUBLIC USE; SPECIAL PRIVILEGES AND IMMUNITIES; CONTROL OF PRIVILEGES AND FRANCHISES. { (a) } No person's property shall be taken, damaged, or destroyed for or applied to public use without adequate compensation being made, unless by the consent of such person, {**and only if the taking, damage, or destruction is for:***
*(1) the ownership, use, and enjoyment of the property, notwithstanding an incidental use, by:***
*(A) the State, a political subdivision of the State, or the public at large; or***
*(B) an entity granted the power of eminent domain under law; or***
*(2) the elimination of urban blight on a particular parcel of property.***
*(b) In this section, "public use" does not include the taking of property under Subsection (a) of this section for transfer to a private entity for the primary purpose of economic development or enhancement of tax revenues.***
*(c) On or after January 1, 2010, the legislature may enact a general, local, or special law granting the power of eminent domain to an entity only on a two-thirds vote of all the members elected to each house.}***
{(d) When a person's property is taken under Subsection (a) of this section,} *except for the use of the State, compensation {**as described by Subsection (a) shall be}* *first made, or secured by a deposit of money; and no irrevocable or uncontrollable grant of special privileges or immunities shall be made; but all privileges and*

franchises granted by the Legislature, or created under its authority, shall be subject to the control thereof.
(Amended Nov. 3, 2009.)

The question is, why would the people vote to restrict their rights? It can only happen in a democracy, and NOT in a republic. Notice how long ago this act happened. Notice the term "urban blight." Notice, in the Bill of Rights, the special provision of the percentage of votes, by the Legislature, can remove more of your rights. Before the manipulation of our rights, they had to deposit money before the taking the people's property; but now, a deposit is NOT needed, except in certain situations. The Bill of Rights was NOT created to ensure more rights to the State.

Some examples of the unconstitutional manipulation are apparent, by reviewing Section 20 of the Texas Constitution that restricts the rights of the people, by the Texas Legislature—after democracy took over, in November of 1985.

Texas Constitution-Original 1876, Article 1
Sec. 20. No citizen shall be outlawed, nor shall any person be transported out of the State for any offense committed within the same.

Texas Constitution, Article 1 { } Added Restrictions
*Sec. 20. OUTLAWRY OR TRANSPORTATION FOR OFFENSE. No citizen shall be outlawed. No person shall be transported out of the State for any offense committed within the same. {**This section does not prohibit an agreement with another state providing for the confinement of inmates of this State in the penal or correctional facilities of that state.**]*
(Amended Nov. 5, 1985.)

Here, the Legislature again violates Section 29 of Article 1, by creating more rights for the State. This gives the State the abilities to take fathers, mothers, sons and daughters away from their families, by moving the convict to another State that was NOT allowed, before. It doesn't look like the people were given more rights; but further restricts their right, to see their loved ones—by the whim of the State.

Section 29 forbids the Texas Legislature from creating any law to restrict the rights of the people. Going around such restriction of the Legislature by suggesting a method that would allowed Fifty-one (51%) percent of the democracy Gang that could restrict any rights of the people found in Article 1 is unconstitutional. The Bill of Rights is NOT supposed to be the Bill of Restricted Rights; but instead, the intention was to keep at arms' length the rights of the people—from the attorneys that were somehow elected to office, unconstitutionally. That's right; attorneys are restricted from running for election, in the Legislative and Executive Branches of government. But evidence of my allegation will be forthcoming.

Those in the Texas Legislature are forbidden by Section 29, to bring matters to the people, to change up the wording of the Texas Constitution that would restrict the rights of the people. Do you see such acts of the Texas Legislature are forbidden, under Section 29 of the Texas Constitution? If not, then you are definitely part of the democracy Gang, and you better hope that Fifty-One (51%) percent of your buddies don't vote to cook you for dinner.

Here is another tidbit for you to mull over in your mind. Get a copy of the Texas Constitution, and a copy of the Constitution For The United States of America (U.S. Constitution); and look closely at the difference in formatting, between the two documents. In the U.S. Constitution, you find amendments at the end of the U.S. Constitution, whereas, amendments to the Texas Constitution are haphazardly done, throughout the document. The reader of the Texas Constitution would likely never know what the amendment had changed or simply been repealed—without doing extensive research. In the U.S. Constitution, you find (mostly) all the words and terms placed in the document, from when it was originally created, up to the time that you are reading this book. In the Texas Constitution, you find the term, "repealed," throughout the document. It takes a lot of research to find out what was really in the Texas Constitution, in times past. Nevertheless, it still gives the reader notice that no matter what changes were made to the Texas Constitution, such changes will NOT affect the vested rights of the people. Now when you give a little thought, to what I just stated above, I would expect that a "What?" should emerge, from your thought processes, sooner or later. As an example, lets say the Texas Constitution had stated, before, you have the right to squat on state land and claim it as your own; and the Texas legislature reasoned such state land had been all been claimed in past years, so there was no need for informing the people of that right; so they convinced the people to vote to remove that right—you know, to give more room to take your other rights, later on.

Texas Constitution-Original 1876
Article 14, Sec. 6. *To every head of a family without a homestead, there* **shall be donated** *one hundred and sixty acres of public land, upon condition that he will select and locate said land, and occupy the same three years and pay the office fees due thereon. To all single men of eighteen years of age and upwards, shall be donated eighty acres of public land, upon the terms and conditions prescribed for heads of families.*
(Repealed Aug. 5, 1969.)

Look at our right above that was repealed by your neighbors. Now think about the term "National Forest". Is that land State land or Federal land? Hmmm.....

Well, when the Texas Legislature gets their consent, from the people, to take their rights away—by repealing them; it seems the Texas Legislature is obligated, in some manner, to give the people a temporary notice—concerning those rights that were removed, by the repeal of certain words in the Texas Constitution. Even though a provision was repealed—where the provision can no longer be read by the public, the Texas Legislature always directs the reader's attention, to look into the back of the Texas Constitution, concerning the right that was "Repealed."

THE TEXAS CONSTITUTION
ARTICLE 9. COUNTIES
Sec. 6. (Repealed Nov. 2, 1999.)
*(TEMPORARY TRANSITION PROVISIONS for Sec. 6: **See Appendix, Note 1**.)*

THE TEXAS CONSTITUTION
***APPENDIX. Notes** on Temporary Provisions for Adopted Amendments*
1.** H.J.R. No. 62, Section 56, 76th Legislature, Regular Session, 1999. Temporary Transition Provisions. **(n) The amendment of any provision does not affect vested rights.

THE TEXAS CONSTITUTION
ARTICLE 8. TAXATION AND REVENUE
Sec. 16. (Repealed Nov. 6, 2001.)
*(TEMPORARY TRANSITION PROVISION for Sec. 16: **See Appendix, Note 3**.)*

Sec. 16a. (Repealed Nov. 6, 2001.)
*(TEMPORARY TRANSITION PROVISIONS for Sec. 16a: **See Appendix, Notes 1 and 3**.)*

Examples, above, can be found in multiple places between the covers, of the Texas Constitution, today—as well as in the past. As stated before, if the people are NOT aware of their rights they had before; it is hard to claim them, today - if you have no knowledge they ever did exist, in the past.

If there were no bad people, there would be no good lawyers.
- Charles Dickens (1812-1870) British novelist.

I think we may class the lawyer in the natural history of monsters.
- John Keats (1795-1821) British poet.

"We are a republic. Real liberty is never found in despotism or in the extremes of democracy."
— Alexander Hamilton

CHAPTER 9
ELEMENTS OF THE CHARGE

When one of your family members, or one of your friends, is charged with committing a crime, the complaint should always contain the Nature and Cause of the accusation. This right is recognized and found under Article 1, Section 10 of the Texas Constitution as well as in the 6th Amendment of the U.S. Constitution. The 'Nature' is the type of law recognized. Example being: admiralty; equity; common law; Transportation Code; Health & Safety Code; etc;... In the 'Cause', there should be elements the prosecutor must prove, beyond a reasonable doubt, the accused (allegedly committed). These separate elements can be the straw that breaks the camel's back, concerning the prosecution's intent to obtain a conviction. Hoping for a conviction is NOT really what the prosecution is striving for. The prosecutor expects a conviction, by whatever means necessary, and when a conviction is NOT likely, then there is the "Lets make a deal"—or a simple suggestion to the judge—to dismiss the charge, for a reason that will be beyond the control of the prosecutor. One of their ready available remedies is to tell the police officer NOT to appear; even though the prosecutor should have contacted the police officer, verified his availability and moved the trial—for the benefit of the cop—and then and only then issue a subpoena, for the cop to show up for trial. Instead, the cop does NOT show up. The case goes away—and the prosecutor does NOT get a demerit for allowing the accused to be found Not Guilty. Have any thoughts of what may happen to a police officer—served a subpoena, who didn't show up on trial day? It's called, "contempt of court." The police officer could easily find himself in jail, for NOT showing up, as indicated in the subpoena. But, if NO subpoena was served, the police officer doesn't even need to be contacted, since the prosecution already has the means to dismiss the case—and NOT lose face.

As stated before, municipal courts and Justice of the Peace courts use, "custom and policy," and charge the accused, with what I call "A Banana Law." It goes something like this: "Mr. Doe, you have been charged with 'Eating Bananas On Tuesday.' How do you plead to the charge, Guilty, Not Guilty, or Nolo Contender?" Now, if a judge or prosecutor said that statement to you, I would hope that you would respond with: "What? There is no such law and I am not required to plead to nonsense." What if instead the judge or prosecutor said: "Mr. Doe, you have been charged with speeding. That is, you have been charged with going 70 mph in a 60 mph zone. How do you plead to the charge, Guilty, Not Guilty, or Nolo Contender?" I would hope that you would respond the same way that I just mentioned, when charged with Eating Bananas on Tuesday. Oh, I know that you believe that speeding is a crime, but I beg to differ—as the term "Speeding" is a vague, non-specific term, found in the Texas Transportation Code. 70 mph in a 60mph zone will NOT be found, in the Texas Transportation Code, anywhere.

Texas Transportation Code
*Sec. 543.010. SPECIFICATIONS OF SPEEDING CHARGE. The complaint **and** the summons **or** notice to appear on a charge of speeding **under this subtitle must specify**:*
*(1) the maximum or minimum speed limit applicable in the district or at the location; **and***
(2) the speed at which the defendant is alleged to have driven.
Acts 1995, 74th Leg., ch. 165, Sec. 1, eff. Sept. 1, 1995.

In fact, if you research the reason that speed limit signs are placed where they are placed, you will eventually run across Section 201.904 of the Texas Transportation Code—giving you the definition of "**Speed Signs**," (check your own State code.)

TEXAS TRANSPORTATION CODE
TITLE 6. ROADWAYS
SUBTITLE A. TEXAS DEPARTMENT OF TRANSPORTATION
CHAPTER 201. GENERAL PROVISIONS AND ADMINISTRATION
SUBCHAPTER K. ROAD AND HIGHWAY USE; SIGNS
Sec. 201.904. **SPEED SIGNS***. The department shall erect and maintain on the highways and roads of this state appropriate **signs** that show the maximum lawful speed* **for** *commercial* motor vehicles*, truck tractors, truck trailers, truck semitrailers,* **and** *motor vehicles engaged in the business of transporting passengers for compensation or hire (buses).*
Acts 1995, 74th Leg., ch. 165, Sec. 1, eff. Sept. 1, 1995.

The question now remains, if the "maximum or minimum speed limit applicable in the district or at the location" only pertains to the type of conveyance mentioned in Section 201.904, above, how could I be charged with "speeding," if I was NOT in such conveyance mentioned above?

Now, if the speed signs you find going down the road are specifically for those that move people or property for hire, then how are you to be noticed how fast that you are allowed to go down the road, on a particular highway, in some other type of conveyance? Good Question. The Transportation Code has a few places that mention the terms "reasonable and prudent." Now the question is, how would you or a jury determine whether you were acting "reasonable and prudent" on the highway, at the time you got a citation for "speeding"? Going faster than some sign suggests can't be an element, to be proven to the jury, because the Texas Legislature has determined that such signs are to regulate those that move people or property, for hire on the highway. Look at Section 201.904 referenced, above. So, there must be something else that would give a jury the ability, to determine that you were NOT acting "reasonable and prudent," on the highway. What about if you ran into someone? What if, you ran a red light and had an accident, or you were texting on your phone and didn't realize that the guy in front of you had to stop and you didn't? Wouldn't that be an element that would show that you did NOT act "reasonable and prudent" on the highway? Well, the Texas Legislature has codified such activity, found in Section 545.351 in the Texas Transportation Code.

Texas Transportation Code
Sec. 545.351. MAXIMUM SPEED REQUIREMENT.
*(a) An **operator** may not drive at a speed greater than is reasonable and prudent under the circumstances then existing.*
*(b) An **operator**:*
*(1) may not drive a vehicle at a speed greater than is reasonable and prudent **under the conditions** and having regard for actual and potential hazards then existing; **and***
*(2) shall control the speed of the vehicle as necessary to **avoid colliding** with another person or vehicle that is on or entering the highway in compliance with law and the duty of each person to use due care.*
*(c) An **operator shall, consistent with Subsections (a) and (b), drive at an appropriate reduced speed if**:*
*(1) the **operator** is approaching and crossing an intersection or railroad grade crossing;*
*(2) the **operator** is approaching and going around a curve;*
*(3) the **operator** is approaching a hill crest;*
*(4) the **operator** is traveling on a narrow or winding roadway; and*
*(5) a special hazard exists with regard **to traffic**, including pedestrians, or weather or highway conditions.*

Above we see the intent of the Texas legislature, to regulate an "Operator."

Texas Transportation Code
SUBTITLE C. RULES OF THE ROAD
CHAPTER 541. DEFINITIONS
SUBCHAPTER A. PERSONS AND GOVERNMENTAL AUTHORITIES
Sec. 541.001. PERSONS. In this subtitle:
*(1) "**Operator**" means, as used in reference to a vehicle, **a person** who drives or has physical control of a vehicle.*

An Operator is a "person."

> (4) **_Person_** means an individual, firm, partnership, association, or corporation.

In the public fool system, we learn that we are individuals. When we individuals get together, we then become something other than an individual. As indicated above, when we get together we could become an association, organization, trust, partnership, or corporation. But, what if there is no definition of "individual," within the Rules of Obedience? Of which there is NOT a definition of "individual," in the Texas Transportation Code. Have you ever heard of the Latin term "ejusdem generis"? It means: "Of the same kind, class or nature." Those attorneys elected to the Texas Legislature and Texas Senate know about the term "ejusdem generis." That is why they define things the way they do. Section 541.001(4) above really means: "**Person**" means an association, organization, trust, partnership, corporation or such other individual entity. If you want to believe that the term "individual" means you, then that is OK with them, as they embrace your consent to be regulated.

Texas Transportation Code
SUBCHAPTER C. VEHICLES, RAIL TRANSPORTATION, AND EQUIPMENT
Sec. 541.201. VEHICLES. In this subtitle:
*(23) "**Vehicle**" means a device that can be used to **_transport_** or draw **_persons_** or property on a highway. The term does not include:*
(A) a device exclusively used on stationary rails or tracks; or (B) manufactured housing as that term is defined by Chapter 1201, Occupations Code.

It is the intent of the Texas Legislature that the above, previous, Section 545.351 statute is to be taken, as a whole. You should NOT be charged with only part of a statute, but the system does this everyday. There are many court cases that have ruled a title of a statute, rule, code or other such regulation, of an activity, plays no relevance, in determining such regulation has been violated. As above, "MAXIMUM SPEED REQUIREMENT" is merely a reference to the regulation, as there is no mile-per-hour indicated, where the reader could determine there is a maximum speed that one should NOT exceed. But, there is an indication, for the reader to understand, the maximum speed had been exceeded. The first indication is that "circumstances then existing" play a part in determining that one should adjust the speed of their conveyance, appropriately. Rain, ice, snow, fog and the amount of visibility of the roadway could play a major part, in determining a lower speed would be "reasonable and prudent;" and to do otherwise would lead people to believe an accident would be more likely, than if the sun was out and the roadway dry. But, just because it is raining, a police officer should NOT be able to pull you over, and give you a ticket—for NOT being "reasonable and prudent," for something you might do. As with cooks in a kitchen, a cake may be constructed in many different ways, and the cake will still be made and taste as good as another constructed differently. I am trying to say that one traveler may be able to travel down the roadway at a much higher speed, safely, where others are an accident waiting to happen. There are many car races that can be viewed on video showing professional racers going at very high speeds, in the rain, and being able to keep their race cars on the track; so, conditions of the roadway affect some more than others. So, there must be some other way for a jury to know, for a fact, that someone was NOT "reasonable and prudent," on the roadway. Looking at subsection (b), above, gives us the answer. The first caution given is that the "operator" should be aware that conditions on the roadway may change, in a matter of moments, due to hazards found on the roadway. This could be a board on the roadway, or a major accident in the roadway—making you take defensive maneuvers, to avoid the hazard. The second condition of subsection (b) is the clear indication that the traveler was NOT "reasonable and prudent," and deserved to be cited for his/her negligence. The traveler failed to avoid colliding with a person or an object. This is most important to understand, because of the term "**and**" found in subsection (b), between the two conditions. Both conditions must be proven beyond a reasonable doubt before a jury could determine that the traveler was NOT "reasonable and prudent," on the roadway. Everything else found in the statute is conditions, of which the traveler needed to be aware, and adjust his/her speed accordingly, to be able to avoid a collision—for which he/she did or didn't do. Now you are ready to sit on a jury, and determine if someone was moving people or property for hire, and went faster than some speed sign; or for those NOT moving people or property for hire, whether they were "reasonable and prudent," on the roadway. But then, are you really ready to determine if someone violated the rules of the road?

What if you sit on a jury, for someone charged for NOT having a driver license? What are the elements that must be proven, beyond a reasonable doubt?

Texas Transportation Code
*Sec. 521.025. LICENSE TO BE CARRIED AND EXHIBITED ON DEMAND; CRIMINAL PENALTY. (a) A person **required** to hold a license under Section 521.021 shall:*
*(1) have in the person's possession **while operating a motor vehicle** the class of driver's license appropriate for the type of vehicle operated; and*
(2) display the license on the demand of a magistrate, court officer, or peace officer.
*(b) A peace officer may stop and detain a person **operating a motor vehicle** to determine if the person has a driver's license **as required** by this section.*

Above is NOT the complete statute you will find, but it contains all the elements that need to be proven, by the prosecutor, for NOT displaying a driver license. As found concerning "Speed Signs" in the Transportation Code above, we find that "motor vehicle" is defined in the United States Code, Title 18, Section 31(6) & (10).

United States Code, Title 18, Section 31
(6) MOTOR. VEHICLE-The term "__motor vehicle__" means every description of carriage or other contrivance propelled or drawn by mechanical power __and__ __used for commercial purposes__ on the highways in the transportation of passengers, passengers and property or property or cargo.

(10) USED FOR COMMERCLIAL PURPOSES.-The term "used for commercial purposes" means the carriage of persons or property for any fare, fee, rate, charge or other consideration or directly or indirectly in connection with any business, or other undertaking __intended for profit__.

Now I know I will have some readers call foul ball, by my citing federal law, instead of a Texas definition in the Texas Transportation Code; but as we will find, all judges should have taken an Oath—to support the laws of the United States. See the Texas Constitution, Article 16, Section 1.

THE TEXAS CONSTITUTION
ARTICLE 16. GENERAL PROVISIONS
Sec. 1. OFFICIAL OATH. (a) All elected and appointed officers, before they enter upon the duties of their offices, shall take the following Oath or Affirmation:
"I, _____, do solemnly swear (or affirm), that I will faithfully execute the duties of the office of _____ of the State of Texas, and will to the best of my ability preserve, protect, and defend the Constitution __and laws__ __of the United States__ and of this State, so help me God."
(b) All elected or appointed officers, before taking the Oath or

Affirmation of office prescribed by this section and entering upon the duties of office, shall subscribe to the following statement:

"I, _____, do solemnly swear (or affirm) that I have not directly or indirectly paid, offered, promised to pay, contributed, or promised to contribute any money or thing of value, or promised any public office or employment for the giving or withholding of a vote at the election at which I was elected or as a reward to secure my appointment or confirmation, whichever the case may be, so help me God."

Anyone heard of the "full faith and credit" clause, found in the U.S. Constitution? Probably not.

Constitution For The United States of America
Article. IV.
*Section. 1. **Full Faith and Credit** shall be given in each State to the public Acts, Records, and judicial Proceedings **of every other State**; And the Congress may by general Laws prescribe the Manner in which such Acts, Records and Proceedings shall be proved, and the Effect thereof.*
*Section. 2. **The Citizens of each State shall be entitled to all Privileges and immunities of Citizens in the several States**. A person charged in any State with Treason, Felony, or other Crime, who shall flee from Justice, and be found in another State, shall on Demand of the executive Authority of the State from which he fled, be delivered up, to be removed to the State having Jurisdiction of the Crime.*

Well, this is the way it works. Let's say your State doesn't require that you get a safety inspection on your conveyance, but you are traveling into a state where the residents there are required to get their conveyance inspected. Why do you think the police officers in this other State don't pull you over and give you a citation, for NOT having a safety sticker on your windshield? It's that full faith and credit clause, found in the U.S. Constitution, allowing you to travel from State to State—without hassle. This same clause allows a Citizen of one State to reach out, and grab a remedy from another State, as YOURS does NOT provide a remedy, in the state where you are domiciled or reside, currently.

Rabbit Trail: I didn't know if you caught the punctuation, of the term "Citizen," found in the U.S. Constitution. If you will go to the Fourteenth Amendment and find the term, "citizen of the United States," you should notice that the term, "citizen," is NOT capitalized; whereas the term, "Citizen," is found throughout the U.S. Constitution—until you get to the Fourteenth Amendment, where the lower-case term, "citizen," appears. I leave it to you to research WHY the term changed, after the War of the Northern Aggression Against The Southern States. Nothing in politics is by accident. {--a cliché often, and incorrectly, attributed to F.D. Roosevelt}

(Jumping off that rabbit trail.)

Let's say, your State doesn't allow you to appeal without an attorney, where if you were living in another State, you would be allowed to appeal without an attorney. Well, reach out to that State and grab that remedy, and piss-off the judges. This is exactly what I am doing when I grab the remedy, of the definition of "motor vehicle," found in federal law. Reasonably, there canNOT be different definitions of a term that provide for a penalty, and if there is, you have the right to be charged with the lesser of the two penalties, if you obtained the knowledge to claim the lesser. If you fail to claim your remedy that is available to you, the system will turn a blind eye. Remedies, as with your rights, are NOT available to those that lack the knowledge they exist.

Let's get back to the Texas Statute Sec. 521.025, of the Texas Transportation Code, above. Your claim is that one of the elements that the prosecutor has to prove, beyond a reasonable doubt, is your conveyance was "used for commercial purposes." Unless the prosecutor can prove this, then any requirement to display a driver license must be dismissed. All elements of any charge must be proven, beyond a reasonable doubt, before a Guilty verdict can be reached—if the system actually recognized the rights of the people and its own laws.

CHAPTER 10
UNCONSTITUTIONAL STATUTES IN TEXAS

Here is another wrinkle, for the State of Texas, concerning our vested rights. The Texas Government Code Section 402.010 provides an avenue to challenge Texas Statutes that violate the Texas Constitution. Or at least, that was the intent of the statute. Let's say the system actually creates the Complaint, and the attorney files the Information in the Court—to give the Court jurisdiction, to hear the case. In the Information, you are charged with violating Section 545.351 of the Texas Transportation Code, which actually gives you the Nature and the Cause of the accusation against you. You pull up the government form associated with the Texas Government Code Section 402.010, and you create a Motion To Dismiss—as the charge is being used unconstitutionally, as it violates Article 1, Section 27, of your right to assemble—since there is no injured party. The system is unconstitutionally applying Texas Statutes that are conditionally used to only regulate commerce, but the road pirates are using it as a means to regulate your right to travel—and mainly to generate revenue that will sustain their job. Article 1, Section 29 forbids the Texas Legislature to make a law to abridge your right to assemble. Using a law, meant for another purpose—to regulate your right to assemble is unconstitutional and would be recognized as such, by the courts—if the judges intended to uphold their Oath to the Constitutions. "By what authority" is the appropriate response, to such a charge claimed against you, by the neighbor known as the prosecutor. In the same sense, you should be able to claim that Article 45.019, of the Texas Code of Criminal Procedure, is unconstitutional—since the Texas Legislature violated your right to know the Nature and Cause of the accusation against you, under Article 1, Section 10 of the Texas Constitution.

Article 45.019 of the Texas Code of Criminal Procedure is unconstitutional, as it allows a complainant to merely state he/she believes that a law was violated, by you.

Rabbit Trail: The complainant or the State's attorney never has to state which law was allegedly violated. Recently, I got this tidbit straight from mouth of Judge Hughes of the Harris County Court at Law #15 that had been elected to her position, since the late 1990's: I have a certified court-reporter transcript, confirming out of the mouth of Judge Jean Spradling Hughes, you have no right to be informed of the actual law that you are being charged of violating.

REPORTER'S RECORD
VOLUME 1 OF 1 VOLUME
CAUSE NO. 2086185

THE STATE OF TEXAS   * IN THE COUNTY CRIMINAL

*

VS.   * COURT AT LAW NUMBER 15

*

BOBIE KENNETH TOWNSEND * OF HARRIS COUNTY, TEXAS
****

PRETRIAL CONFERENCE
****

On the 6th day of June, 2016, the following proceedings came on to be heard in the above-entitled and numbered cause before the Honorable Jean Spradling Hughes, Judge presiding, held in Houston, Harris County, Texas: ...

MR. TOWNSEND: So, if I was charged with eating bananas on Tuesday, all I have to do is find an attorney that could find the law that I was being charged with?

THE COURT: No, if you want a copy of that law, it would be you or your lawyer's responsibility to obtain the copy. **It's not the State's responsibility to provide you a copy of the law that you're violating.**

MR. TOWNSEND: *And if no such law was found, what would be my remedy?*

THE COURT: *Then I would have already thrown them out of court. We wouldn't be standing here today.*

MR. TOWNSEND: *Then why aren't you throwing it out today?*

THE COURT: *Because there is a statute that provides speeding is against the law.*

MR. TOWNSEND: *And that statute would be which one?*

THE COURT: <u>*You have to figure it out. I don't tell you what the law is.*</u> *Remember, I can't help you practice law, okay. You've got to do your own. All right. Anything else? We'll see y'all June 15th, at 8:30 a.m., for trial.*

...

This admission, by a Harris County Judge, absolutely **"Shocks the Conscience."** Judge Hughes clarified the avenue to find out what law you are being charged with, was to hire an attorney and have the attorney research and inform you of the actual law the prosecution has charged you with violating. Judge Hughes gave me assurance, if the attorney found that there was no such law, and the attorney informed her of such fact, she would dismiss the charge. On the other hand, if a *pro se* defendant told her there was no such law, she said she had the discretion to ignore the claim, even if she never seen the actual law herself. Think real hard about what I have said, above. The system believes it is a 'need to know' policy, and it is policy of the courts, the accused does NOT have a right—or 'need to know'— the actual law he or she has been charged with violating, nevertheless Article 1, Section 10 of the Texas Constitution states otherwise.

(Jumping off that rabbit trail.)

The same goes for Article 21.21 of the Texas Code of Criminal Procedure, where the attorney is just directed, "That the offense be set forth in plain and intelligible words." The attorney doesn't have to name the actual Nature and Cause, in the Information filed in Court. Legalese is never stated, in, "plain and intelligible words." It always has to be interpreted by some higher court judge.

1. Article 2.05, of the Texas Code of Criminal Procedure, allows Justice of the Peace court and a municipal court to use a Complaint, as its charging instrument. Such direction, by the Texas legislature, is unconstitutional—since it amends or places conditions on Article 5, Section 12(b), of the Texas Constitution, where only an Information or Indictment gives a Texas Court jurisdiction, to hear a criminal case.

2. Article 44.181 of the Texas Code of Criminal Procedure is unconstitutional, since it violates Article 1, Section 19, of the Texas Constitution, of your right, to due course of the law and it violates Section 10, of your right to know the Nature and Cause. You canNOT be penalized by being forced, into a court of no record, and then have to prove you objected to an invalid complaint, when there is no record of any verbal exchange in the original court.

The Texas Legislature intended, as another tool to fight the oppression, that the form found in Texas Government Code Section 402.010 would be available to the people, to challenge Texas statutes. Use it. As of the writing of this book, I have only found cases concerning the challenging of statutes, in *Ex Parte* filed actions.

Here is the bad news. The judicial branch of Texas government denied the Legislature's mandate, to give the Texas Attorney General Forty-Five (45) days notice, of the claimed unconstitutional statute, before acting upon the claim. The 14th Court of Criminal Appeals, in *Ex Parte Lo*, No. PD–1560–12, (2013), stated the Texas Legislature canNOT screw with the court procedure of the Texas Courts, and Texas Court Clerks could ignore the Forty-Five (45) days notice to the Attorney General. This Court opinion must be unconstitutional, as it creates a conflict separating the powers of the Legislative and Judicial branches of government. The Judicial Branch of government has no authority to create a rule that would suspend a law created by the Texas Legislature. I should think the Attorney General should object to such court mandate, by filing an action, in the Texas Supreme Court—and then escalate the issue all the way to the U.S. Supreme Court, if necessary.

Texas Constitution, Article 1
Sec. 28. SUSPENSION OF LAWS. **No power** *of suspending laws in this State shall be exercised* **except** *by the Legislature.*

If I was in the Texas Legislature, I would propose that the judges' chambers were now in the bathroom, of each court house. Let's see how they liked that mandate. The Texas Constitution has three branches of government; the Legislative that create the laws, the Judicial that interprets the law, and the Executive that enforces the laws. There is a Fourth branch of government called the Administrative Branch, but it really only regulates firms, companies and corporations. That is a book in itself. If you would like to do your own research, go to a search engine on the internet, and search Roosevelt's Fourth Branch of Government—to get yourself familiar with the Administrative Branch of Government, if you so desire.

Absent scandal, a federal judge can serve for decades on the bench, underscoring the importance of appointing judges who have a proper understanding of their constitutional role. - Paul Weyrich

The lie can be maintained only for such time as the State can shield the people from the political, economic and/or military consequences of the lie. It thus becomes vitally important for the State to use all of its powers to repress dissent, for the truth is the mortal enemy of the lie, and thus by extension, the truth becomes the greatest enemy of the State.
Joseph M. Goebbels

CHAPTER 11
DIRECTORY OR MANDATORY

Here is something you weren't taught in the public fool system. If you are told to do something, without having a gun to your head, you usually have a choice whether to perform the act, or NOT. Now the choice may come with consequences, for deciding NOT to perform that act, but then again the consequences may lay upon the director making the demand, if by some means, you are forced to perform over your objections. Here, lies the rub. Is the demand being made, considered 'directory' or 'mandatory' for your performance?

*General or special statutes governing rendition of property for taxes or relating to collection of taxes **are directory**, and cannot, in absence of fraud or wrongdoing, deprive property owner who has **duly rendered property for taxation** of right to vote on taxing district's lending credit or assuming debt. Campbell v. Wright (Civ. App.1936) 95 S.W.2nd 149.*

*A city ordinance making it a penal offense for property owners to fail or refuse to render their property for taxation in the manner designated by Vernon's Ann. Civ. St. art. 1043 did not make article 1043 a "mandatory statute" rather than a "**directory statute**," as respects whether property owners rendering their property for taxation in a manner other than that designated by statute were entitled to vote at city bond election. DuBose v. Ainsworth (Civ.App.1940) 139 S.W.2nd 307, error dismissed.*

*The time fixed for rendition of property to city for taxation by statute, providing that owner "**shall**" hand city assessor and collector complete sworn inventory of property within first three months of each calendar or fiscal year, is **not** mandatory, **but directory**... MARKOWSKY et al. v. NEWMAN et al., 136 S.W.2d, 808 (1940)*

As you see above, Texas judges have determined what a reasonable man may think—that the term, "shall," means an obligation upon the person directed to perform the act—but instead; the strict term, "shall," could involve a different affect, on the person involved—if certain conditions are NOT met.

Most people alive today do NOT know, that once upon a time, only property owners who rendered their property for taxation had the right to vote, on what was to be done—with the property tax money obtained from firms, companies and corporations. You will find, below, the real reason the state allowed the property owners to vote, on the money issue, was to give property owners an <u>incentive</u>, to render their property for taxation. This would increase the coffer for the state agencies, to spend more money. Notice the date, of the *City of Roma* case below.

> *The situation as stated in these two findings is similar to the facts in Hanson v. Jordan, 145 Tex. 320, 198 S.W.2d 262. Justice Brewster, speaking for the Supreme Court, after stating that the purpose of Art. VI, Sec. 3a, Constitution of the State of Texas, limiting voters at a bond election to voters who had **duly rendered their property** for taxes, was **to induce owners of property** to place it upon the tax rolls and become liable for its pro rata share of the taxes levied and assessed by the municipality,...*
> *CITY OF ROMA v. GONZALEZ, 397 S.W.2d 943 (1965)*

As you see above, 1965 was NOT that long ago, when only property owners that rendered their property for taxation could vote, on what was to be done, with the property tax money generated in the system. It should be clear, by now, reading a statute may or may NOT create an obligation upon you, if certain conditions are NOT met.

Example of "directory" and "mandatory" conditions are shown below:

Texas Transportation Code
*Sec. 621.402.   WEIGHING LOADED VEHICLE.   (a)   A weight enforcement officer who has reason to believe that the single axle weight, tandem axle weight, or gross weight of **a loaded** motor vehicle is unlawful may:*
(1) weigh the vehicle using portable or stationary scales furnished or approved by the Department of Public Safety; or
(2) require the vehicle to be weighed by a public weigher.
(b) The officer may require that the vehicle be driven to the nearest available scales.
(c) A noncommissioned employee of the Department of Public Safety who is certified for the purpose by the public safety director and who is supervised by an officer of the Department of Public Safety may, in a port of entry or at a commercial motor vehicle inspection site, weigh a vehicle, require the vehicle to be weighed, or require a vehicle to be driven to the nearest scale under Subsections (a) and (b).
(d) Prior to assessment of a penalty for weight which exceeds the maximum allowable axle weights, the owner or operator is authorized to shift the load to reduce or eliminate such excess axle weight penalties as long as no part of the shipment is removed.
Acts 1995, 74th Leg., ch. 165, Sec. 1, eff. Sept. 1, 1995. Amended by Acts 2001, 77th Leg., ch. 737, Sec. 1, eff. Sept. 1, 2001; Acts 2001, 77th Leg., ch. 941, Sec. 20, eff. Sept. 1, 2001; Acts 2003, 78th Leg., ch. 1275, Sec. 2(136), eff. Sept. 1, 2003.
Amended by:
Acts 2007, 80th Leg., R.S., Ch. 12, Sec. 1, eff. April 23, 2007.

Let's say a police officer pulls you over, in your Eighteen (18) Wheeler, and the officer states he is giving you a citation, for NOT weighing your truck—when you bypassed the scales without stopping. The charge is failing to stop at the weigh station; and you wind up at court, where you are now mandated to defend yourself. Just as usual, the prosecutor does NOT state you have violated Section 621.402, of the Texas Transportation Code—thereby actually giving you notice, of the Nature and Cause of the accusation against you. But instead, you know the friend of a sister who works for the brother of a law firm, who tells you the Section of the Transportation Code, on which the prosecution is relying. See, it pays to know people.

Instead of stating you are NOT Guilty, any reasonable man should realize you are Guilty, by the way the accusation is stated on the complaint. You did NOT stop at the weigh station, as the police officer alleges, so should you plead guilty? No, NOT really. You plead "confession and avoidance."

Confession and Avoidance is a plea, of "Yeah, I did it, So What." Looking above, at Section 621.402 of the Texas Transportation Code, you can plainly see that the statute applies to motor vehicles—that have a maximum weight requirement **and** must be **loaded**. We have previously covered the definition of "motor vehicle". There is also an interesting term, **"loaded,"** found in the statute. Most people should understand an arm can be considered "loaded," by just having one round of ammunition, within the structure of the mechanism. So how would a reasonable man or woman, sitting on a jury, make a determination if the motor vehicle was "loaded" or NOT? Well, by observing Section 621.402, above, we find "Prior to assessment of a penalty for weight which exceeds the maximum allowable axle weights, the owner or operator is authorized to shift the load to reduce or eliminate such excess axle weight penalties as long as no part of the shipment is removed."

Let's say the vehicle was NOT loaded. Would the operator of the vehicle be required to be weighed? Would the order from a police officer, demanding the vehicle be weighed, be directory or mandatory? What would the police officer say to the judge, if you asked the police officer, on the stand, "What gave you the indication the motor vehicle was loaded?" What should the judge do, if the police office said, "I just assumed that the vehicle was loaded"? The judge should dismiss the charge, as one of the elements of the charge was NOT proven to be true, making the order from the police officer directory, instead of mandatory. If the motor vehicle was NOT loaded, then there canNOT be any mandatory obligation to pull into the weigh station. Would it be reasonable an officer may suspect the motor vehicle was loaded, and was required to stop at the weigh station? It would be reasonable the motor vehicle may be loaded, so there is probable cause for a traffic stop, to confirm whether the motor vehicle was loaded or NOT. But, let's say when the driver opened the doors to the trailer, it was empty, or only contained a few items. Would there be a reason to give a citation to the driver, for NOT stopping at the weigh station? I believe it would be reasonable to assume, a jury would NOT find any infraction had occurred, and find the accused Not Guilty—for failing to stop at the weigh station. Here we find the accused Guilty, of the act of NOT stopping; But also NOT Guilty, of such requirement to stop. So, we have learned the term, "shall," found in a statute, does NOT necessarily mean the direction of a statute is mandatory, upon the accused.

"A single, seemingly powerless person who dares to cry out the word of truth and to stand behind it with all of his person and all of his life, ready to pay a high price, has, surprisingly, greater power, though formally disenfranchised, than do thousands of anonymous voters."
--Vaclav Havel

CHAPTER 12
CAN YOU REALLY OWN PROPERTY?

You can only own property a jury will allow you to own. As of the writing of this book, I have NOT found the means to bring this issue before a jury, as the so-called justice system can NOT afford to allow matters in front of a jury that could end the property tax structure that is in place today. The system must violate the guaranteed right, under Article 1, Section 15 of the Texas Constitution, or all is lost for the (tax) system. By the evidence that I have acquired, I have reason to believe and do believe **No One**, who is buying, paid for, inherited or otherwise acquired a piece of land in Texas—even when it contains a structure, to which the owner and others return, from time to time—**owes property tax**, unless the owner of such property renders such property for taxation. My evidence, of this bold statement, can be found at the County Clerk's Office, in downtown City of Conroe, within the boundaries of the County of Montgomery, Texas. For a nominal fee, the County Clerk will provide you with certified copies, of document number PI 145-2012092268-10, document number PI 145-2012092269-5, and document number PI 145-2012092270-4.

Document number PI 145-2012092268-10 is a true and correct copy, of Chapter 157 (CLVII) entitled *"An Act defining what money and property is subject to taxation or exemption, and the mode of listing the same"*, Pages 275 through 281, of the General Laws of the State of Texas—Passed at the session of the Fifteenth Legislature, in the year of 1876. When you acquire a copy of this document, you will find it is certified, by the Texas Legislative Reference Library located in Austin, Texas. As you read all three documents, in series, you can only come to the conclusion it was the intent of the Texas Legislature only firms, companies and corporations are required to pay property tax, in Texas. Every other owner, of property in Texas, is being duped into voluntarily paying a tax that is NOT required, by law. Review the *City of Roma* case, again, as indicated, a few pages, above.

It is just another Gang of Organized Crime stealing from the people who live in their community. It reminds me of a movie showing when the mafia would offer a business, fire insurance. The business that paid the mafia premium would NOT accidentally burn down. Here, the Gang is organized to have one part of the Gang dupe you, in believing you owe a tax you canNOT afford. One part of the Gang gives another part of the Gang a piece of paper, allowing another part of the Gang to physically remove you from your own property—and sell it to some other "person" who agrees to pay the extortion tax, to use the property. The Gang consists of the local courts, the local taxing units, the local county constables' office, the local Tax Assessor/Collector—and the one that ties the scam in a pretty bow, the unconstitutional local central appraisal district.

As stated above, document number PI 145-2012092268-10 is an Act created by the Texas Legislature in 1876. This is the same year the current Texas Constitution was originally created. When you get your own copy, turn to page 278, first paragraph, last sentence, where you will find: "The **term person**, whenever used in this act <u>or any other act regulating the assessment and collection of taxes</u>, shall be construed to <u>include</u> firm, company or corporation."

The term, "include," is specific and canNOT be construed to mean something else than what is listed.

*"**Include**" means: **To confine within**, hold as in an inclosure, take in, attain, shut up, contain, inclose, comprise, comprehend, embrace, involve.*
Black's Law Dictionary, Fifth Edition

(Today we usually say, 'enclosure' with an E, but the old English word was "inclosure" with an I—notably used for fenced lands. E.g., 18th century small farms or lands were inclosed to make one bigger farm—which ceased to be communal common land. But the point is a legal term cannot be reinterpreted, to add something already left out. Whatever is "included" in the legal phrase is also automatically excluding whatever else it didn't say.)

*The Latin term "**inclusio unius est exclusio alterius**" means:*
***The inclusion of one is the exclusion of another.** The certain designation of one person is an absolute exclusion of all others. This doctrine decrees that where law expressly describes particular situation to which it shall apply, an irrefutable inference must be drawn that what is omitted or excluded was intended to be omitted or excluded.*
Black's Law Dictionary, Fifth Edition

That statement above is most specific, as to whom the Texas Legislature intended to regulate. Notice this was intended NOT only for the Act created in 1876; but the intent of the Act is the specific regulation concerning any assessment and collection of taxes, which will apply the same—in any future created Acts of the Texas Legislature.

Further proof, of the intent of the Texas Legislature, can be found when the Acts of the Texas Legislature were codified, in the Texas Revised Civil Statutes, in 1925. Document number PI 145-2012092269-5 is a certified copy, of Article 7149, Pages 2068 and 2069, Volume II of the Revised Civil Statutes of the State of Texas, Adopted at the Regular Session of the Thirty-Ninth Legislature, in the year of 1925. In Article 7149, you find: "The term **"Person"** shall be construed to include firm, company or corporation. (Source)[Acts 1876, 275; G.L. Vol. 8, p. 1111]." What is interesting is under Article 7149, you find the reference of the original Act in 1876, which is document number PI 145-2012092268-10. If I stop at the year of 1925, I have proven that for almost fifty (50) years it was the intent of the Texas legislature that the definition of the term "person," concerning assessment and collection of taxes, was ONLY a firm, company or corporation.

Further proof is found, in document number PI 145-2012092270-4, which is a true and correct copy, of Article 7149, Page 934, Volume 2 of the West's Texas Statutes and Codes, found published by West Publishing Co., in the year of 1977. In Article 7149, you find: ""**Person**."-The term, "person," shall be construed to <u>include</u> firm, company or corporation. (Source)[Acts 1925, S.B. 41]".

There it is. That is preponderance of evidence of more than one hundred years the Texas Legislature's intent was to define the term "person," to be ONLY a firm, company or corporation, when associated with regulating the assessment and collection of taxes in Texas. Later you will see that the 14th Court of Appeals of Texas will conveniently ignore these facts to protect the system, but admit that the term "**person**" is NOT defined in the current Texas Tax Code.

The Texas Tax Code was adopted by the Texas Legislature in 1979, where the definitions of the terms, found in Article 7149 of the Revised Civil Statutes, were relocated in Section 1.04 of the Texas Tax Code. But, for some unexplained reason, the Texas Legislature found it necessary to omit the definition, of the term "Person," from the Tax Code, in 1979 or anytime thereafter. What possible reason would the-powers-that-be find it necessary, to omit the definition of the term "person," in the Texas Tax Code?? It was NOT left out, to deceive anyone, surely. Can You Say "Unjust Enrichment," "Fraud," "Misfeasance," "Malfeasances," "Theft By Deception"?????? Have you lost a right your great-grandparents had, or maybe you just failed to claim it?

I've been told all my life that I had a right to own property. I have a TV that I do NOT have to pay a tax on each and every year, to be able to keep my TV. I have a toaster, but I haven't been required to pay a tax each and every year, to continue to own it. What is it about things placed on dirt—or the dirt itself—changing the status to really own something? You can take a piece of lumber and create a doll house, and NOT be required to pay tax on that wood, each and every year. But, take that same piece of lumber and use it to help build a home—to keep yourself out of the rain; and to keep that home—built with that same piece of wood—they tell you that you must cough up your hard-earned money—each and every year of your life, to be allowed to keep the home you built. Do you see a problem with this? If not, then you are paid with tax payer money, or you have the belief other people owe you things, you never worked for. Lacking critical-thinking skills could allow you to presume it is OK, for some guy in a costume to reach in the pocket of your neighbor's wallet, and give the money to a worthy cause—also known as legalized plunder. This is something that needs to change. You are part of the problem or part of the solution. There is no middle ground. If nothing else, at least ask, "Why," are you required to pay up? Their answer may surprise you.

Some patriots tell me you owe the property tax, due to filing the Homestead Exemption Certificate, in your county clerk's office; but I have yet to find a court case that would confirm that hypothesis. You see, I have a problem with other people changing a definition of the term, "exemption," to mean "discount". If you were simply to research the Homestead Act, whether enacted in the U.S. or in the Republic of Texas, you will find that it came about, because of farming. The people that ran the government concluded people involved in commerce owed the government protection money, for a percentage of the funds received from that commerce. But most of the people that were elected to the different houses of the government were farmers, and NOT just lawyers, like today. These farmers knew it was possible and it was more than likely a farmer could get over his head, in debt, by paying the extortion of the property tax, and lose everything the farmer worked for—and be out on the street, as beggars. So, they come up with this Homestead Act that protected the farmer and his family, from being homeless—for failing to pay this property tax, from the income produced from their property. The people in government passed an act that allowed an exemption, NOT a discount, for the farmers to keep a hundred and sixty acres and a farm house; if the farmer failed to pay the property tax. This allowed enough land and provisions for the farmer to provide for his family, and NOT be beggars in the street. When and if you take a little time, to confirm this information with a little bit of research on the World Wide Web, you will see why I have a problem, with the Homestead Exemption Certificate being the means why people owe the property tax today.

For argument sake, let's say the Homestead Exemption Certificate was really a discount certificate, on the property owned. Looking back in the archives, you find five thousand dollars was the determined value of exemption, in the 1800s. Have you ever calculated what five thousand dollars of twenty-dollar double-eagle gold coins would buy, in land and home, today? Let me tell you, gold coins have a little different value, compared to the five-thousand funny-money Federal Reserve Notes in your pocket today. Let me suggest, five thousand U.S. dollars in gold coin, back in the 1800s, would buy a farm house and one hundred and sixty acres of farm land. That is what I call a discount of property taxes.

In the law library, you will find a volume of books entitled "Words and Phrases". There, if you look up the word "Enjoyment", on page 294 you should find:

Baker v. State, Volume 17 Florida Supreme Court starting at page 406, on page 408:

*Constitution of Florida, Article 9, providing that a homestead, to the extent of 160 acres of land, **shall be exempt** from force sale under **any** process of law, and that this exemption **shall accrue** to their heirs of the party having "enjoyed or taken the benefit of such exemption," means **any one** who has owned and occupied the land with his family, whether he has or has not been threatened with executions or other process, since the enjoyment of a homestead consists in the use and occupation of it with his family.*

Back in the day, courts recognized the rights of the people. Now the judges' pay is diminished by taxes, so they do the bidding of their masters that pay their salary and it is NOT you they recognize as their master. It is your neighbors that take money from you and pay the salaries of the public servants. You are merely the cow that gives up the milk. The public servants get their milk from the company store. Public servants have no knowledge or cares about the source of the milk. The public servants do what the company store tells them what to do, or the milk dries up. If you quit supplying the company store, the public servants will find out where the source of the milk originates and who the true masters are.

I hope that you will come back to this chapter after you read Chapter 30 concerning the 14th Court of Appeals changing the meaning of "person" with the term "includes" and ignoring the evidence I presented showing the intent of the Texas Legislature for over one-hundred years defining the term "person" with the term "include" instead of "includes". Put in a book mark at the end of Chapter 30 to remind you to review Chapter 12 afterwards.

For further research concerning property tax go to the web link:

[www.landgrantpatent.org].

CHAPTER 13
STATE BAR ASSOCIATION
IS UNCONSTITUTIONAL

Now, let us review what happened in 1939 in Texas, and I imagine it happened all over the U.S. of A.; the Texas State Bar Association was created, by the lawyers that were unlawfully elected to office, in both the House of Representatives and the Senate of the Texas government. What I am about to tell you can be confirmed, with little effort on your part, by contacting the Texas Legislative Reference Library; and ask for documentation showing the careers, of the members of the House of Representatives and the Senate, in 1939. What you will find should "**Shock the Conscience.**" Twenty-seven lawyers, out of thirty-one Texas state senators, voted for and created the State Bar Association, in 1939. This would be the same situation if twenty-seven pharmacists voted, to only allow pharmacists to sell vitamins and Kool-Aid. The creation of a monopoly, of self-interest of such matter, is unconstitutional, under Article 3, Section 22 of the Texas Constitution—unless you are an attorney, that is.

THE TEXAS CONSTITUTION
ARTICLE 3. LEGISLATIVE DEPARTMENT
Sec. 22. DISCLOSURE OF PRIVATE INTEREST IN MEASURE OR BILL;
*NOT TO VOTE. A member who has a **personal or private***
***interest** in any measure or bill, proposed, or pending before the*
Legislature, shall disclose the fact to the House, of which he is a
*member, and **shall not vote thereon**.*

Electing attorneys to the Legislative or Executive branch of government is unconstitutional, under Article 2 of the Texas Constitution.

THE TEXAS CONSTITUTION
ARTICLE 2. THE POWERS OF GOVERNMENT
*Sec. 1. DIVISION OF POWERS; THREE SEPARATE DEPARTMENTS; EXERCISE OF POWER PROPERLY ATTACHED TO OTHER DEPARTMENTS. The powers of the Government of the State of Texas shall be divided into **three distinct departments**, each of which shall be confided to a separate body of magistracy, to wit: Those which are **Legislative** to one; those which are **Executive** to another, and those which are **Judicial** to another; and **no person**, or collection of persons, being of one of these departments, **shall exercise any power properly attached to either of the others**, except in the instances herein expressly permitted.*

Article 2, Section 1 above confirms lawyers are required to give up all ties to the Judiciary Branch of government to run and be elected to another branch of government. Today, the attorneys would have to return their membership card to the State Bar Association. It would be similar to a member of the Long Shoremen's Union working with members of the Teamsters' Union job and NOT having to join the Teamsters' Union. The Long Shoremen member would be considered a Scab by the members of the Teamsters. Attorneys elected into the Legislative Branch of government, is a Scab working for the benefit of the State Bar Association and not the people he/she claim to represent.

In fact, before the War of the Northern Aggression Against The Southern States, the several States had created an amendment to the U.S. Constitution, making it unlawful for a lawyer to hold any office.

Constitution For the United States of America
First (original) 13th Amendment
*"If any **Citizen** of the United States shall accept, claim, receive, or retain any title of nobility or honour, or shall without the consent of Congress, accept and retain any present, pension, Office, or emolument of any kind whatever, from any emperor, king, prince, or*

*foreign power, such Person shall cease to be a **Citizen** of the United States, **and shall be incapable of holding any office of trust or profit under them, or either of them**."*
(Ratified March 12, 1819)

With a little bit of research on the World Wide Web, you will find many several States and Territories, before December 6, 1865, would show the above wording, in their State's archive of the U.S. Constitution. It took a war to change history. The First 13th Amendment was replaced with the Second 13th Amendment, as it is found today.

Constitution For the United States of America
Second (present) 13th Amendment
Sect. 1. *Neither slavery nor involuntary servitude, except as a punishment for crime, whereof the party shall have been duly convicted, shall exist within the United States, or any place subject to their jurisdiction.*
Sect. 2. *Congress shall have power to enforce this article by appropriate Legislation.*
(Ratified December 6, 1865 and took the place of the original 13th Amendment)

If you have been around an attorney for very long, you will hear they have a license to practice law. I've never seen a license to practice law and I have asked many attorneys to produce it— and none have, yet. What they do show is their State Bar membership card, which is NOT a license. Show me an operating license that doesn't have an expiration date. When a government issues you some kind of license, they want another license fee, after a short period of time. I want to see the expiration date, of a license to practice law. I have found where the Texas Legislature has allowed the Texas Supreme Court the ability to issue a license to practice law, but I have never seen where the Texas Supreme Court has ever done such act, for anyone. So what is the purpose of the charade? I think it is done to close the shop (guild, like a union), to those learned in law who could compete with those indoctrinated to protect the member brothers and sisters, for screwing their clients over.

I have verified this myth, about attorneys, from various sources; and I expect that you can as well. When an attorney gets his BAR card, the State BAR makes the member take four different oaths to get their BAR card. The first oath is to be loyal to the court, so if the court screws over a member, he is NOT allowed to squeal on the judge. Doing so, the member takes the chance of losing his BAR card and his livelihood, to make money as an attorney. The next oath is to his member buddies of the BAR. He is NOT allowed to squeal on a BAR member, or take the chance of losing his BAR card and his livelihood. The next oath is to the constitution(s). If he doesn't have to turn his head concerning the behavior of his BAR buddies, the judge and other State BAR members, then he will allegedly try and go by the constitution(s). The fourth oath is to the client. The guy that pays him finally gets a little help with a legal matter, as long as he doesn't have to ignore the illegal action of a judge, his fellow attorney that he is allegedly going against and after he ignores the constitution(s), he'll give his best effort to help the client, until the client runs out of money. The State Bar Association is known to protect its members, if they fail in their best effort to help the client. I have reason to believe and do believe, the protection racket and to maintain a closed shop are the main purposes of the State BAR. This is the main reason people who go to court without an attorney never get treated fairly. They are NOT in the club. Believe it or otherwise. I am just trying to pull your head out of the sand.

You can fix the problem by NOT voting for attorneys in the Legislative and Executive Branch of Government.

CHAPTER 14
HOW ALL THIS INFORMATION
CAME TO BE REVEALED TO ME

In the middle 1990s, I met a black man, by the name of Doctor Norris Austin. He was holding classes about the U.S. Constitution, in a Luby's Cafeteria at night. Doctor Austin was a school teacher that had researched the U.S. Constitution, for about fifteen-plus years, prior; and somebody had convinced him to hold a few classes, on the subject. I was one of the fortunate ones that got to hear his words of wisdom. The first words I heard Doctor Austin speak was: "I am here with the desire to help you (white) people be free. If I canNOT get you free, I have no chance of getting free, myself." Everyone in the room laughed. Doctor Norris Austin said: "No Really, I am NOT kidding. I really want you and I to be free, but I can't do it without your help." Doctor Austin was NOT smiling as he made the statement, but then a big grin came upon his face; "Can we get started?" Doctor Austin had a small booklet, for everyone in the room containing the U.S. Constitution, the Declaration of Independence and information about Jury Nullification. Doctor Austin stated that Article One, Section One was the most important paragraph in the whole constitution. Doctor Austin read the paragraph to us:

Constitution For The United States of America
Article. I.
Section. 1. *All legislative Powers herein granted shall be vested in a Congress of the United States, which shall consist of a Senate and House of Representatives.*

Dr. Austin asked for a show of hands, to tell why it was the most important paragraph in the Constitution. There were a lot of suggestions, but none hit home, like Doctor Austin did to us. He read the paragraph again in a different way. "**ALL** Legislative powers **HEREIN GRANTED** shall be vested in a Congress of the

United States." "Do you see **HEREIN GRANTED**?" "Do you see **ALL POWERS**?" "If it is **NOT HEREIN GRANTED,** Congress has **NO POWER** to do anything **NOT GRANTED** by **THIS** constitution."

It was like flipping a switch in my brain. I was being taught the Constitution, by a preacher of the Constitution, and I liked it. I now have nine hours of video, taken back in the 1990s, of Doctor Norris Austin preaching the constitution. Doctor Austin has passed on, about a year or so ago, and he will surely be missed by me and thousands of others that were fortunate to grace his presence and hear him speak. I am NOT going any further concerning Doctor Austin's teaching, possibly you will get to see and hear him on YouTube, one of these days. Because of Doctor Austin teachings, it has led me to further research which has lifted the veil from my eyes, of which I hope to do with you.

"The sacred rights of property are to be guarded at every point. I call them sacred, because, if they are unprotected, all other rights become worthless or visionary. What is personal liberty, if it does not draw after it the right to enjoy the fruits of our own industry? What is political liberty, if it imparts only perpetual poverty to us and all our posterity? What is the privilege of a vote, if the majority of the hour may sweep away the earnings of our whole lives, to gratify the rapacity of the indolent, the cunning, or the profligate, who are borne into power upon the tide of a temporary popularity?" -- *Judge Joseph Story,* 1852

CHAPTER 15
WHY I WENT TO THE LIBRARY OF CONGRESS

I attract, and am attracted to, crazy people. My wife Carolyn is crazy, because she has stayed with me, for over forty years. I have been involved with people that started the "Republic of Texas" movement, back in the 1990's. It seemed to be going well, until one of the members, by the name of Rick McLaren, started scamming some of the other members, by getting them to create silver Republic of Texas Ranger Badges and other services; and paid the vendors, with money he convinced the RT Treasurer to print up. Most members did NOT think that was such a good idea, so the members voted him out of his position he had held, since the movement had started. This did NOT set well with McLaren, so he got a few of his supporters and had a standoff in West Texas, which made national news. Nobody in the movement went to his aid, other than the ones that went with him to West Texas, mainly because of him scamming the other members. The media ran with the story, even though many people tried to show conclusive evidence that McLaren was no longer a recognized member of the movement, which was first started in the mid 90s. A couple of people wound up getting killed, and McLaren and his wife surrendered—after a State of Texas Ranger signed a treaty with McLaren, as a condition of his surrender. That treaty is still a matter of controversy, today. The system gave McLaren twenty-five years, for having bomb-making material, at his so-called compound. I think it was a few gallons of gasoline. Have you noticed how all standoffs are conveniently held at a compound? McLaren is a very dangerous man. NOT that he would physically harm anyone, except by self-defense; rather, McLaren can use a ballpoint pen and destroy a system. I believe that will be the reason the system will never let him out, even after he has served his time. It is my belief McLaren should have never been convicted, and I hope he may be released, as soon as possible. I have reason to believe, and do believe, McLaren's conviction was a void judgment.

One of the other crazy ideas I have is Texas is still a nation, and has <u>never</u> been a state of the union, before or after the War of the Northern Aggression Against The Southern States. Why I say that is because of the documents I have seen, which these members of the Republic of Texas movement have collected, over the years. I personally have hundreds of documents that show Texas is still a nation, as it was, back in 1836. One major proof, of the Republic of Texas still existing today, is easily found—by anyone looking in the current Texas Rules of Civil Procedure, Rule 53.

RULE 53. SPECIAL ACT OR LAW
*A pleading founded wholly or in part on **any private or special act or law** of this State **or of the Republic of Texas** need only recite the title thereof, the date of its approval, and set out in substance so much of such act or laws as may be pertinent to the cause of action or defense.*

Now, surely this is crazy to read, in the Twenty-First Century? Why would we find the laws of the Republic of Texas were still valid, today, if Texas was NOT still the nation it once was? Come on, let's hear some other explanation, from somebody. You canNOT believe how many attorneys I have asked about Rule 53, and try to get them to explain why, or even how it wound up in the rules of procedure. Most just walk away. Others just change the subject. No one gives a reasonable answer. I guess I will be waiting for a while longer, for some other explanation.

Another thing, have you been to the Capital building, in Austin, Texas, and look what is in the middle of the rotunda? Let me be the first to tell you that in the middle of the floor has the Seal of the Republic of Texas, and NOT the seal of The State of Texas. Do you realize the Capital building was built after the War of the Northern Aggression Against The Southern States? Like, almost twenty-five years, afterward. Are you going to tell me, from 1845 to 1878-9, the builders of the Capital building forgot it was supposed to be the capital building of the State of Texas— and NOT the Republic of Texas?

Do you remember the borders of the Republic of Texas extended way up north, but later was broken apart and became several other states, even though the U.S. Constitution states it is unconstitutional, to make a state from a state?

Article. IV.
*Section. 3. New States may be admitted by the Congress Into this Union; but no new State shall be formed or erected **within** the Jurisdiction of any other State; nor any State be formed by the Junction of **two or more** States, or Parts of States, without the Consent of the Legislatures of the States concerned **as well** as of the Congress.*

I know, you see the Consent of the Legislature and Congress, but have you seen the documents allowing the breakup, of the Republic of Texas? Me, neither. Here is something else to ponder over. Is it only a coincidence that all these several states, created out of the land of the Republic of Texas, each have their State Capital located within the boundary that was once the Republic of Texas? Hell of a coincidence.

My family and I went to Washington, D.C., to get a copy of the documents that made the Republic of Texas a state of the union. Surely, we would find it at the Library of Congress. After a few hours searching, one of the Librarians came to us with a smile on her face, and brought us the Treaty of Annexation that Congress considered in 1845, which allegedly made the Republic of Texas a state of the union. My youngest son, Bob, took a look at the document, and handed it back to the librarian; and asked her if she had a copy of the document that was passed by Congress—since the one presented to us was rejected by Congress. The librarian was very puzzled by the last statement on the document showed the proposal had failed to be ratified; and asked for our address, and stated she would mail a copy of it to us, when it was found. That was in November of 2002, and I am still waiting, for the mail to deliver the document.

I expect that any historian can verify that nations being brought into another nation must be accomplished by treaty or by conquest. Since no ratified treaty of annexation exists, then the people of Texas must realize that it is a country under occupation, or it is still an independent nation as it once was and being part of the United States is just an illusion as the masters of illusion has led us to believe. There is a thing called international law, which all countries recognize or should recognize. "The Law" by Frederic Bastiat seems to explain what I have alluded above. Please find a copy on the internet and verify for yourself what is really going on between nations.

If you want government to intervene domestically, you're a liberal. If you want government to intervene overseas, you're a conservative. If you want government to intervene everywhere, you're a moderate. If you don't want government to intervene anywhere, you're an extremist. --Joseph Sobran, Editor of the National Review at one time (1995)

CHAPTER 16
CHEMICAL DUMPERS

Most public servants that I have encountered in my adventure are what I call Chemical Dumpers. I will try and explain my label of such people.

Let's say, you are a young man or woman that gets hired, to do non-skilled work in a company. One day your Foreman comes to you and says he has a job for you, and leads you to a 55-gallon drum of chemical, and tells you to take the drum to the field behind the maintenance building; and dump the contents of the drum on the ground, get a shovel and cover the liquid with dirt, and return the drum to the place that you found it; and report back to him. Now, being a farmer, by trade, you know that the underground water table runs from northwest to southeast; and doing such an act could possibly contaminate the ground water and pollute the water wells, located southeast of the company. Thinking your Foreman may NOT know about the water wells, southeast of the company, you ask if there is another place to dump the chemical. Your Foreman explains to you there are many people, outside the gate, looking to take your job. The fact is, the chemical drum is going to be dumped, where the Foreman said to dump the drum. The question is, "Are you the one that is going to dump the drum, or is it going to be the one that replaces you, as you walk out the gate? The Chemical Dumper dumps the drum. The moral person escalates the problem to the Foreman's supervisor, and from there, further up—until someone directs the Foreman to dispose of the chemical properly; or if that fails, the moral person does what is necessary to see such behavior is stopped, as he looks for another job.

Most, if NOT all, police officers that I have encountered are Chemical Dumpers, when it comes to their job. Most if NOT all judges are Chemical Dumpers, when it comes to their job. Most if

NOT all County and District Attorneys are Chemical Dumpers, when it comes to their job. There could be many reasons that the public servants rape and pillage the public, but I expect the "fear" of losing one's job is at the top of the list, with being a sociopath or a psychopath, while enjoying what their job allows them to do, is a close second. When people fear losing their job, they are as much a slave, as anyone that knows they have a master.

The public servants need to fear for their jobs, because of the people, instead of having fear of those that hired them. As the adventure folds out, below, you will see the public servants being manipulated from behind the scenes, ignoring their duty and responsibility because they believe their fellow brothers and sisters will turn a blind eye, to their rape and pillage of the public. After the adventure pauses, I will show you possible solutions, to our problem with public servants. It will NOT be solved, overnight. But, who knows what a week will bring? Help me stop the Chemical Dumpers.

Up to now, I have jumped around in your mind about things that you have the capability to prove to yourself, if you so desire. From this point forward I will show you why I have No faith or confidence in the Judiciary Branch of government, and neither should you, until there is a reboot to the system. I canNOT reboot the system myself, but with a little help from my neighbors, the system can be rebooted to run the way the founders originally designed.

The following chapters systematically lay the foundation of Judicial corruption and confirms an ordeal that has lasted for over eleven years. I intend for the ordeal to continue for many years, if I cannot find remedy in the current system. I apologize for the progressive legalese that I hope you can and will endure, as I plead my case to you. To combat the absurdities found in the following court opinions, I must speak in their native tongue. For those that are Legally blind, I hate to say it, but you may need to seek an attorney, for interpretation for your complete understanding.

I intend to have a list of solutions that the reader will have access to, so you can inquire what your neighbors are doing, about the lack of faith and confidence in the Judiciary Branch of government, so as to stir the stink to the top. The system full of sharks will eat their own, if you chum the waters correctly.

The speed of exit of a civil servant is directly proportional to the quality of his service. - Ralph Nader

Americans have an automatic responsibility to rebel against authority when that authority is mindless."
Newt Gingrich, 23 July 1998,
at the Young America Foundation Conference

"It's the action, not the fruit of the action, that's important. You have to do the right thing. It may not be in your power, may not be in your time, that there'll be any fruit. But that doesn't mean you stop doing the right thing. You may never know what results come from your action. But if you do nothing, there will be no result."
-Gandhi

CHAPTER 17
MY WIFE'S DREAM HOUSE

This is a major crossroad in my life. This is where I name names and show you buying a home may turn a corner in your life—that will educate yourself more than any college course you could ever find.

Back in 2004, my wife Carolyn had the bug to get away from Channelview, Texas, one of the main petrol-chemical-industrial communities in the Houston, Texas area. I got fired from the best job I ever had because of IRS problems (the IRS events would take another book). I had depression kicking in at the time, and to make matters worse, my wife had "new house fever," which added to her desire to change up our surroundings, by finding another house, elsewhere. She finds her dream house and I find my nightmare.

In the small community of Conroe, Texas, my wife finds a mansion for $124,900. There must be a catch. I walk in and I can't believe my eyes. I am thinking to myself, "I do not deserve a house like this. It is too fine, for me." (Maybe I materialized my ongoing problem, by thinking that way; search the web for "The Secret.") When you walk through the etched-glass, front, double doors, you come to an arched entry that opens up to a living room that has a seventeen (17) foot ceiling. Everything is freshly-painted white, except the fireplace. On each side of the fireplace are two very-large, clear windows that reach up to that seventeen (17) foot ceiling. You walk into this huge living room, then turn right through this large entry, you come to a large dinning area, next to a very large kitchen that has more cabinets than I have ever seen, in a kitchen. I find out the house is over 3,300 square feet of living space. The House is on three-quarters of an acre. It has Huge trees and a circle drive in the front. "I do not deserve a house like this!!!". My wife is swooning. I tell my Realtor friend,

Tom Maxton (call him (713-858-3657) he'll get you a great deal), to see if he could get it for us, and he did. Just my luck, Tom comes through for me, again. In fact, it seems that my Realtor is so good, he gets the contract locked in, about five (5) or ten (10) minutes before this other couple could get it finalized. So as you can see, this was meant to happen. Fate is having no choice.

Now, I made a few mistakes NOT checking out the property, of which, if I had it all over to do again, I would have gotten another house and paid more for it—I would have been better for it. But, did I tell you, it was my wife's Dream House? The first mistake was NOT getting my own house inspector. I used the one the seller's Realtor suggested, since he was in the area. He missed a lot, it turns out, which is just the tip of the iceberg money pit.

Here is part of the contract I and my wife agreed to accept, since it was my wife's Dream House:

II. Special Provisions - continued
*4. Toxic Mold. THE PROPERTY MADE THE SUBJECT OF THIS CONTRACT IS CURRENTLY THE SUBJECT OF A **TOXIC MOLD** RELATED INSURANCE CLAIM. Prior to the execution of this Contract, Seller provided Buyer with a copy of the investigation report prepared by ENVIROTEST dated 8-8-01, 9-01, and 7-3-02 & 2/4/03 and report by McDowell Owens dated 8-8-01. Buyer has read and does understand its content. BUYER ALSO EXPRESSLY ACKNOWLEDGES THAT SEI.LER HAS D1SCLOSED THE EXISTANCE AND SCOPE OF TOXIC MOLD IN THE PROPERTY. BUYER AGREES THAT SELI.ER SHALL HAVE NO LIABILITY OR RESPONSIBILITY FOR TOXIC MOLD IN THE PROPERTY OR FOR THE REMEDIATION Of SAME. BUYER EXPRESSLY ASSUMES ALL RISKS ASSOCIATED WITH THE TOXIC MOLD IN THE PROPERTY. BUYER RELIVES SELLER OF ALL COST OR EXPENSE RELATED TO ITS REMEDIATION. **AND ALL DAMAGES BUYER MAY SUFFER FROM THE MOLD, INCLUDING ALL PERSONAL INJURIES MAY BE CAUSED BY THE MOLD.***

Did I mention that the house had **Black Toxic Mold** in the structure? I had a plan to get rid of the **Black Toxic Mold**, I convinced myself that I knew what I was getting my self into. At least, if nothing else, the property taxes would stay low, because of the damage of the **Black Toxic Mold**, and I could use the savings on the property tax, to attempt the repair in the house. Surely, a Stewart Title Co. report would NOT lie to me, about what to expect the property taxes to increase, after I purchased the property, right?

Taxes

	2003 Tax Rates	
Tax Entity/Collector	Tax Rate (per $100.00)	Estimated Tax Before Exemption
CITY OF CONROE	0.43350000	$133.39
CONROE ISD	1.73250000	$533.09
MONTGOMERY CO	0.48280000	$148.56
MONTGOMERY CO HOSP	0.10820000	$33.29
NO HARRIS CO JR CLGE	0.11450000	$35.23
Total:	2.87150000	$883.5

http://www.propcrtyinfo.comlHARlReportslrptDetail.aspx?Key=HAR &Pin=6955-00-00200-001&C... 5/29/04

Records showed that the previous property owners paid less than $700 a year property tax, for three prior years, allegedly because of the current **Black Toxic Mold**. Surely, the estimate shown above, of $883.50 per year, would be a reasonable amount to expect the property tax could increase. The closing documents did NOT reflect any attempt, by the previous owners, to remediate the **Black Toxic Mold**. What possibly could go wrong? What I didn't realize was that the previous owners may have been kissing cousins with Mark Castleschouldt, the chief appraiser with the Montgomery Central Appraisal District, when I was not.

At closing, my half of the property tax turns out to be $335.00 on July 1, 2004. On or about January 1, 2005 I received a property tax appraisal from the Montgomery Central Appraisal District for over $4,000, because they appraised the property well-over $160,000. I thought to myself: "What happened to the $109,000 variance that was applied to the property the last four (4) years?" "There must be a mistake." What the Montgomery Central Appraisal District did was to make my property unsellable. If there was any way I could have realized the appraisal district could do this, I would NOT have touched that property, with a hundred (100)- foot pole.

I now had no extra money to do the repairs that I envisioned, and now I had no incentive to do the repairs. My efforts may turn out to be futile, and be pissing money down a well, never to be seen again.

Since it looks like my family would be living in a **Black Toxic Mold** environment, for some time, I purchase many Hepa Filter Machines at $300, or more, a piece. I soon found out that all the filters needed to be cleaned, about every two (2) weeks. I would kick myself, if it would do any good.

"I am only one, but I am one. I cannot do everything, but I can do something. And because I cannot do everything, I will not refuse to do the something that I can do. What I can do, I should do. And what I should do, by the grace of God, I will do." - *Edward Everett Hale*

CHAPTER 18
MY WAR BEGINS

I call down to the appraisal district and get the low down, of protesting the appraisal of my property, in Montgomery County. It's NOT my first rodeo. I protested my property tax in Harris County, Texas, back in the early 1990s. When I sold my house in Channelview, Texas, my home had the lowest appraisal value in a three block area, putting the home in a lower property-tax bracket. Even back then, I knew something was up, when I found out the appraisers had no authority, to go in your home to inspect. The appraisers supposedly had the duty to determine the market value of property, but how could they do their job, if they had no access to the inside of a piece of property? Doesn't the inside of a house reflect what the market value of the property is? Would a potential home buyer want to see the inside of the home before considering purchasing it? My war led me to the answer to the dilemma with the appraiser, and one of the main reasons that caused me to write this book. Did you know writing a book gives credibility to be an Expert Witness, in court? Well, it does. Go figure.

On or about June, 2005, I get my property protest hearing, at the Montgomery Central Appraisal District. I determined I had to find out 'By What Authority' these people running this appraisal district could make my property unsellable. The first thing they do is get you, with one of the peon appraisers, to play "Lets Make a Deal." He/She shows you few comparisons, of certain Apples, he/she would like to compare with your Orange. I tried to explain, to the appraiser, my situation, and he stated he was willing to lower the appraisal, to the amount I had paid for the property; but he was NOT willing to grant the variance—that was previously on the property, for the last few years. After I tell him I am NOT taking the deal, he/she tells me to go back, up front, and the receptionist will call me, when I can get in front of the Appraisal Review Board (ARB). This ARB is a weird animal. After you go in front of them a few times, you realize that they are just, "Yes Men," "Boot Lickers" of the appraisal district; and have little, if any, concern, with your wishes or desires—or evidence, for that matter. I sat around, with another group of people, waiting for my turn with the ARB. When the receptionist calls your name, you go in front of a panel of people that seem to be occupied with something else than what you are there to do. The guy or gal that sits next to you, at the ARB hearing, is one of those peon appraisers that you may have previously met, in the back room.

The Chairman of the ARB runs the show. "Good evening Mr. Townsend. We are the independent council of the Appraisal Review Board of the Montgomery Central Appraisal District and we are here, to hear your protest of your appraisal. We will first swear you and Mr. Flowers in, before we begin. You will then sign a document stating that you have been sworn in." The ARB Chairman let the Rep for the MCAD to go first. Mr. Flowers had some computer-generated printout, of comparisons of property, to justify why the MCAD determined my property should be appraised, at over $160,000. We go through the dog and pony show, where the Chairman of the ARB listens, to the spill of Mr. Flowers comparing his Apples, to my Orange. Then, they let me have my turn.

"Mr. Chairman, can I ask a couple of question, before I get started? Thanks. How did you get your job?" The Chairman, a gracious man, acting as though he has nothing to hide says that he put in a resume, and the Board of Directors of the Montgomery Central Appraisal District looked it over and appointed him to serve on the ARB, then the members got together and selected a Chairman out of the group; and here we are. "How do the members of the Board of Directors get their job?" The Chairman stated that the board of each Taxing Unit appoints a member of the Board of Directors (BOD) and the members of the BOD vote in who they would want to be Chairman of the Board—just like the members of the ARB vote who they want to be Chairman of the ARB. "Who is the elected official that oversees the functions of the appraisal district?" The Chairman of the ARB said he did NOT understand the question. "I am asking which elected official I need to talk to, that can get one of you people involved with the appraisal district fired?" The Chairman of the ARB asked if anyone knew and it seemed no one did; and he said that would probably be a question for the BOD. "Mr. Chairman, it sounds like you are telling me that everyone's job that is associated with this appraisal district is dependent, upon on an increase of appraisals in the district, or their pay or even their job may be cut, since <u>everyone</u> is appointed to their position?" Silence in the room.

I gave the members of the ARB a few documents, showing where my wife and I had to acknowledge the property contained Black Toxic Mold, when it was purchased. I showed the ARB where we paid a little over $300 for our half of the property tax at closing; and then I asked Mr. Flowers, how many of those properties, that were compared to my property, had Black Toxic Mold in their structures. Mr. Flowers stated he did NOT know. But, Mr. Flowers then gave the revelation of the MCAD's policy— that I, and I would expect thousands of others, did NOT know. Mr. Flowers stated that it was <u>the policy of MCAD</u> all damaged property purchased in Montgomery County was considered repaired, by the simple act of purchasing the property. Please read that last sentence again. "**It Shocks The Conscience**". MCAD expected all new owners of damaged property would repair any damages, as soon as possible, as to increase its selling price. I asked where I could find this policy of the MCAD, and Mr. Flowers stated that <u>it was an unwritten policy</u>. I tried to explain I was led to believe the property tax would NOT exceed $900, per year, until repairs were completed—if they could be completed. I showed the ARB the Steward Title estimate. The ARB stated they would be willing to go back down, to the purchase price of

$124,900, but that was the best they could do. "Meeting is over. You will get our determination in the mail." Welcome, to *The Twilight Zone*. I decide to pay the extortion, of the $3,346.45, under protest. This yearly sum amounted to over five years-worth of property tax paid, by the previous owners, of the same property, in the same condition I received it. I stated their decision made my property unsellable, and I would NOT have purchased the property, if I had known about the unwritten policy of the MCAD. I left.

It's not given to people to judge what's right or wrong. People have eternally been mistaken and will be mistaken, and in nothing more than in what they consider right and wrong.
— Leo Tolstoy, War and Peace

One has a right to judge a man by the effect he has over his friends.
— Oscar Wilde

"Power is the great evil with which we are contending. We have divided power between three branches of government and erected checks and balances to prevent abuse of power. However, where is the check on the power of the judiciary? If we fail to check the power of the judiciary, I predict that we will eventually live under judicial tyranny." - Patrick Henry

CHAPTER 19
NOT A REPUBLICAN FORM OF GOVERNMENT

I was informing you it seems that no one involved, with the central appraisal districts in Texas, created in 1979, are elected by the people, and all are appointed, by the so-called taxing units in the county; and it seems there is no elected official that oversees the on goings and doings of this Gang. If you believe, after reading this book, that I have proven that the central appraisal districts were not created as a republican form of government, then everything that they have done since 1979 was/is done unconstitutionally and the taxing units owe you a property tax refund. You are the potential jury to set on this case.

Rabbit Trail: Review the above again, about when the Texas Tax Code came into existence in 1979. Before 1979, the Tax Assessor/Collector was the one that put out the appraisals and collected the money; and he was elected to that position, where you could get him unelected (fired) from the position he held. Today, the Tax Assessor/Collector is just the guy who sends you a tax statement. It's NOT even a tax bill. Looks like a Bill, but just pull up the document he sends you, and find, "Statement," at the top of the document. Have you every received a Bank Statement from your Bank? Did you think it was a Bill? Why would you? It had the term, "Statement," at the top of the document. Why do we think the "Statement," sent by the Tax Assessor/Collector, is a Bill? Do the words, "Amount Due," make it a Bill, even though it has "Statement," at the top of the document? How would you know? If you assume something, are you always right? Did you know that there is a big difference between an assumption and a fact? Well, there is. Is it a fact you were sent a Tax Bill, consisting of a document that has Statement at the top of the document? Don't you think you should find out? Let's review the Texas Tax Code, and see what the Tax Assessor/Collector's duty is.

TAX CODE
TITLE 1. PROPERTY TAX CODE
SUBTITLE E. COLLECTIONS AND DELINQUENCY
CHAPTER 31. COLLECTIONS
Sec. 31.01. ___**TAX BILLS**___.
(a) Except as provided by Subsections (f) and (i-1), the assessor for each taxing unit **shall prepare and mail a** ___**tax bill**___ *to each person in whose name the property is listed on the tax roll and to the person's authorized agent. The assessor shall mail tax bills by October 1 or as soon thereafter as practicable....*
(c) **The** ___**tax bill**___ **or a** ___**separate**___ **statement** ___**accompanying the tax bill**___ **shall**:
(1) identify the property subject to the tax;
(2) state the appraised value, assessed value, and taxable value of the property;...

Go get your last-year's Tax Bill sent to you, by the Tax Assessor/Collector, and see what the title of the document is. Does it state, "Statement," or does it state, "Bill"? Doesn't the Tax Code state, above, that if there is a "statement," it must be "**accompanying**" a "tax bill"? Does the term "**accompanying**" mean "part of the same form"? I don't think so. Where is the "tax bill"? Did your bank pay the "statement" before it received a "tax bill"? Did you pay the "statement" before you received a "tax bill"? Why doesn't the Tax Assessor/Collector send you a Tax Bill, instead of a Statement? There you go being an adult again, and forgetting to ask, "Why?" There has to be a reason, because it is the duty of the assessor to send a tax bill, NOT just a statement.

Surely, Article 1, Section 10 of the U.S. Constitution couldn't have anything to do with that, or could it?

Constitution for the United States of America
Article 1
Sect. 10. ___**No State shall**___ *enter into any Treaty, Alliance, or Confederation; grant Letters of Marque and Reprisal; Coin Money; emit Bills of Credit;* ___**make any Thing but**___ *gold and silver Coin a* ___**Tender in Payment of Debts**___; *pass any Bill of Attainder, ex post facto*

Law, or Law impairing the Obligation of Contracts, or grant any Title of Nobility.

***No State shall**, without the **Consent** of the Congress, lay any ImPosts or Duties on Imports or Exports, except what may be absolutely necessary for executing its inspection Laws; and the net Produce of all Duties and ImPosts, laid by any State on Imports or Exports, shall be for the Use of the Treasury of the United States; all such Laws shall be subject to the Revision and Control of the Congress.*

***No State shall**, without the **Consent** of Congress, lay any Duty of Tonnage, keep Troops, or Ships of War in time of Peace, enter into any Agreement or Compact with another State, or with a foreign Power, or engage in War, unless actually invaded, or in such imminent Danger as will not admit of delay.*

If the federal government took away the gold, in 1933, and then took away the silver, in 1965, how can the State lawfully demand something other than gold and silver, as a payment of the property tax? The dilemma occurs, when the elected and appointed officers in the several states take that Oath of Office, found in Article 16, Section 1 (see Chapter 9). If the public servants have to go by the U.S. Constitution, then how can the State send you a Tax Bill when the state canNOT accept any Thing, but gold and silver Coin as Tender, in Payment of Debts? Maybe they send you or your bank a tax statement, and allow you to voluntarily pay the tax, with Federal Reserve Notes that they can spend, as well. **It Shocks the Conscience**, doesn't it? If the U.S. Constitution—and/or the Texas Constitution—is just a piece of paper, and has no binding effect on the public servants; then where do you think they claim to get their authority from? They can't have it both ways; but it seems they can, with your help and consent.

Double Rabbit Trail: Speaking of consent, back when I was 16 years young, I went on a quest asking different Christian denominations, for the interpretation of the Bible Verses: Daniel 7-21 & Revelation 13-7. Both Bible verses state the devil will make war upon the saints, and he will overcome them.

The Bible: Daniel 7

15   "As for me, Daniel, my spirit within me was anxious and the visions of my head alarmed me.

16   I approached one of those who stood there and asked him the truth concerning all this. So he told me, and made known to me the interpretation of the things.

17   'These four great beasts are four kings who shall arise out of the earth.

18   But the saints of the Most High shall receive the kingdom, and possess the kingdom for ever, for ever and ever.'

19   "Then I desired to know the truth concerning the fourth beast, which was different from all the rest, exceedingly terrible, with its teeth of iron and claws of bronze; and which devoured and broke in pieces, and stamped the residue with its feet;

20   and concerning the ten horns that were on its head, and the other horn which came up and before which three of them fell, the horn which had eyes and a mouth that spoke great things, and which seemed greater than its fellows.

*21   <u>As I looked, this horn made war with the saints, and prevailed</u>
<u>over them,</u>*

22   until the Ancient of Days came, and judgment was given for the saints of the Most High, and the time came when the saints received the kingdom.

23   "Thus he said: 'As for the fourth beast, there shall be a fourth kingdom on earth, which shall be different from all the kingdoms, and it shall devour the whole earth, and trample it down, and break it to pieces.

The Bible: Revelation 13

1   And I saw a beast rising out of the sea, with ten horns and seven heads, with ten diadems upon its horns and a blasphemous name

94

upon its heads.

2 And the beast that I saw was like a leopard, its feet were like a bear's, and its mouth was like a lion's mouth. And to it the dragon gave his power and his throne and great authority.

3 One of its heads seemed to have a mortal wound, but its mortal wound was healed, and the whole earth followed the beast with wonder.

4 Men worshiped the dragon, for he had given his authority to the beast, and they worshiped the beast, saying, "Who is like the beast, and who can fight against it?"

5 And the beast was given a mouth uttering haughty and blasphemous words, and it was allowed to exercise authority for forty-two months;

6 it opened its mouth to utter blasphemies against God, blaspheming his name and his dwelling, that is, those who dwell in heaven.

*7 **Also it was allowed to make war on the saints and to conquer them.** And authority was given it over every tribe and people and tongue and nation,*

8 and all who dwell on earth will worship it, every one whose name has not been written before the foundation of the world in the book of life of the Lamb that was slain.

9 If any one has an ear, let him hear:

10 If any one is to be taken captive, to captivity he goes; if any one slays with the sword, with the sword must he be slain. Here is a call for the endurance and faith of the saints.

I asked many preachers: "How can the devil overcome the saints?" If anyone should be able to rebuke the devil, it should be the saints. I only found one preacher, who looked about 80-years young, and gave me the most reasonable answer I could believe. He told me: "Well son, there can only be one way the devil will be able to overcome the saints; the saints will have to give the devil consent to overcome them." Are WE being overcome by consent? Time will tell.

(Jumping off those rabbit trails.)

Before I was so rudely interrupted, I was telling you about how the central appraisal districts in Texas are NOT a republican form of government. There is NOT an elected person associated with the central appraisal districts in Texas since their creation in 1979.

I got a meeting with the BOD of the MCAD and I asked what I need to do to get the current Chief Appraiser Mark Castleschouldt (Castleschouldt) fired. I told the board that Castleschouldt granted a variance to the previous owners, and then took it away from me, when I bought the same property, in the same condition. I told the board Castleschouldt made my property unsellable for what he did, so at least they could fire him for making my property unsellable. The members of the BOD said there was nothing I could do about getting Castleschouldt fired, and there was nothing I could do which would place the variance back on the property, if Castleschouldt didn't want to reinstate the variance on the property. The BOD told me to go fish, so I thought maybe the Montgomery County Commissioner's Court could get me remedy.

I noticed two of the elected county commissioners, who sit on the Montgomery County Commissioner's Court, were also appointed members of the Montgomery Central Appraisal District's Board of Directors. Since I wanted to find a way to fire the Chief Appraiser Castleschouldt, and the MCAD BOD would NOT do it for me, I needed to find another way. I got with the secretary for the Montgomery County Commissioner's Court, and found out when the next meeting was going to be held; and asked that I could be placed on the agenda, in that meeting. I was allowed to get 10 minutes of the Commissioner's Court time, to speak my say.

Rabbit Trail: Did you know in every county in Texas there is one, and only one, Constitutional County Judge elected?

Texas Government Code
CHAPTER 26. CONSTITUTIONAL COUNTY COURTS
Sec. 26.005. SEAL. (a) Each county court shall be provided with a seal that has a star with five points engraved in the center. The seal must also have "County Court of _____ County, Texas" engraved on it.

(b) The impress of the seal shall be attached to all process other than subpoenas issued out of the court and shall be used to authenticate the official acts of the county clerk and county judge.
Sec. 26.015. VISITING JUDGE TO TAKE OATH. In addition to any oath previously taken, a person appointed as a visiting judge of __a__ __constitutional county court__, including a person who is a retired, former, or active judge, __shall take the oath of office required by the__ __constitution__.

All the other county judges are called statutory county judges, and are NOT considered a Constitutional County Judge.

As of the writing of this book, the Constitutional County Judge of Montgomery County, Texas, has been indicted. Is this a great country or what?
(Jumping off that rabbit trail.)

At the meeting, I told the Constitutional County Judge who sits as the chairman of the commissioner's court, I had a problem with the MCAD and I wanted him to fire the Chief Appraiser. The constitutional county judge informed me he had no authority, to make anyone on the MCAD to do anything. In fact, the constitutional county judge informed me even if I sued the MCAD and won, it would NOT cost Montgomery County any funds. I got further confused, as to where the MCAD authority originated and where their funding comes from. It seems that the taxing units pay funds, to the central appraisal districts. I looked at the budget of the MCAD for a few years back, and it looks like there is a division of the percentage of each taxing unit that pays the MCAD each year, from the property tax they receive from the Tax Assessor/Collector. The auditor of the MCAD swears up and down that increasing the appraisal of properties, in the appraisal district, does NOT increase the amount of funds going to the MCAD—from the taxing units. Just do a little critical thinking and ask yourself, if there is any possibility to increase the budget of a central appraisal district, by increasing the appraisal of the properties in the district? It doesn't take a brain surgeon to figure out the central appraisal districts have incentive, to increase the amount you pay in property tax, and no incentive at all to reduce it. Look up "conflict of interest." You will come to the conclusion that there definitely is a conflict of interest, if the budget of a central appraisal district is determined, whether there is an increase in property tax that is received by the taxing units.

Rabbit Trail: This is called legalized plunder. Pirates plunder by robbing other ships, of their cargo, on the high seas. Public servants plunder the public, to increase their chance of getting a raise, increase in benefits and getting a better retirement—off the bounty collected from the victims. Public servants don't really care about paying taxes, since it winds back in their own pocket, eventually. The more tax they pay, the bigger their paycheck. Remember that people who work and receive funds from the State canNOT afford to allow their fellow man to be free, from plunder; or the public servant would be forced to find a job, in the private sector, where they must produce something the public wants or needs. If they are NOT capable of doing this, they will become wards of the State, but then receive less than they would, by being active in legalized plunder against his fellow man. Our job is to make the system contract its functions, to the private sector, and get out of this Ponzi scheme that is doomed to fail. Taxes will have to increase, to a point where people will lose everything they have worked for, to pay the retirement of their public servants, or the system will go broke and fail, to meet its obligations, to pay for the retirement of the public servants. This cycle can be avoided by simply contracting with companies in the private sector, to do the functions of the public servants, now. There will be no incentive for the contractors to plunder the public, as their contract is fixed, but it also creates a liability, to perform the functions that were agreed upon. The budget of the municipality will be easier to be managed, and no need to adjust for retirements that will NOT take place. Being a public servant used to be serving the public, and NOT a means to a career. Elect the people that will put it back the way it is supposed to be.

(Jumping off that rabbit trail.)

Through research, I found that the central appraisal districts were created by the Texas Legislature, in 1979. Before 1979, each separate taxing unit appraised the same property and gave a different report to the elected Tax Assessor/Collector; and he/she sent out a bill to the property owners showing different appraisals according to the separate taxing units. My War led me to find out the process that was used in the past, but for now, I will focus upon the result of the creation of the central appraisal districts.

In the original Texas Constitution of 1876, the one we read today, directed the people who worked for the Texas government agencies, under Article 1, Section 2, that every agency created was mandated to be a "republican form of government," whatever that means.

*Texas Constitution, **Article 1, Section 2***
*"All political power is inherent in the people and all free governments are founded on their authority, and instituted for their benefit. The faith of the people of Texas stands pledged to **the preservation of a republican form of government**, and, subject to this limitation only, they have at all times the inalienable right to*

99

alter, reform or abolish their government in such manner as they may think expedient."

Being guaranteed, under **Article 1, Section 2** of the organic 1876 Texas Constitution, a republican form of government guarantees the Texas people the ability to control their public servants' conduct, through the use of a ballot box.

Republican government. *One in which **the powers of sovereignty are vested in the people** and are exercised by the people, either directly, or through representatives chosen by the people, to whom those powers are specially delegated. [In re Duncan, 139 U.S. 449, 11 S.Ct. 573, 35 L.Ed. 219; Minor v. Happersett, 88 U.S. (21 Wall.) 162, 22 L.Ed. 627.]*
Black's Law Dictionary, Fifth Edition, p. 626.

*By the Constitution, **a republican form of government** is **guaranteed** to every State in the Union, and the distinguishing feature of that form is **the right of the people** to choose their own officers for governmental administration, and pass their own laws in virtue of the legislative power reposed in representative bodies, whose legitimate acts may be said to be those of the people themselves; but, while the people are thus the source of political power, their governments, National and State, have been limited by written constitutions, and they have themselves thereby set bounds to their own power, as **against the sudden impulses of mere majorities**.*
In re Duncan, 139 US 449 - Supreme Court 1891

*It may be concluded, therefore, that a fundamental principle associated with **our republican form of government** is that every public officeholder remains in his position at the sufferance and for the benefit of the public, subject to removal from office **by edict of the ballot box** at the time of the next election, or before that time by any other constitutionally permissible means.*
Tarrant County v. Ashmore, 635 SW 2d 417 - Tex: Supreme Court, 1982

There has NOT been any election in any district that has elected any member or any employee of any central appraisal district, in Texas, for the position they currently hold. Apparently the central appraisal districts, created in 1979, are NOT a republican form of government. Through further research and by use of the Public Information Request, I found that Castleschouldt, the chief appraiser of the Montgomery Central Appraisal District, has no Oath of Office or Statement of Officer (some call the bribery statement). If a chief appraiser claims authority over the public, then Article 16, Section 1, of the Texas Constitution, mandates the taking of the Statement of Officer and then the Oath of Office.

THE TEXAS CONSTITUTION
ARTICLE 16. GENERAL PROVISIONS
Sec.A1.AAOFFICIAL OATH. (a) **All** *elected and appointed officers,* **before** *they enter upon the duties of their offices, shall take the following Oath or Affirmation:*
"I, _____, do solemnly swear (or affirm), that I will faithfully execute the duties of the office of _____ of the State of Texas, and will to the best of my ability preserve, protect, and defend the Constitution and laws of the United States and of this State, so help me God."
(b) **All** *elected or appointed officers,* **before** *taking the Oath or Affirmation of office prescribed by this section and entering upon the duties of office, shall subscribe to the following statement:*
"I, _____, do solemnly swear (or affirm) that I have not directly or indirectly paid, offered, promised to pay, contributed, or promised to contribute any money or thing of value, or promised any public office or employment for the giving or withholding of a vote at the election at which I was elected or as a reward to secure my appointment or confirmation, whichever the case may be, so help me God."
(c) Members of the Legislature, the Secretary of State, and **all other** *elected and appointed state officers shall file the signed statement required by Subsection (b) of this section with the Secretary of State* **before** *taking the Oath or Affirmation of office prescribed by Subsection (a) of this section.* **All other** *officers shall retain the*

signed statement required by Subsection (b) of this section with the official records of the office.

(Amended Nov. 8, 1938, and Nov. 6, 1956; Subsecs. (a)-(c) amended and (d)-(f) added Nov. 7, 1989; Subsecs. (a) and (b) amended, Subsecs. (c) and (d) deleted, and Subsecs. (e) and (f) amended and redesignated as Subsec. (c) Nov. 6, 2001.) (TEMPORARY TRANSITION PROVISION for Sec. 1: See Appendix, Note 3.)

Rabbit Trail: I have a good friend that I will call Mr. Phillips. I could devote a complete chapter of the book on Mr. Phillips' escapades, but I will only bring up a single event that involved Mr. Phillips. Mr. Phillips is one of the few people I am acquainted with that knows his rights. Mr. Phillips is one of these fellows that had no Driver License, no Registration, no Safety Sticker; and was pulled over by the local establishment more than a few times as he enjoyed his right to assemble and to be left alone. On one of the occasions, Mr. Phillips was taken to jail, over a Class C Misdemeanor, and the city jailer, doing the custom and policy of the city, was to take prisoners out of their cell and take their picture and their finger prints, before putting them back in their cell. When Mr. Phillips is taken out of his cell, Mr. Phillips informed the city jailer that he didn't consent for his property to be taken by the city. Mr. Phillips informed the city jailer that his image, his finger prints, along with other bodily functions are his personal property, and that Article 1, Section 17 forbid the taking of such property, without compensation or his consent. The city jailer called for help and when help arrived, the city jailer informed Mr. Phillips they were going to take his finger prints, or break his fingers in the attempt. Mr. Phillips said: "I know that you have the ability to do anything to me that you are physically capable of doing. I just know that you haven't got the authority to do it. Do what you will." The city jailer put Mr. Phillips back in his cell.

(Jumping off that rabbit trail.)

Texas Constitution Article 1
*Sec.A17. TAKING, DAMAGING, OR DESTROYING PROPERTY FOR PUBLIC USE; SPECIAL PRIVILEGES AND IMMUNITIES; CONTROL OF PRIVILEGES AND FRANCHISES. (a) **No person's property** shall be taken, damaged, or destroyed for or applied to public use without adequate compensation being made, **unless by the consent** of such person,...*

The correlation between the story of Mr. Phillips and the chief appraiser is the assumption the chief appraiser acts, upon some authority that apparently does NOT involve the Texas Constitution. Having no Oath of Officer, there can never be a claim from anyone Castleschouldt violated his Oath of Office, since he has none. The real question is: "Where does the authority originate that allows the chief appraiser to use his discretion that would affect the public?" I really can't find the answer to this question as, of the writing of this book. As we go along, you too will see that the judicial system does what is necessary to keep that information hidden from the public, and to never confirm or deny that the central appraisal district(s) are NOT a republican form of government.

So, the creation of the central appraisal districts is unconstitutional, since they have no oversight, by any elected official that could lose his position for their bad behavior. I have found no ballot box available to get the Chief Appraiser fired, from his appointed position. Article 1, Section 2, of the Texas Constitution, is secured by Article 1, Section 29 of the Texas Constitution, where is states that the Texas Legislature is without power to create a law that would abridge the right to preserve the republican form of government, but apparently the Texas Legislature did violate their Oath of Office—by creating an unconstitutional entity, called the central appraisal district that is NOT fazed by any ballot box. How do unconstitutional acts affect my rights and your rights?

It cannot be presumed that __any clause__ in the constitution is intended to be without effect; and therefore such construction is inadmissible, unless the words require it. [5 U.S. 137, 175]

Thus, the particular phraseology of the constitution of the United States confirms and strengthens the principle, supposed to be __essential to all written constitutions__, that a law __repugnant__ to the constitution __is void__, and that courts, as well as other departments, are bound by that instrument. [5 U.S. 137, 180]

MARBURY v. MADISON, 5 U.S. 137 (1803)

As we see above, the Supreme Court of the United States of America does NOT, or at least didn't, look kindly to unconstitutional acts by legislators. If such acts were looked at, as though they never were enacted in the first place, then what does that say about the tax statement sent by the Tax Assessor/Collector, concerning information he acts upon, by an unconstitutional entity called the Montgomery Central Appraisal District? Sounds like I need for the system to take me to court, and prove that I owe the tax.

"There is a principle which is a bar against all information, which is proof against all arguments and which cannot fail to keep a man in everlasting ignorance -- that principle is contempt prior to investigation." -- Herbert Spencer

Having your fate rest in the hands of a jury is the same as entrusting yourself to surgery with a mentally retarded doctor.
-Bill Messing, quoted in Dream World, by Fred Woodworth

Judges are but men, and are swayed like other men by vehement prejudices. This is corruption in reality, give it whatever other name you please. - David Dudley Field

CHAPTER 20
I DIDN'T PAY THE 2006 PROPERTY TAX

By the time January 2006 rolled around, I had done a lot of research, concerning how the previous owners had received the variance of the property tax, for the previous three years before I purchased the property. I found out the previous owners were on first-name basis with the Chief Appraiser, Castleschouldt. I have correspondence between Castleschouldt and the previous owners, talking about their children getting sick from the Black Toxic Mold. I sent a public information request looking for documents in the appraisal district's possession concerning the property I just bought. I received a document, <u>from the appraisal district</u> showing the property should have been torn down, to the slab, and rebuilt.

David and Angela Davis
1504 Memorial Lane
Conroe. TX 77304
No one from Allstate ever said for us to move, not to go into the house, or went over the reports with me.
05-16-01 filed mold claim in person with Allstate agent George Noel. My son Marshall was throwing up two - three times per day during this time.
06-01-01 Don Hildabrandt, (adjustor) came and inspected the home and said he didn't see a problem but will send a company out anyway. For two weeks I searched for a rental home with no previous pets or smokers. Allstate didn't, help, I got sicker.
*02-13-02 TexPowcrVac **remediation bid** is $76K plus verbal of $80K-$100K **for rebuild**.*
*02·25·02 Tommy agreed to pay $153K house, **demo fee**, 3 month lease and clean items that arc salvageable. Gave me demo companies numbers.*

I received documents, <u>from the MCAD</u>, showing that Allstate Insurance Company was going to pay for the removal of the structure, and rebuild the house. But instead, the previous owners may have decided to take the insurance money, and sell the damaged property to me. This is their right, under the law of contracts. This, in itself, did NOT bother me, as I thought I knew what I was doing—when I purchased the property. I knew the repairs that I planned may NOT have worked, and that I may have to sell the property, to someone else, like me that was willing to take the chance of becoming sick, from the property. I just did NOT expect I would be blindsided by the MCAD, so I decided NOT to pay the extortion money, and make them take me to court to get it. I kept the funds in a separate area that was allocated to pay the property tax, if I lost in court. My logic determined that being the defendant, I didn't have to prove I didn't owe the amount of property tax, the system had to prove that I owed the amount claimed. I went to the 2006 protest hearing with the same results, but I still was naïve about appealing the ARB decision, so I waited on the system, to take me to court.

Giving money and power to government is like giving whiskey and car keys to teenage boys. --P.J. O'Rourke, Civil Libertarian

The most absurd apology for authority and law is that they serve to diminish crime. Aside from the fact that the State is itself the greatest criminal, breaking every written and natural law, stealing in the form of taxes, killing in the form of war and capital punishment, it has come to an absolute standstill in coping with crime. It has failed utterly to destroy or even minimize the horrible scourge of its own creation. - Emma Goldman, Anarchism

CHAPTER 21
2007 ASSESSMENT LOST IN THE MAIL

Here it is, in 2007, and no word from the system, about taking me to court—for past property tax I refused to pay. But now, I have two years I haven't paid the property tax. NOT only that, I don't realize the MCAD didn't send me the assessment for 2007, so I do NOT send in a protest letter—like I did last year.

Finally, I receive a threat letter, dated July 9, 2007, from Linebarger, Goggan, Blair, & Sampson, LLP, 103 W. Phillips St., Conroe, Texas 77301; telling me I had ten days to cough up $4,439.98—or they would file suit, to recover the funds. I responded to the threat letter, stating I requested all further correspondence to be sent to us, in our proper name, using the upper and lower case letters—as indicated in my response.

Rabbit Trail: Our study group found out that the Administrative Code, Section 79.31—in 2003 and before—states only All Capital Letters, in a name, will be recognized as a corporation. After 2003, the legislature tried to get tricky, by stating that all Capital Letters, "or" All Lower letters, would be recognized as a corporation. Notice it does NOT say, Upper case with lower case letters will be recognized as a corporation. The recognition of a corporation is by one (all caps), or the other (all lower case), and NOT both. Does a email address have all lower letters?

(Jumping off that rabbit trail.)

Back to the attorneys: I summed up the letter to the attorneys with:

First: *Please provide me with any documentation that would be from J. R. Moore, Jr. Tax Assessor/ Collector that would indicate verification that J. R. Moore has give you authorization to represent the interest of J. R. Moore.*

Next: *Please provide me with any documentation that would indicate that you are qualified to represent J. R. Moore, Jr. Tax Assessor/ Collector by providing your Texas Bar Association's Bar Card number and **a copy of your license to practice law** in the State of Texas.*

Next: *Please provide me a copy of **the actual Bill** that is associated with the Texas Property Code sec. 31.01. (see attached) Your letter provided a Statement that does not indicate to adhere to the Texas Tax Code sec. 31.01 (c) that should **accompany** the Tax Bill of which I have not yet received.*

Next: *Please provide me with a copy of the document entitled "appraisal card" as described by the Texas Administrative code (see attached §9.3001) for the property and years associated with your letter.*

Next: *Please provide me with a copy of the rendering forms for the property and years associated with you letter. Please reference the Administrative Code sec. 9.3031 & 9.3003(b)(3) (see attached).*

Next: *Please provide for me any documentation that would indicate that the property associated with your letter **is "located in this state"** in accordance with the Texas Supreme Court rulings.*

Being a third party debt collector, you must adhere to the Fair Debt Collection Practices Act and provide me with proof as requested above of the alleged tax debt due as indicated by your letter.

Failure to provide me with the requested information, should you file a suit against me, may lead to a counter claim against you and your law firm.

Sincerely,

Bobie Kenneth Townsend

The only response I got back from the law firm was, on September 6, 2007, stating that penalty and interest had increased the amount, to $4,515.23; and that they would be seeking a court order—to sell my property. The law firm never sent the requested documents, which indicates that most of this may be a bluff. But time would tell. I was getting ready for court.

While waiting, for the law firm to start the process, on me; I sent in a public information request, on or about November 1, 2007, to the Tax Assessor/Collector, asking for a copy of the Tax Bill, concerning my property for the years 2006 and 2007, as found in reference under sec. 31.01(a) of the Texas Tax Code. Second, I asked for a copy of the "separate statement" that may or may NOT have accompanied the "tax bill," as found in reference under Section 31.01(c) of the Texas tax Code. Third, I asked for a copy of the document entitled "appraisal card," as described by RULE §9.3001 of the Texas Administrative code, for the years of 2006 & 2007. Fourth, I asked for a copy of the rendering forms associated with my property, during the years of 2006 & 2007. I informed the Tax Assessor/Collector he could reference the Administrative Code Sections 9.3031 & 9.3003(b)(3), concerning the rendering documents. Fifth, I asked for a copy of the assessment that would have applied to my property, for the years 2000 through 2007. What I received was most interesting.

Response to my first request—asking for a copy of the Tax Bill by the Tax Assessor/Collector, I was sent a document entitled, "Statement of 2006 Taxes Due for Montgomery County, et. al." The other document had the same title, other than it was for 2007. Both documents indicated the same "Statement Date," and both had the same "Statement Number." The term, Tax Bill, was nowhere to be found.

Response to my second request—where I was asking for any "separate statement" that may or may NOT have accompanied the "tax bill," I received a couple of documents entitled, "A Comparison of Taxes For The Current Year Verses The Previous 5 Tax Years." Nowhere on either responsive document had the term, "Statement," been indicated.

Response to my third, fourth and fifth requests was, I would have to get such documents, from the MCAD. But along with what I had requested, The Tax Assessor/Collector sent a responsive document, a Statement showing the tax owed and paid, for the years 1995 through 2007. The document indicated the previous owners had paid $10,256.58, from 1995 through 2004 (9 years), when the property was sold to my wife and I. The same statement indicated property taxes, owed from 2005 through 2007 (3 years), equaled $10,968.26. It apparently means a lot to the pocket book, when you know the Chief Appraiser. **It Shocks the Conscience,** to know what they get away with.

"Blessed are those that struggle, for oppression is worse than the grave, tis better to die for a noble cause, than to live and die a slave"
Last Poets

There is no such thing as justice — in or out of court.
- Clarence Darrow, 1936

If the jury have no right to judge of the justice of a law of the government, they plainly can do nothing to protect the people against the oppressions of the government; for there are no oppressions which the government may not authorize by law. - Lysander Spooner, Trial by Jury

CHAPTER 22
LENDER BECOMES THE TAX COLLECTOR

I heard nothing from the law firm, through March of 2008. For obvious reasons, the law firm decided it was better NOT to take me to court, for back taxes, and instead it was better for them to contact Countrywide Home Loans, Inc.—and let them know that property tax was owed, letting them deal with the situation.

I received a letter, dated March 12th, 2008, in the mail—from Countrywide Tax Services Corporation informing me they just paid the property tax indicated, owed on the property. I called Countrywide, and asked if I was NOT allowed some kind of notice, before the taxes were paid by Countrywide. The person on the phone stated it was their policy to give a thirty day notice, before they paid the taxes. I asked for a copy of the notice sent to me. The person checked their records, and then stated it looked like no notice was sent, prior to the payment. Typical. No Administrative due process—just have the banking system become the tax collector, if a mortgage is still attached to the property. It apparently does NOT mean anything the Deed of Trust allows me to defend all liens that occur on the property. How am I allowed to defend a lien, if the bank pays the amount allegedly owed?

Townsend's Deed of Trust
4. Charges; Liens.
Borrower shall promptly discharge any lien which has priority over this Security Instrument unless Borrower: (a) agrees in writing to the payment of the obligation secured by the lien in a manner acceptable to Lender, but only so long as Borrower is performing such agreement; **(b) contests the lien in good faith by, or defends against enforcement of the lien in, legal proceedings** *which in*

*Lender's opinion operate to prevent the enforcement of the lien while those proceedings are pending, but only until such proceedings are concluded; or (c) secures from the holder of the lien an agreement satisfactory to Lender subordinating the lien to this Security Instrument. If Lender determines that any part of the Property is subject to a lien which can attain priority over this Security Instrument, **Lender may give Borrower <u>a notice identifying the lien</u>. Within 10 days of <u>the date on which that notice is given</u>, Borrower shall satisfy the lien or take one or more of the actions set forth above in this Section 4.***

The bank and the law firm both know I could NOT claim to be defending anything, as the matter was settled according to the law firm and the tax collector/assessor. But now, I have a problem with the mortgage servicer. We have no meetings of the mind, of what had just occurred. Let's run a rabbit trail scenario.

Rabbit Trail: Let's say you and another decide to go have lunch. After a great meal, you decide you need to go to the restroom. When you return, your luncheon associate hands you a copy of your bill, and states he just paid your bill to the waitress (You say, "Thanks"); and now you hear you owe him $15.26, plus $3.00 tip. Do you legally owe your associate any money? Could he sue you if you did NOT reimburse him what he paid in your behalf? When you went to the restroom, you did NOT tell the associate to pay the waitress—if she showed up while you was gone. He took it upon himself to pay your bill. Let's NOT go down the moral road. But instead, let's go down the legal road. Could he sue you, for NOT paying him back, what he voluntarily paid? We all know he could sue you, but what chances does he have to prove you legally owed him—for voluntarily paying your bill? Do you think the judge would ask the associate to prove there was a contract, whether verbal or written? He could lie and say that there was an understanding; and you could be the bad guy and tell the truth, that the associate did the act voluntarily—but then changed his mind and wanted to be reimbursed. But, legally, could the associate convince the judge to Order you, to reimburse him what he paid in the restaurant—and now also, the court cost the associate spent, by suing you? I think NOT.

(**Jumping off that rabbit trail.**)

So, such reasoning, on my part, has me paying the mortgage servicer the same monthly payment I was always paying, before this property tax issue got out of hand. I consider the payment of the property tax voluntary on the servicer's part, and it could sue me to recover funds it voluntary paid, as if in my behalf. We all know what that will lead to, don't we?

The Bible: 2 Corinthians 13
Verse 1: This is the third time I am coming to you. Any charge must be sustained by the evidence of two or three witnesses.

The Bible: Proverbs 22
Verse 1: A good name is to be chosen rather than great riches, and favor is better than silver or gold.

The Bible: Ecclesiastes 7
Verse 1: A good name is better than precious ointment; and the day of death, than the day of birth.

CHAPTER 23
NON-JUDICIAL FORECLOSURE

Non-Judicial Foreclosure should be outlawed throughout the several states for any mortgage company that intends to sell their interest in the property during the life of the mortgage contract creating clouds on titles throughout the country remaining forever until found, corrected or forgiven by a quiet title action.

The non-judicial foreclosure procedure was reasonable when people got a mortgage loan from a single source. At closing, the borrower received a warranty deed recorded in the county records, showing the borrower owned the subject property. The borrower and the lender signed a loan agreement, which conditioned the amount of payments paid, to a third party escrow company—known as the mortgage servicer; whereby, the mortgage service would transfer the borrower's payments, to the lender—minus a service fee. At closing, the borrower would sign over a special warranty deed, in favor of the lender, and it was held by the mortgage servicer; and the escrow company was under contract, to give such special warranty deed document to the lender, on the condition the borrower got behind a certain amount of payments. The lender receives the loan payments, from the mortgage servicer, which it got from the borrower. This is NOT to say that the lender could NOT sell an amount of future payments to a third party as to generate cash flow for the lender, but the lender still remained the "person entitled to enforce" (PETE) the non-judicial foreclosure, if a default were to occur by the borrower. When the loan is completely paid off, the mortgage servicer returns the original loan document (The Note), the special warranty deed and a release of lien to the borrower. The borrower has a mortgage and special-warranty-deed papers-burning party—to see the negotiable documents go up in flames. If there is a record in the county records showing a lien was against the property, the release of the lien is filed in the county clerk's records. That was that.

But, let's say the borrower fell on hard times, and missed a payment to the lender. The mortgage servicer is obligated, in behalf of the lender, to notice the borrower a payment was late; and now a late charge was owed to the lender, as well. The borrower, still on hard times, is late, again. And then, the mortgage servicer notifies the borrower a default had occurred, and a final default will occur—if accrued payment, interest and late fee are NOT offered in good faith, by such and such date, or the subject property will be non-judicially foreclosed—and the special warranty deed would be transferred, to the lender. The lender would then file the special warranty deed, in the county clerk's office, transferring the property back to the lender, without having to go to court.

What would become of the special warranty deed made out to the lender if the lender sold the loan, to another? Think of the problem the one who bought the loan would have, if there was a default. It definitely would turn into a judicial matter.

Today's non-judicial foreclosure creates clouds, on titles, throughout the United States of America. There is no special warranty deed associated, with getting a loan from the banking institutions. But rather, a Deed of Trust is created, worded clearly against the borrower, with no accountability, to the lender or its assignees. Ninety-Nine point Ninety-Nine (99.99) percent of all bank loans are NOT associated with the original lender, either days before, or days after, closing on the subject property. Yes, I did say, 'days before closing on the subject property.' A cloud on the title of the subject property probably occurs, at the time of the signing of some of the closing documents—before the day of the actual closing. A cloud on the title of property occurs, when someone claims interest in a piece of property, and has NOT recorded such claim in the county records; but such documentation is generated and does exist, of such claim creating the cloud.

"The illegal we do immediately. The unconstitutional takes a little longer." -- Henry Kissinger

*Here is the often expressed understanding from the United States Supreme Court, that "in common usage, the term **"person"** does not include the Sovereign, statutes employing the **person** are ordinarily construed to exclude the Sovereign." Wilson v. Omaha Tribe, 442 U.S. 653, 667 (1979) (quoting United States v. Cooper Corp., 312 U.S. 600, 604 (1941)). See also United States v. Mine Workers, 330 U.S. 258, 275 (1947).*

In our country the people are sovereign and the Government cannot sever its relationship to the people by taking away their citizenship. Our Constitution governs us and we must never forget that our Constitution limits the Government to those powers specifically granted or those that are necessary and proper to carry out the specifically granted ones. Afroyim v. Rusk, 387 U.S. 253 (1967).

"...and it is the duty of the courts to be watchful for the constitutional rights of the citizen, and against any stealthy encroachments thereon." Byars v. U.S., 273 US 28 (1927)

"The makers of our Constitution undertook....to protect Americans in their beliefs, their thoughts, their emotions, and their sensations. They conferred, as against the Government, the right to be let alone - the most comprehensive of rights and the right most valued by civilized men. To protect that right, every unjustifiable intrusion by the Government upon the privacy of the individual, whatever the means employed, must be deemed a violation of the Fourth Amendment." Olmstead v. U.S., 277 US 438 (1928)

CHAPTER 24
COUNTRYWIDE HAVING PROBLEMS

The original Lender concerning my property in Conroe, Texas, was Countrywide Home Loans, Inc. Countrywide had many different branches of the corporation, which performed different functions in the banking system, for many years. During 2008 and years to come, Countrywide had problems concerning its loaning standard operating procedure (SOP). The news was full of lawsuits, concerning Countrywide and other banking institutions. The Federal Government got into the scheme of things. There are many sources showing the CEO of Countrywide, Angelo R. Mozilo, being compensated as CEO—to the tune of 470 million dollars. Mr. Mozilo settled lawsuits against him, personally, to the tune of 67.5 million dollars. One can only wonder, how Mr. Mozilo got by, with only 400 million left, to scrap by on. One, of such lawsuits, involved MBIA.

__MBIA Sues Countrywide:__ Part of the Solution to Clean Up the Lies
link: http://seekingalpha.com/article/98383-mbia-sues-countrywide-part-of-the-solution-to-clean-up-the-lies
Oct 3, 2010
Yesterday MBIA (MBI) sued Countrywide, now part of Bank of America (BAC), __alleging fraud, misrepresentation and breach of contract__ in connection with over 14 billion worth of MBS-containing Countrywide mortgages and insured by MBIA. MBIA has already __incurred $459 million in losses__. This is the beginning of what may be a long battle by the bond insurers MBIA and Ambac (ABK) to recover part of their losses __from those responsible__, a process they refer to as remediation.
*****

During further research, concerning Countrywide, I found interesting documentation recorded, with the Texas Secretary of State. I have, in my possession, a document I received from the Texas Secretary of State indicating a mortgage service company, called "Countrywide Home Loans Servicing LP," name was changed, to, "BAC Home Loans Servicing, LP"—on April 27th, 2009, by Jack W. Schakett, President and Chief Executive Officer, for Countrywide GP, LLC. Keep in mind, it was NOT an officer of Bank of America who made the name change.

CHAPTER 25
MERS 1 & 2

The following will test the reader's resilience, in really wanting to know about MERS. But, if you have a mortgage, or plan to get a mortgage someday, this is where you will really learn. When you read the term, "MERS," in your Deed of Trust, the wool is being pulled over your eyes—by the one that has you sign the Deed of Trust.

*In re Mitchell, Case No. BK-S-07-16226-LBR (Bankr. D. NY 2009): There is **no evidence of the alleged relationship** of the principal of which MERS#1 assumes to act.*

*In re Vargas, 396 B.R. 511, 517 (Bankr. C.D. CA 2008): MERS#1 **failed to identify the source of the authority to assign the Note** making such assignment improper.*

*Mortgage Electronic Registration Systems, Inc. v. Graham and Martinez, 229 P.3d 420 (KS Ct.App. 2010): "... there is **no evidence** that MERS received permission **to act as an agent for Countrywide**."*

*OneWest Bank v. Drayton, 2010-20429 (NY S.Ct. 2010): "MERS as 'nominee' **has no independent authority** and must prove its authority on behalf of the true owner of the note and mortgage."*

*Saxon Mortgage Services, Inc. v. Hillery, 2008 WL 5170180 (USDCt. N.D. CA 2008): Being **no evidence** that MERS#1 **was ever the holder of the Note** or given authority to assign, the assignment and recordation of the assignment was ineffective.*

Most, if NOT all, Federal National Mortgage Association (Fannie Mae)-associated loans involve something called MERS. Most Deed of Trusts name MERS, as something that's called a "nominee," for the original Lender of the so-called loan. MERS is NOT what most people will tell you it is, especially from the courts or attorneys. MERS is like a blind octopus that does NOT know what each of its tentacles is touching.

> *Townsend' Deed of Trust*
> *DEFINITIONS*
> *Words used in multiple sections of this document are defined below and other words are defined in Sections 3, 11, 13, 18, 20 and 21. Certain rules regarding the usage of words used in this document are also provided in Section 16. **Borrower is the grantor** under this Security Instrument.*
> *(C) **"Lender" is** COUNTRYWIDE HOME LOANS, INC.*
> *(E) **"MERS" is** Mortgage Electronic Registration Systems, Inc. MERS is a separate corporation that is **acting solely as a nominee** for Lender and Lender's successors and assigns. **MERS is the beneficiary** under this Security Instrument. MERS is organized and existing **under the laws of Delaware**, and has an address and telephone: number of Post Office Box 2026, Flint, Michigan 48501-2026, tel. (888) 679-MERS.*

I have found that MERS canNOT be a beneficiary of anything or obtain interest in any Note; and MERS can and does mean more than one entity.

> *This Court finds that **MERS's theory** that it can act as a "common agent" for undisclosed principals **is not supported by the law**. The relationship between MERS and its lenders and its distortion of its alleged "nominee" status **was appropriately described** by the Supreme Court of Kansas as follows: "The parties appear to have defined the word [nominee] **in much the same way that the blind men of Indian legend described an elephant - their description depended on which part they were touching at any given time**."*
> *Landntark Nat 'l Bank v. Kesler, 216 P .3d 158, 166-67 (Kan. 2010).*

It is common knowledge among the ranks of the banking associations "MERS" means, "Mortgage Electronic Registration System, Inc." (I'll call this MERS#1.) But, I found, through research, "MERS" may also mean, "MERSCORP, Inc." (I'll call this MERS#2.)

> *"As a requirement for mortgages that were securing loans or promissory notes that were sold to securitize trust, the rating agencies would only allow mortgages MERS — well let me step back. They required that **a bankruptcy remote single purpose entity** be created in order for transactions holding loans secured by MERS, by mortgages MERS served as mortgagee to be in those pools and receive a rating, an investment grade rating without any changes to the credit enhancement. They required that to be **a bankruptcy remote single purpose subsidiary of MERS, of Merscorp.**"*
> *Secretary and treasurer of MERS: deposition of WILLIAM HULTMAN - (page 32, lines 9-20): BANK OF NEW YORK AS TRUSTEE FOR THE CERTIFICATE HOLDERS CWABS,INC. ASSET-BACKED CERTIFICATES,SERIES 2005-AB3 Vs. UKPE, Case No. F-10209-08, Superior Court of New Jersey (April 20, 2010)(DEPO WH)*

As you go through my research of MERS, you run across a term, **"bankruptcy remote single purpose entity."** Then, you find out MERS has claimed that status. In layman's terms, my understanding, of **"bankruptcy remote status,"** is that it holds no assets, where lacking such assets could cause a bankruptcy. This shows to be confirmed, by *MERS v. Estrella*, 390 F.3d 522, 524-525, where, in this case, you can find the transcript of the Secretary and Treasurer of MERS, Mr. William Hultman (Mr. Hultman), giving a deposition concerning the business practices of MERS. The following statements, given by Mr. Hultman, will be designated, as "DEPO WH – Page #-#".

> *MERS#1 **does not** list as an asset on its books any mortgage and it **carries no insurance** to protect any interest in a mortgage. (See DEPO WH - Page 134-135)*
> *MERS#1 is **not entitled** to any proceeds of a Note. (See DEPO WH - Page 138)*

MERS#1 has __no monetary interest in a Note__. (See DEPO WH - Page 150)
MERS#1 has __no entitlement to money paid under the Note__. (See DEPO WH - Page 151)
MERS#1 has __no beneficial interest in a Note__ even if it is said to be the note-holder. (See DEPO WH - Page 153)

The above term, "Note," references the negotiable instrument the Borrower signs, at closing—commonly known as a "Promissory Note."

I have found, MERS#2 has documented Rules the members of MERS#1 have to go by. The June 2009 "MERSCORP, Inc. Rules of Membership" (MERSCORP Rules) show, specifically, members of the MERS system are members of "MERSCORP, Inc."—and NOT those of Mortgage Electronic Registration Systems, Inc.. MERSCORP Rules, Rule 1, § 1 defines MERSCORP, Inc., as "MERS."

MERSCORP Rules fail to state Mortgage Electronic Registration Systems, Inc. has any members.

MERSCORP Rules fail to reference any term in the document, to the Uniform Commercial Code (UCC); and such terms canNOT be presumed, to mean the same thing found in the UCC.

MERSCORP Rules fail to have a requirement either MERS#1 or MERS#2 or its members should comply with, or even know of, the UCC—as they purport to transfer interest, on the Note and Deed of Trusts, under the name of MERS#1.

MERSCORP Rules were apparently created in a fashion to mislead judges—knowing the "MERS" designation is really MERSCORP, Inc., and NOT Mortgage Electronic Registration Systems, Inc.

MERSCORP Rules, Rule 3, § 3(a)(ii)
*"..., assign the lien of any mortgage naming MERS as the mortgagee when the Member is also the current promissory note-holder, or if the mortgage is registered on the MERS® System, **is shown to be registered to the Member**,..."*

MERSCORP Rules, Rule 3, § 3(a)(ii) describes a situation that never existed.

MERSCORP Rules, Rule 2, § 5(a) specifically states MERSCORP, Inc. is defined as the wholly-owned subsidiary of Mortgage Electronic Registration Systems, Inc.; or, in other words, 'MERS is the owner and subsidiary of MERS'.

MERSCORP Rules Rule 2, § 4(b) confirms MERS#1 does NOT make decisions or give instructions, pertaining to the Note and Deed of Trust, indicating MERS#1 could NOT be a nominee or agent, for the "Person Entitled To Enforce" (PETE).

MERSCORP Rules Rule 2, § 6 indicates MERS#2 will abide by the PETE, but if there is no instruction from the PETE, then MERS#2 will rely upon what the loan servicer says to be done.

MERSCORP Rules Rule 2, § 6 also indicates that instructions from the PETE must be given to MERS#2 as well as MERS#1, again showing MERS#1 will NOT act as a nominee or agent, for the PETE.

MERSCORP Rules show MERS#1 never owns any legal ownership or economic interest, in a Note.

MERSCORP Rules Rule 2, § 7 show it is the responsibility, of the members of MERS#2, to track Notes, and NOT by MERS#1 or MERS#2—if any such tracking takes place.

MERSCORP Rules Rule 3, § 1 shows MERSCORP, Inc.—and NOT Mortgage Electronic Registration Systems, Inc.—has the obligation of performance.

MERSCORP Rules confirm, if MERS#1 does NOT perform its functions, MERS#2 is obligated to see such performance is done.

MERSCORP Rules Rule 3, § 3 shows MERSCORP, Inc. can give its members, "a corporate resolution designating one or more officers of such Member, ... as "certifying officers" of Mortgage Electronic Registration Systems, Inc."

MERSCORP Rules, Rule 3, § 3(a), last sentence, shows MERSCORP, Inc. is indemnified of any wrong doing, by the so-called "certifying officer;" confirming MERS#1 and MERS#2 have no control over such actions, which the members, or their so-called "certifying officers," may do—in the name of MERS#1.

Since the "certifying officer" is NOT directed by MERS#1 or MERS#2, then such assignments must state who has designated such action to take place—making such alleged assignment vague and improper and creating a cloud, on the title of who the PETE was, at the time of the assignment; and whether the PETE did actually delegate such assignment, to another, with 100% of the rights, as per the UCC.

UCC § 3-203(d) does NOT allow a "certifying officer," in possession of a Note and Deed of Trust, to make the determination to enforce the right to foreclose—as the "certifying officer" would NOT be able to convey 100% of the interest, in the Note, nor transfer it—pursuant to UCC § 3-203(a).

MERSCORP Rules, Rule 8 encourages the violation of the UCC, as indicated above, by NOT requiring any identification of, or permission from, the PETE—for any foreclosure-related dealings.

MERSCORP Rules, Rule 9 confirms information, placed in the MERS System by the members themselves, does NOT belong to MERS#1 or MERS#2, but to the members who entered the information. Federal Rules of Evidence (F.R.E.) § 804(b)(3) allows 'statements against interest,' concerning the admissibility of the MERSCORP Rules and any content of (Link:) www.mersinc.org, which any Defendant Bank might claim to be in force—at the time of the alleged assignment—be made available.

Saying all that, we all should conclude, as mentioned, MERS is a blind octopus that does NOT know what each of its tentacles is touching. Again, MERS does NOT add one record in its so-call electronic system. Only the members can and do all entries found, in the record. So, there is no independent record-keeping system that shows the chain of title, in any assignment of a Note and Deed of Trust. The problem with that is.... Such so-called assignments NOT recorded in the Texas County Clerk's Office are a violation of State law.

Texas Local Government Code
*Sec. 192.007. RECORDS OF RELEASES AND OTHER ACTIONS. (a) To release, transfer, assign, or take another action relating to an instrument that is filed, registered, or recorded in the office of the county clerk, **a person must file, register, or record another instrument relating to the action in the same manner as the original instrument was required to be filed, registered, or recorded**. (b) An entry, including a marginal entry, may not be made on a previously made record or index to indicate the new action.*

The chain of title is necessary, to eliminate a cloud on a title. The Deed of Trust indicates there is an original Lender, and it is usually recorded, into a Texas County Clerk's Office. The Texas Legislature finds it necessary, if there was an assignment of the Note and Deed of Trust, then the Texas County Clerk needs to record the assignment that would effect the chain of title, of the particular piece of property.

This MERS system, of recording the so-called assignments of the Note and Deed of Trust, through the Mortgage Electronic Registration System, is NOT done by any credible person who could be held accountable the transaction actually occurred;

whereby the electronic log could be printed out, certified and recorded in a Texas County Clerk's Office. There is no one employed, by MERS, who would have first hand information an assignment actually occurred and was documented, in the electronic record. It was only employees of law firms or banks that made the entries in the MERS data log; and as far as I can find out, there is no paper trail created that would support the reason, for the MERS data entries. Later on, I will name people and corporations pretending to be employees of MERS who create fraudulent documentation, record the invalid assignments in the County Clerk's Office and steal property from people—using unauthorized behavior, in the name of MERS.

One major Fact, concerning MERS in Texas, is: I have a record named, "The Certificate of Amendment," dated December 3rd, 2010, from the Texas Secretary of State showing "Mortgage Electronic Registration Systems, Inc." stopped doing business in Texas, on September 15th, 2009—by changing its name, to "Altec Properties, Inc." The Certificate of Amendment changing the name of MERS was signed, by a "Robert Jacobsen" claiming to be an authorized Officer, of MERS. The Certificate of Amendment document I have displays a Filing Number, 801128564, & a Document Number, 274759530002. Check it out for yourself, by getting one of your own, from the Texas Secretary of State.

Saying all that above, keep in mind that most of the judges and attorneys I encounter have knowledge of the above information about MERS, and more. Nevertheless, the judges ignore this information about MERS, as though the information is irrelevant—when a case is marked for dismissal.

For those that desire to learn more about MERS and non-judicial foreclosures, I recommend **"Fighting the Foreclosure Machine"** by Robert M. James B.B.A., M.P.A., J.D.. Mr. James also has a research paper called "Shellgame-MERS" that you can acquire that goes into MERS in more detail.

CHAPTER 26
MY FIRST APPEAL TO A TEXAS DISTRICT COURT

In 2009, I believed that I had my ducks in a row, concerning the MCAD; and I was ready to see what I could do, in a Texas District Court. On or about December 30th, 2009, I filed my petition in Conroe, Texas; and it was assigned to the 359th District Court, the Honorable Judge Kathleen A. Hamilton presiding. The case is styled: *Bobie Kenneth Townsend vs. Montgomery Central Appraisal District*, Cause Number: 09-12-12429. I had also sued Mark Castleschoultd, the Chief Appraiser, in his official capacity. I really wanted to get this guy fired. My causes of action were as follows: negligent hiring; breach of fiduciary duty; theft of property; and fraud. Since this was my first rodeo, I had little experience dealing with court stuff, so I logically went through the well known *O'Conner's Texas Causes of Action* book, and looked up anything that seemed to relate to the taking of my property, by the MCAD.

Negligent Hiring had only a few elements that I needed to prove: 1) Defendants owed the plaintiff a legal duty to hire, supervise, train, or retain competent employees. 2) Defendants wantonly, maliciously, and knowingly breached that duty. This sounded like a pretty simple thing, for me to prove to a jury. Now claiming that MCAD breached their fiduciary duty, to me, may be a hit or miss. The elements that I had to prove were the defendants has the duty of full disclosure; that is, a duty NOT to conceal matters that might influence a fiduciary's actions, to the principal's prejudice. MCAD wantonly, maliciously, and knowingly failed, to notice plaintiff, purchasing a piece of damaged private property, in Montgomery County, would be considered repaired—under the policy or custom of the defendants. Logically to me, at the time, MCAD has an obligation to notice the public buying damaged property (in Montgomery County) would make it considered brand-spanking-new—right after closing on the property. If the custom and policy of MCAD would be considered unreasonable, then the public was due notice of its unreasonableness.

Theft of Property can be accomplished in a variety of different ways. Most people think of the criminal aspects of the claim. I was NOT claiming that MCAD did a criminal act of theft, but rather a civil breach of theft. Classifying a piece of property as commercial, when in fact it is private and non-income producing, is a type of theft—by conversion. I claimed the defendants wantonly, maliciously, and knowingly appropriated the private real property, by taking it without the plaintiff's effective consent. The defendants created the illusion plaintiff had somehow rendered his private real property, for taxation, giving defendants dominion, over plaintiff's private real property. The defendants submitted false documentation, to the Montgomery County Tax Assessor/Collector, as to insinuate plaintiff had duly rendered the said property for taxation; as to establish plaintiff's private real property, on the appraisal roll—creating a theft of property and no benefit to plaintiff, by such action. That is exactly what the appraisal district did.

The claim of fraud is very hard to prove, in court. I found multiple cases showing different elements that were to be proven, and all the defendant needs to disprove is just one of the elements. I found a few cases where the trial judge made up elements, and simply claimed that such mystery element was NOT proven by the claimant. The elements I found in O'Conner's were: 1. There was a transaction involving real estate. Plaintiff purchased the property based specifically on information provided by defendants, on their web site, (Link:) http://www.mcad-tx.org. 2. During the transaction, the defendants made a false representation of fact. The defendants' web site, (Link:) http://www.mcad-tx.org, showed the previous owners of said property were granted a variance, due to the damage of the said property, for 3 years prior to plaintiff purchasing the property. 3.

Defendants failed to inform plaintiff purchasing a damaged piece of property (within Montgomery County) made the property considered repaired—by the simple act of purchasing the property. 4. The false representation was made for the purpose of inducing the plaintiff, to enter into a contract. Omission of defendants' policy or custom, as to the repair of damaged property—on defendants' web site, (Link:) http://www.mcad-tx.org—was to increase the amount of tax donations, of damaged property. 5. The plaintiff relied, on their false representation—by entering into the contract. All this I could prove, which amounted to a cause of action, of fraud—or as I thought, at the time.

I really did NOT know I was on a road that could remove all property tax, from private property. At the time, I just wanted the variance placed back on the property, so that I could attempt to repair the property; and if all my effort was futile, I could at least sell the property—to someone else that could attempt to repair it—and get my money back. But that was NOT meant to be. Instead, I found out "firms, companies and corporations" were the only things, in Texas, required to actually owe property tax—unless a private owner(s) rendered their property, for taxation. Go back and review Chapter 12, "**Can You Really Own Property**?" I never realized the deceit required by the judicial system, to keep this information under wraps. It is my hope that the information that I will reveal to you about the Judicial Branch of the system will **Shock the Conscience** as it has mine. Shinning light upon the actions of certain judges and justices may start the snowball rolling to remove the rot and replace with moral fiber. I had no idea at what lengths attorneys would go to protect the system that they have created.

My first attempt lasted, from December 30th, 2009 to June 15, 2010, when Judge Hamilton dismissed my case, for "lack of subject-matter jurisdiction." The system does NOT allow a *pro se* to know why his case has been dismissed. When you look at the pleadings, from the attorney representing the defendants, you find he claims by the Texas Tax Code blah, blah, blah .... The attorney never mentions the jurisdictional statement from my Original Petition.

Townsend's Jurisdictional Statement:
"That the jurisdiction of this court is invoked under the provisions of Article 5, Section 8 of the Texas Constitution."

Article 5, Section 8 of the Texas Constitution is pretty straight forward as to the issues the District Court can hear.

Article 5 *of the Texas Constitution*
Sec. 8. *JURISDICTION OF DISTRICT COURT. District Court jurisdiction consists of exclusive, appellate, and original jurisdiction of* **all** *actions, proceedings, and remedies, except in cases where exclusive, appellate, or original jurisdiction may be conferred by this Constitution or other law on some other court, tribunal, or administrative body. District Court judges* **shall have the power** *to issue writs necessary to enforce their jurisdiction. The District Court* **shall have** *appellate jurisdiction and general supervisory control over the County Commissioners Court, with* **such exceptions** *and under such regulations as may be prescribed by law.*
(Amended Aug. 11, 1891, Nov. 6, 1973, and Nov. 5, 1985.)

Do you think Judge Hamilton does NOT know what the term, "all," means? I really think she does; but if you really do NOT want to deal with some issue, just claim you lack jurisdiction; and let the appellate court deal with it—if the plaintiff can or will spend the extortion fees to appeal. The intention was to get rid of the case, as soon as possible, so Judge Hamilton dismissed the case, for lack of jurisdiction. Problem was, the attorneys forgot to serve me, with their motion to dismiss special exceptions.

I had previously filed a motion for default judgment, since the attorneys did not answer the petition. I put in a motion for reconsideration, since I was not served with the defendant's answer. Attorneys said, 'oops,' and filed their "Defendant's Motion To Set Aside Order and Request For New Submission Date." Judge Hamilton found rules are just a guide line, and granted their motion; and set aside her Order dismissing the case—ignoring my motion for default judgment. Defendants' attorney file their "Defendant's Second Supplemental Original Answer, Plea To The Jurisdiction, Special Exceptions, Special Denials, Affirmative Defenses and Counterclaim."

Since the defendant's document covered so much, I decided to respond with: "Plaintiff's Response to Defendants' Plea to the Jurisdiction," "Plaintiff's Response to Defendants' Special Exceptions," "Plaintiff's Response to Defendants' Affirmative Defenses," "Plaintiff's Original Answer To Defendants Counterclaim," & "Plaintiff's Notice of Lack of Oath of Office." Throwing in the kitchen sink, I also filed my, "Notice of Bobie Kenneth Townsend Proof of Sovereignty," where my genealogy was attached—showing the seed where I came from. I could not understand how an entity, like the central appraisal district, got jurisdiction over a son of the land and still don't.

I filed many more pleadings, where the attorneys felt it necessary, to file their: "Defendant's Third Supplemental Original Answer, Plea To The Jurisdiction, Special Exceptions, Special Denials, and Affirmative Defenses," but left off the counterclaim. They did feel it necessary, to file a Verification document by Castleschouldt, which had no firsthand information to verify. The attorneys filed a lot of separate responses to my other documents. Judge Hamilton got tired of the case file getting filled up, so she dismissed the case—for lack of jurisdiction, once more. I filed my motion for reconsideration, and a request for findings of fact and conclusions of law, but Judge Hamilton ignored it all— and let me appeal.

The appeal went to Ninth Court of Appeals, at 1001 Pearl St., Beaumont, Texas 77701. The case number is 09-10-00394-CV. The court fee was $175.00, and it was paid on September 9th, 2010. The District Court Clerk fee, to send the record to the appellate court, was $375.00. Judge Hamilton refused to allow one open hearing, to discuss anything, so there was no transcription fee. Lucky me.

It took almost a year, for the Appellate Court Justices McKeithen, C.J., Kreger and Horton, JJ, to screw over a *pro se*. On July 28, 2011, Justice Hollis Horton gave the opinion of the court that the justices affirmed Judge Hamilton's lack of subject matter jurisdiction, due to the fact that I did NOT file my petition, in a timely manner. The justices, parroting the attorney for the defendants, claimed I did NOT file my petition timely, as the Tax Code mandates in §42.21(a). The justices stated I had only sixty (60) days, to file my petition; but I filed my petition after that time, to challenge the increase in market value, of my property. The Justices skipped over the Article 5 Section 8 jurisdictional statement, using the "other court" provision, stating Section 8 would have allowed the District Court to hear my other claims, if the appellant just would have filed his petition, within the 60 day window. So, if you want to claim "fraud" against an appraisal district, be sure to file the claim within the 60 day window—that is, if you protest your property tax. The Great and Powerful OZ has spoken. What a four-slice stack of baloney, in black robes.

I filed a Motion for Reconsideration, pointing out the tax code did NOT give any District Court Judge directions, how to address the causes of action that I had claimed. I pointed out Article 5, Section 8 specifically gave jurisdiction to District Courts, for ALL actions. The response I received, from the Appellate Court, was "Motion Denied." No other response. They might as well said: "What are you going to do about it, if we don't reconsider it? Because we never will."

I appealed to the Supreme Court of Texas, on or about September 28th, 2011, and it was assigned case number 11-0777. I actually thought the case number (777) was a sign things would be different. Apparently I did NOT follow the Appellate Rule 53.6, and my petition for review was too long—so I was Ordered to redraft my Petition for Review, and I did, on or about October 21st, 2011. On January 6, 2012, the Texas Supreme Court decided NOT to hear my petition. As with the Ninth Court of Appeals, my Motion For Reconsideration was met with "Motion Denied."

The following year, Appellate Rule 53.6 was deleted.

At this point in time, I had reservations maybe things may have been different, if I had just followed the rules found in the Tax Code, but as you will discover, "rules are just a guide line" that are easily ignored, if needed. **It Shocks the Conscience.**

People today enslave themselves when all that freedom requires is the word "No."
Wendy McElroy, 1995

"The truth is, all might be free if they valued freedom, and defended it as they ought. ...If therefore a people will not be free; if they have not virtue enough to maintain their liberty against a presumptuous invader, they deserve no pity, and are to be treated with contempt and ignominy."
-- Samuel Adams

CHAPTER 27
MY SECOND LAWSUIT

On or About August 20th, 2010, I filed another appeal, from the farce of the ARB hearing, at the MCAD. Here again, I did NOT follow the rules found in the Tax Code, and I sued the wrong party.

I again filed my petition in Conroe, Texas; and was again assigned to the 359th District Court, and again the Honorable Judge Kathleen A. Hamilton was presiding. The case is styled: *Bobie Kenneth Townsend vs. Appraisal Review Board of Montgomery County, Texas*, Cause Number: 10-08-09020.

Through the research at that time, I found that the ARB is the problem and NOT the solution, to get my property off the appraisal roll. The ARB refused to reinstate the variance, again. I sued, using four different causes of action; but looking back, cause of actions 3 & 4 were the same cause of action.

The ARB is NOT a republican form of government, even though they have sworn an oath to guarantee same. 1) There is no official elected, by the body politic within Montgomery County, that oversees the official, or otherwise, actions by the ARB. 2) Members of the ARB have taken an Oath of Office, as required by Article 16, Section 1 of the Texas Constitution, to guarantee a republican form of government. 3) The ARB is without authority (jurisdiction), under the Texas Constitution, to confirm non-income producing private property, to be placed on the appraisal roll.

The ARB failed to address, in the hearing, whether plaintiff's non-income producing private property **should NOT be taxed in Montgomery County**—the actual subject of the protest plaintiff had filed, in the Property Tax – Notice of Protest Form 50-132.

The ARB failed to address, in the hearing, whether or NOT plaintiff's non-income producing private property **exemption was denied, modified or canceled**—the actual subject of the protest plaintiff had filed, in the Property Tax – Notice of Protest Form 50-132.

I claim that the ARB failed to address, in the hearing, whether my non-income producing private property **should NOT be taxed in this appraisal district—or in one or more taxing units**—the actual subject of protest I had filed, in the Property Tax – Notice of Protest Form 50-132.

I claimed the ARB failed to order the Chief Appraiser to produce the rendering document which rendered my non-income producing private property for taxation. The failure of the ARB, to do their fiduciary duty, caused a violation of Article 1, Section 19, of the Texas Constitution. The ARB failed to give plaintiff due process by denying his right to examine the documents that the Chief Appraiser relied upon to place plaintiff's non-income producing private property on the appraisal roll.

What actually occurred, at the ARB hearing, was just comparing Apples and Oranges, again. Market value was the only issue discussed, by the ARB members and the appraiser representing the MCAD; and none of the issues were discussed from my Notice of Protest Form 50-132.

This matters little, when you do NOT know what the rules are, when it comes to names of entities. When you look at structure, of the Montgomery Central Appraisal District (MCAD), how could you possibly know the ARB is NOT considered part of the MCAD? This is something hard for me to get right, in my mind, even today.

When you look at the Final Order issued by the ARB, concerning the property protest hearing, you find the address and the phone number, of the ARB, are exactly the same address and phone number, of the MCAD; but the system claims no relationship, between the two. The ARB final order is mandated, by Section 41.47 of the Tax Code, to inform the property owner, "**in clear and concise language** of the property owner's right to appeal the board's decision to district court." People without an attorney should reasonably conclude **clear and concise language** would be found in the Order, stating who needed to be sued, in the appeal.

Texas Tax Code
Sec. 41.47. DETERMINATION OF PROTEST.
*(a) The appraisal review board hearing a protest **shall determine** the protest and make its decision by written order.*
*(e) The notice of the issuance of the order **must contain** a prominently printed statement in **upper-case bold lettering** informing the property owner **in clear and concise language** of the property **owner's right to appeal** the board's decision to district court. The statement **must describe** the deadline prescribed by Section 42.06(a) of this code for filing a written notice of appeal, and the deadline prescribed by Section 42.21(a) of this code for filing the petition for review with the district court.*

But, I found out later, the courts have already determined the ARB and the MCAD are, in some manner, separate entities that canNOT be considered one and the same. How would you know? How would I know? I'm supposed to be clairvoyant, and know about and understand Section 42.21(b) before being aware of its existence?

Texas Tax Code
Section 42.21(b) "...Any other petition for review under this chapter must be brought against the appraisal district. A petition for review **is not required** *to be brought against the appraisal review board,* **but may be brought against** *the appraisal review board in addition to* **any other required party, if appropriate.***"*

How anyone would obtain the knowledge to look in Section 42.21(b) of the Tax Code, the court did NOT elaborate. Do you see the term, "if appropriate," above? If the MCAD and the ARB are separate entities, and the ARB will NOT be considered part of the appraisal district, then for what purpose is the term, "if appropriate"? As you will see, by the opinion of the Ninth Court of Appeals, since the ARB canNOT be considered part of the appraisal district; shouldn't Section 42.21(b) state the ARB canNOT be the only defendant? The term, "if appropriate," leads non-attorneys to believe the ARB can be the only party of the appraisal district, in the appeal of the Final Order—as I did think so—at the time.

Below is a representation, of a Final Order of the ARB. Notice the reference, "Tax Code, Section 42.08(D)." That subsection of the Tax Code does NOT exist, "in" or "at" law.

Rabbit Trail: Did you ever think about you are "in" a lawsuit, but if you hire an attorney he/she is "at" a lawsuit? I would rather hire an attorney that was "in" it, with me. But, it seems that you can ONLY find an "Attorney at Law" to hire. Go review, again, those four different Oaths an attorney takes, when they get their Bar Card.
(Jumping off that rabbit trail.)

There is no (D) subsection, of Section 42.08. I requested, in writing, Judge Hamilton of the 359th District Court have the ARB correct their Final Order, and direct the property owners where to find out how, to appeal their decision. I also wrote and informed the MCAD the Final Order of the ARB was incorrect; and asked the MCAD to require the ARB to correct their Final Order. I believe the ARB Final Orders still show the same invalid subsection of the Tax Code—that does NOT exist, even today.

APPRAISAL REVIEW BOARD
MONTGOMERY COUNTY TEXAS
109 GLADSTELL - P.O. BOX 2233
CONROE, TEXAS 77305
(936) 756-3354 CONROE (936) 441-2186 METRO

TOWNSEND, B KENNETH & CAROLYN
1504 MEMORIAL DR
CONROE, TX 77304-1647

Re: 6955-00-00200 R120293 TOWNSEND, B KENNETH & CAROLYN
MCDADE ESTATES 01, LOT 2

NOTICE OF ISSUANCE OF FINAL ORDER

*The Appraisal Review Board has made a final decision on your protest. The order determining the protest is indicated below. You have the right to appeal this order to the District Court. If you want to appeal, **you should consult an attorney immediately**. You must file a petition with the District Court within 60 days of the date you receive this notice. If you do appeal and your case is pending, **except as provided under Tax Code, Section 42.08(D)**, you must pay lesser of this amount of taxes not in dispute or the amount of taxes due on the property under the order from which the appeal is taken, **to each taxing unit** before taxes for the year become delinquent.*

*You may have the right to appeal this order through binding arbitration if the value determined by the order is $1 million or less; the property in dispute is real property; the ARB order determining protest concerns **either the appraised or market value of the property**; taxes have been timely paid; and a lawsuit has not been filed in district court. A request for binding arbitration including the appropriate arbitration fee must be filed with the appraisal district* within 45 days of the property owner receiving the ARB order determining the protest. If a property owner files a request for binding arbitration, the property owner may not file a suit in district court. A copy of a request for binding arbitration form is included with this notice.

ORDER DETERMINING PROTEST

On 6/21/2010, the Appraisal Review Board of Montgomery County, Texas, heard the above protest **concerning the appraisal record** for tax year 2010.

The taxpayer and **chief appraiser appeared**. A summary of the chief appraiser's testimony, a list of witnesses and a list of evidence submitted appear as part of the records of this case.

The taxpayer's notice of protest was filed in time. The Appraisal Review Board found that it had jurisdiction over the case. The Appraisal Review Board delivered written notice of the hearing in the manner required by law.

VALUE IS OVER MARKET VALUE, VALUE IS UNEQUAL COMPARED WITH OTHER PROPERTIES

Having heard the evidence and arguments from both sides, the Appraisal Review Board with quorum present determined that:

The appraisal records are incorrect and should be changed.

The Appraisal Review Board therefore ORDERS that:

The 2010 value is $ 124,900

Terry F Bowie, Chairman
Appraisal Review Board

Looking at the above Final Order, you see the ARB states the Chief Appraiser was at the hearing, well, Mark Castleschouldt was NOT at the hearing, even though Section 41.45(c), of the Texas Tax Code, states the chief appraiser will be at every protest hearing.

Tax Code
Sec. 41.45. HEARING ON PROTEST.
(c) The chief appraiser **shall appear at each protest hearing** before the appraisal review board to represent the appraisal office.

Also, the Final Order labels me, as a "taxpayer," so let's see what a definition, of a "taxpayer," is according to the Texas Legislature.

Ch. 566   60TH LEGISLATURE - REGULAR SESSION
MULTISTATE TAX COMPACT
H. B. No. 365
*An Act relating to adopting the Multistate Tax Compact; providing for membership on the Multistate Tax Commission, consultation with local government representatives, and creation of the Multistate Tax Compact Advisory Committee; **and declaring an emergency**.*
Be it enacted by tile Legislature of tile State of Texas:
Adoption of Compact
Section 1. The Multistate Tax Compact is adopted and entered into with all jurisdictions legally adopting it to read as follows:
"MULTISTATE TAX COMPACT
•Article I. Purposes.
"The purposes of this compact are to:
*"1. Facilitate proper determination of State and local tax liability of multi state **taxpayers**, including the equitable apportionment of tax bases and settlement of apportionment disputes.*
"2. Promote uniformity or compatibility in significant components of tax systems.
*"3. Facilitate **taxpayer** convenience and compliance in the filing of tax returns and in other phases of tax administration.*
"4. Avoid duplicative taxation.
"Article II. Definitions.
"As used in this compact:
*"3. **'Taxpayer' means** any corporation, partnership, firm, association, governmental unit or agency or person acting as a business entity in more than one State.*

In the current Tax Code, under Chapter 141, Section 141.001, Article II, DEFINITIONS; we find the exact same definition, of "**Taxpayer**"—as was created, on June 13th, 1967, as shown above. It would seem the ARB labeling me a "taxpayer" is incorrect, if the records do NOT show the owner, of the property, is a "corporation, partnership, firm, association, governmental unit or agency or person acting as a business entity in more than one State." But, the courts have no incentive to address the issue if there is a chance such determination may minimize the cash flow to the State.

Without allowing me an Open Hearing during the entire first and second case before her, Judge Hamilton dismisses my case, for want of jurisdiction, once again (**It Shocks The Conscience**). I appeal her decision.

My notice of Appeal was filed, on or before February 24th, 2011. The case number is 09-11-00089-CV. The Ninth Court of Appeals admits the ARB Final Order did NOT inform me of whom to sue—in an appeal of their decision. The case was before Justices McKeithen, C.J., Gaultney and Horton, JJ; and the opinion was given by Justice Horton, on August 31, 2011.

Ninth Court of Appeals Opinion NO. 09-11-00089-CV
*"The information required to be included in **the Board's final order does not include information on how service of the petition is perfected**, as that information **is found in section 42.2l(b)**. See id. **We conclude** that the Board's final order contained the information required by section 41.47(e). See id. § 41.47(e). **We overrule issue one**."*

The appellate court found I could have amended my Petition, to include the MCAD, even though the attorneys' pleading stated I had no opportunity, after the 60 day window. The appellate court could have as easily remanded the case, back—to the trial court—and Ordered the trial court to allow the amendment; but instead it was the *pro se's* fault, for NOT knowing the rules are just a guide line—and can be ignored by the courts, at any time.

Ninth Court of Appeals Opinion NO. 09-11-00089-CV
*"**We conclude** that Townsend **had the opportunity** to amend his petition to make the District an additional party to his suit **before the trial court dismissed his suit for lack of jurisdiction**. See Levatte v. City of Wichita Falls, 144 S.W.3d 218, 225 (Tex. App.-Fort Worth 2004, no pet.); see also Haddix v. Am. Zurich Ins. Co., 253 S.W.3d 339, 346-47 (Tex. App.-Eastland 2008, no pet.)"*

I filed a Motion For Reconsideration, and brought up a few errors of the court. 'Clear and concise language,' of a property owner's right to appeal, should contain the proper direction to a party, who is NOT an attorney, of any particulars to appeal NOT found in the Texas Rules of Civil Procedure—and included in the final order of the Appraisal Review Board (ARB), of Montgomery County, Texas, where such direction would be found.

*For more than a century the central meaning of procedural due process has been clear: "**Parties whose rights are to be affected are entitled to be heard**; and in order that they may enjoy that right they must first be notified." Baldwin v. Hale, 1 Wall. 223, 233 [17 L.Ed. 531]. See Windsor v. McVeigh, 93 U.S. 274 [23 L.Ed. 914]; Hovey v. Elliott, 167 U.S. 409 [17 S.Ct. 841, 42 L.Ed. 215]; Grannis v. Ordean, 234 U.S. 385 [34 S.Ct. 779, 58 L.Ed. 1363]. It is equally fundamental that **the right to notice and an opportunity to be heard "must be granted at a meaningful time and in a meaningful manner**." Armstrong v. Manzo, 380 U.S. 545, 552, 85 S.Ct. 1187, 1191, 14 L.Ed.2d 62.*
Brown v. McLennan County, Etc., 627 SW 2d 390 - Tex: Supreme Court 1982

I had a proper (& property!) interest, in knowing the procedures necessary, to appeal a decision of the ARB—and to be noticed, of those required procedures. But, where is the incentive for district court judges and appellate court justices to go by the mandates of the Texas Supreme Court? There is no incentive and there is no penalty for ignoring such mandates until the Texas Supreme Court remands the case back to the inferior court.

> **The distinction between** substantive limitations and procedural protections is consistently recognized by federal appellate courts. In Goodisman v. Lytle, 724 F.2d 818, 820 (9th Cir.1984), the court stated:
> **Procedural requirements** ordinarily do not transform a unilateral expectation into a constitutionally protected property interest. A constitutionally protected interest has been created **only** if the procedural requirements are intended to be a "significant substantive restriction" on... decision making. If the procedures required impose no significant limitation on **the discretion of the decision maker,** the expectation of a specific decision **is not enhanced enough** to establish a constitutionally protected interest in the procedures.
> Grounds v. Tolar Indep. School Dist., 856 SW 2d 417 - Tex: Supreme Court 1993

I pointed out the Supreme Court—of the United States of America, finds *pro ses* need instructions, and have the right to know.

> "...court errs if court dismisses the pro se litigant **without instruction of how pleadings are deficient and how to repair pleadings.**"
> Platsky v. C.I.A., 953 F.2d. 25 (2nd Cir.1991)
> (See Haines v Kerner, 404 U.S. 519(1972))

The only response that I received, from the Ninth Court of Appeals, was, "Motion Denied." I appealed the decision, on or about October 21, 2011, to the Supreme Court of the State of Texas; and was assigned the case, No. 11-0861. Soon after filing the appeal, the case was disposed of, without explanation. The Texas Legislature has allowed Texas courts to take a filing fee, with the foreknowledge of having no intention to hear a case from a *pro se*. This is just another form of plunder, "unjust enrichment," caused by our neighbors. This is another reason NOT to elect attorneys where they can create laws to benefit themselves.

THE JUDICIAL SYSTEM * The most expensive machine ever invented for finding out what happened and what to do about it.
- Judge *Irving Kaufman*

The more corrupt the state, the more numerous the laws.
- *Tacitus* (55-117 A.D.)

CHAPTER 28
MY THIRD LAWSUIT

By this point, it's 2010, and I had NOT paid property tax—since 2006. Bank of America started foreclosure procedures. I received a letter from Bank of America Home Loans, P.O. Box 650070, Dallas, TX 75265-0070, and dated April 16, 2010; BAC Home Loans Servicing, LP was the Mortgage Servicer acting for the new Lender—by the name of "Loan Servicing," located, at P.O. Box 7532, Van Nuys, CA, 91406-9998. Remember in Chapter 24, **"Countrywide Having Problems,"** where I showed how Countrywide Home Loans LP was renamed, to BAC Home Loans, LP? Remember also, where the Texas Local Government Code makes it mandatory **any** assignment, of the Note and Deed of Trust, needs to be filed in the County Clerk's Office. I checked with the County Clerk's Office, and there was no evidence of any assignment, to an entity called "Loan Servicing." I received a letter from a Law Firm, by the name of Barrett Daffin Frappier Turner & Engel, LLP (BDFTE), 15000 Surveyor Boulevard, Suite 100, Addison, Texas 75001; stating they were representing BAC Home Loans Servicing, LP FKA Countrywide Home Loans LP (BAC); and were accelerating the debt of the Note and Deed of Trust. This apparently meant "Loan Servicing" had sold the Note and Deed of Trust, to BAC. I checked with the County Clerk's Office, and found there was an Appointment, of a Substitute Trustee, made on August 24th, 2010—by a Steve Porter that works for BDFTE, who filed it with Montgomery County Clerk's Office, on September 13, 2010. I also found an Assignment of Note and Deed of Trust, dated September 24, 2010, filed in Montgomery County Clerk's Office on, October 7, 2010. Now, do you find a problem with the Assignment document, and the Substitute Trustee document—knowing the information I just provided to you? Let me point it out.

There has to be an assignment of the Note and Deed of Trust, before an Entity has the authority to appoint someone, as a substitute trustee. What was done by the law firm is called, "The Cart Before The Horse." The screw-up, of the BDFTE law firm, only gets better as we go along.

You may need to review Chapter 23 on Non-Judicial Foreclosures, but this non-judicial procedure is what I am about to go through, for the first time. I received a copy, of a "Notice of Substitute Trustee Sale," on or about August 30th, 2010, indicating an auction will commence—on October 5th, 2010, at 1:00PM, at the West Entrance of the Montgomery County Court House, located in Conroe, Texas. I told my wife to stop making house payments, since I had been informed they were accelerating the debt and demanded the entire balance allegedly owed.

On or about October 1st, 2010, I file a Petition and a Temporary Restraining Order; and it is assigned to, you guessed it, the 359th District Court—presided by Judge Hamilton. The case is cited as: *Bobie Kenneth Townsend v. BAC Hone Loans, LP FKA Countrywide Home Loans LP*, Case No. 10-10-1065. The Court Clerk walks my Petition to the chambers of Judge Hamilton; and for some unexplained reason, Judge Hamilton signed my Temporary Restraining Order (TRO). That was the first and last time I got to physically see Judge Hamilton concerning one of my cases. I faxed a copy to the BDFTE law firm; and on October 5th, 2010, my youngest son served the substitute trustee, with a copy of the TRO—and the substitute trustee's sale was stopped, for the time being.

On or about October 12th, 2010, I was informed my state case was moved, to Federal Court. It was assigned to the United States District Court, Southern District of Texas, Houston Division, in the court of the Honorable Kenneth M. Hoyt, United States District Judge. The case is cited as: *Bobie Kenneth Townsend v.*

BAC Hone Loans, LP fka Countrywide Home Loans LP, Civil Action NO. 4:10-cv-3751.

OK, let's take a break. You are going to need it, to get through this Chapter. If you have been reading for some time, you need to place a bookmark here and return after a good night's sleep. The details stated below may cause a headache and possibly a migraine by the time you reach the next Chapter. Saying that, I will give you a short "Chapter Trailer" so that you can flip pages to the next Chapter, if your brain goes into overload over the legal crap stated.

Chapter 28 Book Trailer: The author files suit against an evil bank in State Court, where an evil law firm moves the author's case to Federal Court where a Federal Judge hates pro ses and never reads the pleadings of pro ses. The evil law firm tells lies about the plaintiff, makes up quotes that don't exist in court cases. The evil law firm cites court cases that have been nullified by changes in law. The Federal judge that hates pro ses creates an Order where almost ever sentence is a lie and just dismisses the plaintiff's case without a valid reason.

Now, take a break. Don't forget the bookmark.

Got your glass of water and sandwich?

OK, here we go.

The law firm representing BAC was AKERMAN SENTERFITT, LLP (Akerman), Plaza of the Americas, Suite S1900, 600 North Pearl Street, Dallas, Texas 75201. This law firm was one of the largest law firms in the U.S. The attorneys of record were C. Charles Townsend, SBN: 24028053, FBN: 1018722 and Elizabeth Mazzarella, SBN: 24069320, FBN: 1085533. I could NOT find any relation between myself and the attorney C. Charles Townsend, but you canNOT pick your relatives. What I did find out was the attorney C. Charles Townsend was a former executive officer of Countrywide, before becoming an employee of Akerman; so he had first-hand knowledge, of the custom and policy of Countrywide's operation.

A flag should be sent up the flag pole, since Akerman was in Dallas, and there are plenty of law firms in the Houston, Texas area. This was my first indication the banking institutions did NOT pick the law firms that would represent them, in foreclosure lawsuits. As we go along, it looks like there is a "punch bowl" somewhere—where law firms grab a current lawsuit against a bank, and claim to represent the party; and there is no separate contract between the banks and the law firms. The system is designed to just dismiss, rather than to resolve, a dispute. I will support this idea, further down the road.

I never got a face-to-face hearing, in from Judge Hoyt. We had one telephone conference call, for an initial pretrial and scheduling conference, on January 24, 2011 at 09:30 AM. Judge Hoyt denied me all forms of discovery. It appears most-all Republican Federal Judges do NOT allow *pro ses* discovery, while Democrat Judges will allow some discovery. I have no explanation for it; it is just what happened to me.

Judge Hoyt's Order after the telephone conference
The following schedule shall govern the disposition of this case:
Discovery to be completed by: *June 6, 2011*
Dispositive motions due by: *June 30, 2011*
Docket call to be held at 11:30 a.m. on: *September 12, 2011*
Estimated trial time: 8 hours   *Bench*

At the beginning, the attorneys asked for more time, to answer my petition. Judge Hoyt first granted their motion for extension of time; and extended their time to November 8th, 2010. Then Judge Hoyt granted even more time to answer, until November 29, 2010.

On or about November 29th, 2011, the law firm filed a Motion to Dismiss, stating "Plaintiff Merely States Legal Conclusions Insufficient to Plead a Claim for Negligent Hiring"; Plaintiff Has No Claim for Breach of Fiduciary Duty Because There is No Fiduciary Relationship; Theft of Property is Inapplicable Because Plaintiff Did Not Plead Factual Allegations to Show A Theft or Any Damages Occurred; Plaintiff's Fraud Allegations Fail to Show BAC Had a Motive to Commit Fraud; Plaintiff's DTPA Claim Fails Because He Is Not a Consumer and His Claim is Not Actionable; BAC Has Standing to Act Upon the Note and Deed of Trust."

This is called, 'going through the motions.' The attorneys need merely to make some statements and cite some various court cases; and this gives the dismissal court the alleged reason to dismiss a state case—that has been moved to Federal Court. I have cited many court cases that show pleadings from attorneys mean little, if anything, without something credible to support the allegations. If there are no affidavits, no witness on the stand, such pleadings are smoke in the wind by law; but to pull the wool over *novas* attorneys or *pro ses*, such type of maneuvering is all that is needed for a hanging judge.

Rabbit Trail: If you are thinking about hiring an attorney, here is a question for the attorney: "What is an example of a factual allegation, compared to an allegation that is merely a conclusion?" If the attorney can NOT give you an actual example of both where you can clearly understand the difference, then apparently you do NOT want the attorney arguing in front of a judge, in your behalf. As of the writing of this book, I have yet to find an attorney that can give me an example. I must be cursed with bad luck, when it comes to finding a competent attorney. It may be because I want them all to take a drug test. But, on the other hand, it may be what Judge Robert Bork said in his book, "The Tempting of America", that 99.9% of all attorneys are incompetent? Might it be that? Judge Bork was recommended by President Reagan to be placed on the U.S. Supreme Court, but the Senate would not confirm him because he was a constitutionalist.

"The truth is that the judge who looks outside the Constitution always looks inside himself and nowhere else."- Judge Robert Bork

(Jumping off that rabbit trail.)

I served my Request for Discovery, on or about February 18th, 2011. The attorney, C. Charles Townsend, attempted to answered my requested discovery, personally, instead of "**by any officer or agent;**" but none of it was verified by anyone that had first-hand information, concerning the information provided. It was as though no answer was provided, by any credible person.

Federal Rules of Civil Procedures
Rule 33. Interrogatories to Parties
(b) ANSWERS AND OBJECTIONS.
(1) Responding Party. The __interrogatories must be answered__:
(A) by the party to whom they are directed; or
(B) if that party is a public or private corporation, a partnership, an association, or a governmental agency, by any officer or agent, who must furnish the information available to the party.

In fact, nothing was actually provided, to me. The attorneys have a standard response for production of documents to pro ses:

*"Defendant objects to this request for the reason, and to the extent, **it is not relevant** to any claim or defense at issue in this litigation and **is not reasonably calculated** to lead to such information and, as such, **imposes an undue burden and unreasonable costs** upon Defendant."*

*"Defendant further objects to this request for the reason, and to the extent, **it is vague and ambiguous**."*

*"Defendant further objects to this request for the reason, and to the extent, that **it assumes facts which are misleading, false or in dispute**. Subject to, and without waiving, the foregoing objection, **no items have been identified which are responsive to this request**."*

My youngest son pointed out to me, in the latest "The X-Files" TV Series, where Agent Fox Mulder said, "... the devil is just one man with a plan, but evil, true evil, is a collaboration of men, which is what we have here today. ... liars do not fear the truth; if there are enough liars."

The motion for dismissal was NOT appropriate to be heard, until June 30th, 2011, as indicated by the Scheduling Order of Judge Hoyt. We needed to go through Discovery, first. But, Judge Hoyt doesn't read my pleadings; and instead filed an Order for me to do something I had already done. This is just a tidbit of evidence Judge Hoyt did NOT read my pleadings.

Judge Hoyt's Order

ORDER

*Before the Court is the defendant, BAC Home Loans Servicing, LP f/k/a Countrywide Home Loans Servicing, LP's, motion to dismiss the plaintiff's petition for failure to state a claim, alternatively, motion for a more definitive statement [Doc. No. 13]. Although **the plaintiff has failed to respond to the defendant's motion**, even after an extension of time [Doc. No. 16], the Court, **nevertheless**, **ORDERS the plaintiff to amend his pleadings** on or before February 7, 2011, pursuant to FRCP 12(e) and the rules of pleadings. Failing, the Court will have no alternative but consider the defendant's motion to dismiss **as unopposed**.*

It is so Ordered.

SIGNED at Houston, Texas this 26th day of January, 2011.

When you look at the record [Doc. No. 23], you will see I did respond to BAC's Motion to Dismiss, on January 18th, 2011— with a 35-page response, entitled "Plaintiff's Response To Defendant's Motion To Dismiss Plaintiff's Petition For Failure To State a Claim." In my response, on line #73, I specifically address Judge Hoyt's threat of dismissal:

Townsend Response:"73. Plaintiff found in "Collins" that a motion to dismiss is rarely granted."

"Opinion in Collins v. Morgan Stanley Dean Witter
*A motion to dismiss under rule 12(b)(6) "is viewed with disfavor **and is rarely granted**." Kaiser Aluminum & Chem. Sales v. Avondale Shipyards, 677 F.2d 1045, 1050 (5th Cir. 1982).*

*The complaint must be liberally construed in favor of the plaintiff, and all facts pleaded in the complaint **must be taken as true**. Campbell v. Wells Fargo Bank, 781 F.2d 440, 442 (5th Cir. 1986).*

*The district court may not dismiss a complaint under rule 12(b)(6) "**unless it appears beyond doubt** that the plaintiff can prove **no set of facts** in support of his claim which would entitle him to relief." Conley v. Gibson, 355 U.S. 41, 45-46 (1957)."*

More legalese. What determines a "set of facts"—more than one fact? Does making a statement "allege" a fact? Do two statements make a "set of facts"? Can you get a set of dishes for two? I think NOT. So, maybe it has to be a minimum of four facts—to make a set. Like a set dishes.

What happened to: "I'll show the jury mine, and you show the jury yours; and then we will let the jury decide?" No, no, no, your right to a trial by jury only happens, if the judge will let you. Paying a fee, to a court, to have a **right to a jury** is apparently NOT a contract. It is just part of the "unjust enrichment" the court system uses, for cash-flow enhancement. "It's NOT like buying a ticket to a Baseball Game and expecting to be allowed in the stadium to actually watch the game. Where did you get that idea? You Idiot, You Moron, You *Pro se.*"

Texas Constitution Article 1
*Sec. 15. RIGHT OF TRIAL BY JURY. The right of trial by jury **shall** **remain inviolate.** The Legislature shall pass such laws as may be needed to **regulate the same**, and **to maintain its purity and** **efficiency**.*

Below are just some of the points I argued, in my response, to give BAC a more definite statement of my claims.

Townsend Response:"34. The defendant claims that "under Texas law, the elements of a cause of action for breach of fiduciary duty are: (1) that the plaintiff and defendant had a fiduciary relationship; (2) the defendant breached its fiduciary duty to the plaintiffs; and (3) the defendant's breach resulted in injury to the plaintiff." Jones v. Blume, 196 S.W.3d 440 (Tex. App.-Dallas 2006). Plaintiff found in "Jones" that the defendant is responsible and has the duty to control the Escrow Agent, Trustees and has an informal fiduciary relationship toward plaintiff."

"Opinion of Jones v. Blume

Fiduciary Duty of Escrow Agent

An **escrow agent must be appointed** through a specific legal document that imparts a specific legal obligation. Bell v. Safeco Title Ins. Co., 830 S.W.2d 157, 160 (Tex. App.-Dallas 1992, writ denied). **An escrow agent's duties are strictly limited to those set forth in the escrow agreement.** Equisource Realty Corp. v. Crown Life Ins. Co., 854 S.W.2d 691, 697 (Tex. App.-Dallas 1993, no writ).

Fiduciary Duty as Trustee

The Texas Trust Code provides that a trust is created "**only** if the settlor manifests an intention to create a trust." Tex. Prop. Code Ann. § 112.002 (Vernon 1995). A court has no authority to impose a trust and trustee duties unless **the prerequisites of a trust** are satisfied. See Chapman Children's Trust v. Porter & Hedges, L.L.P., 32 S.W.3d 429, 438 (Tex. App.-Houston [14th Dist.] 2000, pet denied).

Informal Fiduciary Relationship

An informal fiduciary relationship may arise where one person trusts in and relies upon another, **whether the relationship is** a moral, social, domestic, or purely personal one. Meyer, 167 S.W.3d at 331; Schlumberger Technology Corp. v. Swanson, 959 S.W.2d 171, 176 (Tex. 1997)."

Townsend Response: "36. The defendant's claim: Texas courts have held that the relationship between a borrower and lender is not a fiduciary one. 1001 McKinney Ltd. v. Credit Suisse First Boston Mortgage Capital, 192 S.W.3d 20 (Tex. App.-Houston [14th Dist] 2005)."

In "McKinney Ltd.," the defendant quoted the dissenting opinion of Justice Frost, but still omitted the word, 'Generally,' when Justice Frost stated the relationship between a borrower and lender is NOT a fiduciary one. The defendant does NOT claim to have standing, as the lender, until September 24, 2010, shown by the defendant's Exhibit A. As a servicing agent, there is a fiduciary duty to the plaintiff seeing his monthly payments are accounted, correctly. Claiming to be formally-known as Countrywide Home Loans Servicing LP is irrelevant, if the relationship to Countrywide Home Loans Servicing LP has not been established, prior to becoming BAC. Plaintiff did NOT have the luxury to select the servicing agent, but the fiduciary relationship existed, nevertheless.

> "Opinion in 1001 McKinney Ltd:
> To determine whether the tort actions can be maintained, we look to the substance of the cause of action rather than the manner in which it was pleaded. Jim Walter Homes, Inc. v. Reed, 711 S.W.2d 617, 617-18 (Tex.1986). **Tort obligations are those imposed by law when a person breaches a duty that is independent from promises made between the parties to a contract**; contractual obligations are those that result from an agreement between parties, which is breached. Southwestern Bell Tel. Co. v. DeLanney, 809 S.W.2d 493, 494 (Tex. 1991)."

Townsend Response "38. The defendant doing business in Texas takes on the obligation of the Texas Constitution creating a fiduciary duty toward customers that are required to accept their services. This obligation consist under charter where by such requirement is to abide by the constitution and laws of this state."

> "Texas Probate Code
> Sec. 105A. Appointment and Service of Foreign Banks and Trust Companies in Fiduciary Capacity.
> (b) Before qualifying or serving in the State of Texas **in any fiduciary capacity**, as aforesaid, such a foreign corporate fiduciary **shall file** in the office of the Secretary of the State of the State of Texas (1) **a copy of its charter, articles of incorporation or of association, and all amendments thereto, certified by its secretary under its corporate seal**;…"

Townsend Response "41. The defendant's claim that "a formulaic recitation of the elements, because of its conclusory nature, is not entitled to the usual presumption of truth. Moreover, a complaint must offer more than an "unadorned, the defendant- unlawfully-

harmed-me accusation."" Ashcroft v. Iqbal, 129 S. Ct 1937 (2009)."

In "*Ashcroft*," the opinion of the court stated detailed factual allegations were NOT required, but it was required the reviewing court draw on its own experience and common sense.

> "*Opinion in Ashcroft v. Iqbal*
> *Under Federal Rule of Civil Procedure 8(a)(2), a complaint **must contain** a "short and plain statement of the claim **showing that the pleader is entitled to relief**." "[D]etailed factual allegations" **are not required**, Twombly, 550 U. S., at 555, but the Rule does call for sufficient factual matter, accepted as true, to "state a claim to relief that is plausible on its face," id., at 570. **A claim has facial plausibility when the pleaded factual content allows the court to draw the reasonable inference that the defendant is liable for the misconduct alleged.** Id., at 556. Two working principles underlie Twombly. First, the tenet that a court must accept a complaint's allegations as true is inapplicable to threadbare recitals of a cause of action's elements, supported by **mere conclusory statements**. Id., at 555. Second, determining whether a complaint states a plausible claim is context-specific, **requiring the reviewing court to draw on its experience and common sense**. Id., at 556.*"

Townsend Response "61. The defendant claims that a plaintiff, even a pro se one, see Taylor, 296 F.3d at 378, must instead plead facts, and those facts "must be enough to raise a right to relief above the speculative level." Bell Atlantic v. Twombly, 127 S. Ct 1955 (2007).

Remember the question, to ask an attorney: "What is an example of a factual allegation, compared to an allegation that is merely a conclusion?" In the judge's opinion, below, factual allegations must "**possess enough heft**" to "sho[w] that the pleader is entitled to relief."   Now, we know factual allegations not only contain "heft," but there must be enough of it to matter. I found "*Twombly*" has to do with the Sherman's Act, but the case shows to be still in favor of plaintiff, since my pleadings contain enough "heft."

> "Opinion in Bell Atlantic v. Twombly
> Factual allegations must be enough to raise a right to relief
> **_above the speculative level_** on the assumption that all of the
> complaint's allegations are true.
>
> Asking for plausible grounds does not impose a probability
> requirement at the pleading stage; **_it simply calls for enough
> fact to raise a reasonable expectation that discovery will
> reveal evidence of illegal agreement_**. The need at the pleading
> stage for allegations plausibly suggesting (not merely consistent
> with) agreement reflects Rule 8(a)(2)'s threshold requirement
> that the "plain statement" **_possess enough heft to "sho[w] that
> the pleader is entitled to relief_**.""

Townsend Response "65. Defendant claims that "however, even if
the injury "would not have happened but for the defendant's
[hiring], the connection between the defendant and the plaintiff's
injuries may be too attenuated to constitute legal cause."" City of
Gladewater v. Pike, 727 S.W.2d 514 (Tex. 1987).

I have found many instances, where attorneys and
paralegals cut and paste quotes, from other documents—instead
of the actual case, itself. When attorneys cite court cases or other
sources, it is best to verify the case or the source states what the
attorney says it does. But, when you clarify and verify, you will
find attorneys leaving off part of a sentence, to make their case
stronger—or even creating a quote you will NOT be able to find,
in the case cited.

I soon realized the defendant's *"Gladewater"* quote,
above, is NOT found in the actual case cite of *"Gladewater;"* but I
did find a quote, in *"Gladewater,"* that was in my favor:

"Opinion in City of Gladewater v. Pike

Negligence *requires the presence of **three basic elements: duty** on the part of one person to another; **breach** of that legal duty; and **injury** to the person to whom the duty is owed as a proximate result of the breach. Bell Helicopter Co. v. Bradshaw, 594 S.W.2d 519, 531 (Tex. Civ. App. - Corpus Christi 1979, writ ref'd n.r.e.)*

*Thus, **the two elements of proximate cause are cause-in-fact and foreseeability**. Williams v. Steves Industries, Inc., 699 S.W.2d 570, 575 (Tex. 1985); McClure v. Allied Stores of Texas, Inc., 608 S.W.2d 901, 903 (Tex. 1980); Missouri Pac. R. Co. v. American Statesman, 552 S.W.2d 99, 103 (Tex. 1977). **Cause in fact means that the omission or act involved was a substantial factor in bringing about the injury and without which no harm would have occurred.** McClure, 608 S.W.2d at 903. **Foreseeability requires that the actor, as a person of ordinary intelligence, would have anticipated the danger that his negligent act created for others.** Nixon v. Mr. Property Management Co., Inc., 690 S.W.2d 546, 549-50 (Tex. 1985). **Foreseeability does not require that a person anticipate the precise manner in which injury will occur once a negligent situation that he has created exists.** Southwest Forest Industries, Inc. v. Bauman, 659 S.W.2d 702, 704 (Tex. App. - El Paso 1983, writ ref'd n.r.e.). In applying these rules of law, however, we are dependent upon the facts of the case.*

*Like any other **ultimate fact**, however, **proximate cause need not be supported by direct evidence**, as circumstantial evidence and inferences therefrom are a sufficient basis for a finding of causation. Farley v. MM Cattle Co., 529 S.W.2d 751, 755 (Tex. 1975)."*

It is very important I point out again, the quote the attorney used, in his Motion to Dismiss, does NOT exist—in the case cite, of **City of Gladewater v. Pike**. I have found many quotes, by many judges, do NOT exist in the case cite of which they are allegedly citing. Judges create BAD "case law" precedents, by using quotes that do NOT exist in the opinion of the case site. **It Shocks the Conscience**.

Please understand there are many, many more pages, of this same type of information, responding to BAC's Motion to Dismiss. Through my studies, it is my conclusion Briefing Attorneys, which work for any judge, just read the pleadings of one of the attorneys; in a lawsuit or if a *pro se* is involved, just the attorney's pleadings that represent the party the *pro se* is against. I will support this conclusion, with lies from appellate court judges—in their Opinions, later on.

Since it is obvious Judge Hoyt did NOT read my response, to BAC's Motion to Dismiss, Judge Hoyt could NOT wait to get rid of the case; and ordered the dismissal of the case, on January 31st, 2011.

Judge Hoyt's Order
ORDER GRANTING DEFENDANT'S MOTION TO DISMISS
Defendant BAC Home Loans Servicing, L.P.'s motion to dismiss is GRANTED.
*Plaintiff **may file** an amended complaint within 7 days of the entry of this order, **except as to his** claims for negligent hiring, breach of fiduciary duty, theft of property, violation of the Texas Deceptive Trade Practices Act, and standing, **those claims are dismissed with prejudice**.*
SIGNED: Judge Hoyt, Jan. 31, 2011

Notice the issues were dismissed, **with prejudice**. This is legalese, for: "You can never bring up these causes of action against this same party concerning this same incident ever again."

The Deceptive Trade Practices Act is intended to permit the adversely affected plaintiff to recover the greatest amount of "actual damages" alleged and established as caused by the defendant. Woo v. Great Southwestern Acceptance Corp., 565 S.W.2d 290, 298 (Tex.Civ.App.- Waco 1978, writ ref'd n.r.e.). **Actual**

159

damages means those recoverable at common law. Brown v. American Transfer & Storage Co., 601 S.W.2d 931, 939 (Tex. 1980).

Knowing NOT what to do, I again searched "O'Conners... Causes of Action" and found: "Plaintiff claims defendant committed Common-Law Fraud against plaintiff"; "Plaintiff claims that defendant committed Statutory Fraud against plaintiff"; "Plaintiff claims defendant committed Conspiracy to Commit Fraud against plaintiff"; "Plaintiff, claims Breach of Contract by the defendant"; "Plaintiff, claims Negligent Misrepresentation by the defendant"; and "Plaintiff, claims defendant violated the Truth in Lending Act (15 U.S.C. §1601 et seq.)." I filed my [Dkt#26] "Plaintiff's First Amended Complaint," on or about February 7th, 2011.

I show, where "the defendant now claims to be the current Lender the purported original Note and Deed of Trust, whereby just a few months before acted in the capacity of a Servicing Agent for some unknown previous Lender."

UCC 3.405
Sec. 3.405. Employer's Responsibility for Fraudulent Indorsement by Employee
    (a) In this section:
    *(1) "**Employee**" **includes** an independent contractor and employee of an independent contractor retained by the employer.*
    *(2) "**Fraudulent indorsement**" **means**:*
    *(A) in the case of an instrument payable to the employer, **a forged indorsement** purporting to be that of the employer; or*
    *(B) in the case of an instrument with respect to which the employer is the issuer, **a forged indorsement** purporting to be that of the person identified as payee.*

I show, where "there is **no** evidence before the court that an indorsement has occurred conforming that the defendant is holder of the note" (older spelling of 'endorsement').

UCC 3-203

*(c) **Unless otherwise agreed**, if an instrument is transferred for value and the transferee does not become a holder because of lack of indorsement by the transferor, the transferee has a specifically enforceable right to the unqualified indorsement of the transferor, **but negotiation of the instrument does not occur until the indorsement is made**.*

I show, where "the assignment was done **without** a corporate seal giving a technical defect of defendant's Exhibit A."

Texas Civil Practices and Remedy Code
CHAPTER 16. LIMITATIONS
SUBCHAPTER A. LIMITATIONS OF PERSONAL ACTIONS
*16.033. **Technical Defects in Instrument***
*(a) **A person with a right of action for the recovery of real property** conveyed by an instrument with one of the following defects must bring suit **not later than four years after** the day the instrument was recorded with the county clerk of the county where the real property is located:*
(1) lack of the signature of a proper corporate officer, partner, or company officer, manager, or member;
(2) lack of a corporate seal;
(3) failure of the record to show the corporate seal used;
(4) failure of the record to show authority of the board of directors or stockholders of a corporation, partners of a partnership, or officers, managers, or members of a company;
(5) execution and delivery of the instrument by a corporation, partnership, or other company that had been dissolved, whose charter had expired, or whose franchise had been canceled, withdrawn, or forfeited;
*(6) **acknowledgment of the instrument in an individual, rather than a representative or official, capacity;***
*(7) **execution of the instrument by a trustee without record of the authority of the trustee or proof of the facts recited in the instrument;***
*(8) **failure of the record or instrument to show an acknowledgment or jurat that complies with applicable law;** ...*

I show (am I showing too much?), where the "Plaintiff received a response dated September 28, 2010 from the defendant of its intention to continue with the auction of plaintiff's home and that there would be no TILA discovery as the matter was final."

> *Before a lien holder forces sale of a homestead, **the homestead's exempt portion must be ascertained** and, if possible, the excess segregated from the homestead. **The forced sale of an unsegregated homestead is a nullity.** Crowder, et al. v. Benchmark Bank, No. 93-01939-CV (Dallas), 10/17/94, 11 pp.; Mallou v. Payne & Vendig, 750 S.W.2d 251 (Tex.App.-Dallas 1988, writ denied).*

"Plaintiff's Exhibit K shows that the defendant is actually the same agency that was called **Countrywide Home Loans Servicing, LP** that was directed by the original Lender, by which have direct knowledge of the past actions against plaintiff and whereby the defendant is directly responsible for any harm that was done to plaintiff."

> *"**Party in interest may become liable for fraud by mere silent acquiescence** and partaking of benefits of fraud." Bransom v. Standard Hardware, Inc., 874 S.W.2d 919, 1994*

I show, where the defendant violated the Texas Business and Commerce Code, Section 27.01.

Texas Business and Commerce Code
Sec. 27.01. FRAUD IN REAL ESTATE AND STOCK TRANSACTIONS.
*(a) **Fraud in a transaction involving real estate** or stock in a corporation or joint stock company consists of a*
*(1) **false representation** of a past or existing material fact, when the false representation is*
*(A) made to a person for the **purpose of inducing** that person to enter into a contract; and*
*(B) **relied on** by that person in entering into that contract; or*

162

(2) ***false promise*** *to do an act, when the false promise is*

(A) *material;*

(B) *made with the intention of not fulfilling it;*

(C) *made to a person for the purpose of inducing that person to enter into a contract; and*

(D) *relied on by that person in entering into that contract.*

(b) *A person who makes a false representation or false promise commits the fraud described in Subsection (a) of this section and is liable to the person defrauded for actual damages.*

(c) *A person who makes a false representation or false promise with actual awareness of the falsity thereof commits the fraud described in Subsection (a) of this section and is liable to the person defrauded for exemplary damages. Actual awareness may be inferred where objective manifestations indicate that a person acted with actual awareness.*

(d) *A person who (1) has actual awareness of the falsity of a representation or promise made by another person and (2) fails to disclose the falsity of the representation or promise to the person defrauded, and (3) benefits from the false representation or promise commits the fraud described in Subsection (a) of this section and is liable to the person defrauded for exemplary damages. Actual awareness may be inferred where objective manifestations indicate that a person acted with actual awareness.*

I show, where "the defendant falsely convinced me that in plaintiff's original deed of trust it states: 'The beneficiary of this Security Instrument is MERS.'"

*"By engaging in a pattern of racketeering activity, specifically **mail or wire fraud**,' the Defendants subject to this Court participated in **a criminal enterprise affecting interstate commerce**." (Compl. para. 231) Foster, et al. v. MERS, et al., Case No. 3:10-cv-00611 (W.D. Ky. filed Sept. 28, 2010).*

The class action complaint—in **Foster** against MERS, LPS, and other conspirators—is 124 pages long.

I show the court, "Plaintiff has the right to protest any property tax donation before paying."

Original Deed of Trust – Sec. 4
*Borrower shall promptly discharge any lien which has priority over this Security Instrument **unless Borrower**: (a) agrees in writing to the payment of the obligation secured by the lien in a manner acceptable to Lender, but only so long as Borrower is performing such agreement; (b) **contests the lien in good faith by, or defends against enforcement of the lien in, legal proceedings which in Lender's opinion operate to prevent the enforcement of the lien while those proceedings are pending, but only until such proceedings are concluded**; or (c) secures from the holder of the lien an agreement satisfactory to Lender subordinating the lien to this Security Instrument. If Lender determines that any part of the Property is subject to a lien which can attain priority over this Security Instrument, **Lender may give Borrower a notice** identifying the lien. Within 10 days of the date on which that notice is given, Borrower shall satisfy the lien or take one or more of the actions set forth above in this Section 4.*

I show the court, where "the defendant breached the contract by NOT applying plaintiff's monthly mortgage payment in the correct order."

Original Deed of Trust – Sec. 2
*2. Application of Payments or Proceeds. Except as otherwise described in this Section 2, **all payments accepted and applied by Lender** shall be applied **in the following order of priority**: (a) interest due under the Note; (b) principal due under the Note; (c) amounts due under Section 3. Such payments shall be applied to each Periodic Payment in the order in which it became due. Any remaining amounts shall be applied first to late charges, second to any other amounts due under this Security Instrument, and then to reduce the principal balance of the Note.*

I show the court, my home can NOT be sold by anyone, other than the one that possesses the Note and Deed of Trust.

*Furthermore, the evidence indisputably shows that **the defendant sheriff and substitute trustee was not possessed of the original deed of trust, or of the promissory note** secured thereby, or of the refusal of the named trustee to act, **which instruments clothed the defendant sheriff with the power to act in the premises**, but that such instruments were at the time in the exclusive custody and possession of Mr. Pitts, the attorney and representative of the beneficiary of the deed of trust, and were securely deposited in the safe in his office.*
WEST v. AXTELL et al, 322 Mo. 401, 17 S.W.2d 328 (1929)

I show the court, where it has the power to give me remedy.

Damages for injury to real property *are typically calculated and awarded as the lesser amount of the decline in fair market value versus the cost of restoring the property to its state before the trespass, in other words, the injured party is entitled to recover the amount by which the property has been devalued, Hartshorn v. Chaddock 135 NY 116, 31 NE 997 (1892) Slavin v. State 152 NY 145, 46 NE 321 (1897).*

*In instances where the conduct complained of **is willful, wanton or egregious**, the Court is vested **with the power to award exemplary damages**. Exemplary damages may lie in a situation where it is necessary not only to effectuate punishment but also **to deter the offending party from engaging in such conduct in the future**. Such an award may also be made to address, as enunciated by the Court of Appeals in Home Insurance Co. v. American Home Products Corp. 75 NY2d 196, 550 NE2d 930, 551 NYS2d 481 (1989) "...**gross misbehavior** for the good of the public...on the ground of public policy". **Indeed, exemplary damages are intended to have a deterrent effect upon conduct which is unconscionable, egregious, deliberate and inequitable.** I.H.P. Corp. v. 210 Central Park South Corp. 12 NY2d 329, 189 NE2d 812, 239 NYS2d 547 (1963).*

*Since **an action to foreclose a mortgage is a suit in equity**, Jamaica Savings Bank v. M.S. Investing Co. 274 NY 215, 8 NE2d 493 (1937), **all of the rules of equity are fully applicable to the proceeding,** including those regarding punitive or exemplary damages, I.H.P. Corp. v. 210 Central Park South Corp. , supra .*

The attorney for BAC, Elizabeth A. Mazzarella, SBN: 24069320; FBN: 1085533 with AKERMAN SENTERFITT, LLP; untimely (8 days late) filed [Dkt#34] their typical response.

Take a deep breath, before trying to read the next paragraph.

Please take notice that the following is just the titles of paragraphs found in the attorney's response: "Plaintiff's First Amended Complaint Should Be Dismissed For Failure To State A Claim Upon Which Relief Can Be Granted;" "Plaintiff's Common Law Fraud Claim is Barred By the Statute of Limitations;" "Plaintiff's Statutory Fraud Claim is Barred by Limitations and is Inapplicable;" "Plaintiff's Conspiracy Claim Fails Because He Cannot State A Viable Tort Claim Against BAC;" "Plaintiff's Breach of Contract Claim Fails Because His Pleadings Show BAC Did Not Breach the Deed of Trust and Because He Cannot Enforce A Contract He First Breached;" "Plaintiff Did Not Contest the Tax Assessment or Resulting Lien Through a Legal Proceeding Which In Lender's Opinion Operated to Prevent the Enforcement of the Tax Lien;" "Plaintiff Was Not Entitled to Notice of BAC's Payment of the Property Taxes, and Even if He Was, He Cannot Enforce a Contract He First Breached;" "Plaintiff's Negligent Misrepresentation Claim is Also Barred By the Statute of Limitations;" "Plaintiff's Claim For Rescission and Damages Under TILA Fails as A Matter of Law Because Those Remedies Are No Longer Available to Plaintiff;" "Plaintiff Cannot State a Claim for Violation of the FDCPA Because BAC is Not a Debt Collector;" and "Conclusion," "Plaintiff's second attempt to plead plausible claims against BAC fails as a matter of law. All but two of these claims are time barred; leaving only his breach of contract claim and violation of the FDCPA And these two claims are demonstrably lacking in merit. Because all of plaintiff's claims fail as a matter of law, the court should dismiss the action with prejudice."

The attorneys provide nothing to support their allegations. Just stating such things appear to be sufficient for the court to act against a pro se.

"Lacking in Merit." This is legalese-magical term, for "I do NOT have to explain the reason," wink, wink, nod, nod. Saying so is good enough, for a *pro se* case.

Take another breath... I respond [Dkt#38] with my: "Plaintiff's Response To Defendant's Motion To Dismiss Plaintiff's First Amended Complaint For Failure To State A Claim." I start off with: "Plaintiff states as a fact that the defendant never answered plaintiff's first amended complaint." "The record shows that defendant never denied any of plaintiff's allegations, but instead just defended its actions by claiming plaintiff did not complain sooner." "Plaintiff states for the record that plaintiff objects to Defendant's Motion To Dismiss Plaintiff's First Amended Complaint For Failure To State A Claim pled as a means to deprive plaintiff of a fair trial by use of case cites which were either misquoted or obsolete as the record shows was also done in the defendant's previous Motion to Dismiss and served the defendant's attorneys so well." "The defendant's pleading concerning Rule 12(b)(6) is irrelevant as this is not before the court as a general motion." "An affirmative defense claim by the defendant is not a bar to prosecution." "Plaintiff objects to the defendant having in the record two different Exhibit 1's, two different Exhibit 2's, two different Exhibit 3's, two different Exhibit 4's and a Defendant's Exhibit A of which plaintiff has a different Exhibit A." "Plaintiff's First Amended Complaint is based upon facts giving plaintiff the right to a evidentiary hearing." "Defendant's Motion To Dismiss Plaintiff's First Amended Complaint For Failure To State A Claim is based upon misrepresentation, mistakes, and lies supporting fraud in the inducement, fraudulent conveyance, constructive fraud, intrinsic fraud and extrinsic fraud by employing dishonesty to deprive plaintiff of money, property and right of property."

Even my brain goes into overload, after reviewing my edited response from the attorney's cut-and-paste BS. My pie in the sky reply to their BS was done with hope, as though it could make the judge reconsider his made up mind. I know that it was gullible on my part back then; but during that time frame, I still thought Federal U.S. District Judges were credible, honorable people.

Take another breath.

I further state: "The defendant is an associate of Bank of America and is pleading confession and avoidance in hopes that court will agree that the damage and injury of plaintiff was years ago to avoid any liability to the current injury of the plaintiff. The defendant claims there is a statute of limitation upon the cause of actions plead by plaintiff but in fact when harm is continuous to the point of recognition, defendants argument is moot."

*37 Am Jur 2d at section 8 states, in part: "**Fraud vitiates every transaction and all contracts**. Indeed, the principle is often stated, in broad and sweeping language, that **fraud destroys the validity of everything into which it enters, and that it vitiates the most solemn contracts, documents, and even judgments**."*

Rabbit Trail: When you research American Jurisprudence, you find that the Am Jur books were written by Justices, of the Supreme Court of the United States of America. Back when, possibly but NOT probably, the Supreme Court Judges believed in their job to protect and defend the Constitution For the United States of America. Back when you appealed there was a response, from a judge, other than "Motion Denied" or "Petition for a Writ of Certiorari Denied." Court-case opinions seemed more credible, in the early 1800s, but now I question them all. So, when you read a statement out of the Texas Jurisprudence, know that a Justice of the Texas Supreme Court, or of the Texas Court of Criminal Appeals, had some input in what is found in the many volumes. Saying all that, I truly believe all of the lower-court judges do NOT care what the Justices of the Supreme Court think, or have thought in the past. They only care if the Justices review one of their cases, and remand the case back to them. Then they care. Otherwise, they do NOT care. It will be obvious to you, too, when you finish reading this book.

(Jumping off that rabbit trail.)

I show where: "it is a fact that the defendant was required to give plaintiff 10 days notice before paying any claim against the property or there is no obligation upon the borrower to do anything about it. The defendant's Motion to Dismiss under Section "D" **left off the last sentence** that is found in paragraph 118 of plaintiff first amended complaint."

It was the attorneys who worked for the law firm, AKERMAN SENTERFITT, LLP, Plaza of the Americas, Suite S1900, 600 North Pearl Street, Dallas, Texas 75201, that took out the relevant parts of contracts, to make their clients look better. The attorneys are supposed to be governed by ethical behavior, but it seems that Mr. C. Charles Townsend, SBN: 24028053, FBN: 1018722, *Attorney-in-Charge*; & Mr. Michael J. McKleroy, SBN: 24000095, FBN 576095 & Elizabeth A. Mazzarella, SBN: 24069320, FBN: 1085533 don't have to worry about ethics—when dealing with *pro ses*.

Townsend's Original Deed of Trust – Sec. 4 –Last Sentence
*"**Within 10 days of the date on which that notice is given**, Borrower shall satisfy the lien or take one or more of the actions set forth above in this Section 4."*

Virtually all the cases cited, by the attorneys for BAC, are in my favor. I could go on point-by-point, citing the errors by the attorneys for BAC; but I want to point out one particular issue that is very disturbing: when attorneys cite cases that no longer apply—because the law had changed. The case cited, by the attorneys, is **Perry v. Stewart Title Co., 756 F.2d 1197 (1985)**. This case is cited by most, if NOT every attorney, representing a banking institution. Here was my response, to the attorney citing the "**Perry**" case:

> *Townsend's response:*
> *"The defendant claims that it is not subject to the Fair Debt Collection Practices Act as Congress had declared them __not to be__ a debt collector, especially citing Perry v. Stewart Title Co. and Williams v. Countrywide Home Loans, Inc. as a bases for the claim. It is a fact that Perry v. Stewart Title Co. is a 1985 case, but __in 1986 Congress amended Section 1692a__ cited by this case __and confirmed that attorneys were considered debt collectors__ and removed mortgage servicing companies as exempted. Perry v. Stewart Title Co. is not a viable case to cite and Williams v. Countrywide Home Loans, Inc. based its decision upon the Perry case as well. 15 U.S.C. § 1692a(6)(G) does not exist."*
>
> *"TITLE 15--COMMERCE AND TRADE*
> *CHAPTER 41--CONSUMER CREDIT PROTECTION*
> *SUBCHAPTER V--DEBT COLLECTION PRACTICES*
> *Sec. 1692a. Definitions*
> *Amendments*
> *1986--Par. (6). Pub. L. 99-361 in provision preceding cl. (A) substituted ``clause (F)'' for ``clause (G)'', struck out cl. (F) which excluded any attorney-at-law collecting a debt as an attorney on behalf of and in the name of a client from term ``debt collector'', and redesignated cl. (G) as (F)."*

I have seen many cases, afterward, in the Federal Courts, dismissing actions, against banking institutions, merely based upon the "***Perry***" case. I expect it still goes on today. **It Shocks the Conscience**.

Why did United States District Court Judge Hoyt rule against my case? Lets review Judge Hoyt's Memorandum & Order (M&O), signed on March 29th, 2011 [Dkt#45]. When a reviewer looks at the pleadings—of the attorneys for BAC, and the M&O of Judge Hoyt, you will see parroting of the attorneys' pleading. I responded to the M&O, with my "Plaintiff's Motion For Reconsideration of Memorandum and Order and Final Judgment" [Dkt#47].

[Dkt#47] "The Court's Memorandum states on page 2: "the plaintiff does not dispute the accuracy of the facts as related by BAC."

"The above statement is false as plaintiff has disputed and objects to everything that has been alleged by the defense counsel without presenting clear and convincing proof of such allegations."

"The Court's Memorandum states on page 2: "Yet, to avoid the dismissal of his case based on limitations, the plaintiff presents, without stating facts to support it, the "discovery rule."

"The above statement is false concerning plaintiff failing to state facts supporting his request to supplement his amended complaint to bring forth the discovery rule concerning affirmative defenses claimed by the defendant. Plaintiff shows in Plaintiff's Motion To Amend or Supplement Plaintiff's Complaint the opinions of *Bell Atlantic v. Twombly,* 127 S. Ct. 1955, 1964–65 (2007); *Woods v. William M. Mercer, Inc.,* 769 S.W.2d 515, 517 (Tex. 1988); *Wise v. Anderson,* 163 Tex. 608, 359 S.W.2d 876 (Tex.

1962); *Sherman v. Sipper*, 137 Tex. 85, 90, 152 S.W.2d 319, 321 (1941); *Liles v. Phillips*, 677 S.W.2d 802, 808-809 (Tex. App.--Fort Worth 1984, writ ref'd n.r.e.); and *Hendricks v. Thornton*, 973 S.W.2d 348, 364 & n.19 (Tex. App.—Beaumont 1998, pet denied) concerning the ability to invoke the discovery rule. The above case cites should be considered facts as they state that acts of fraud have been known to be reveled in the present by use of the discovery rule even 'if the fraud is concealed' today."

> *"The Court's Memorandum states on page 2: "Here, __the plaintiff__ __fails__, even after supplementing his amended pleading, __to state__ __when__ he discovered that the Loan Origination Agent committed the negligence, fraud and other acts of tort. Therefore, __the defense is__ __meaningless__."*

"The above statement is false as it states that plaintiff had already supplemental his amended complaint, when in fact plaintiff had only amended his complaint and had asked for leave of the Court to supplement or amend his complaint to request the discovery rule since the defendant had just recently claimed an affirmative defense which allows for the discovery rule request. Plaintiff, NOT being an attorney, was NOT aware that a specific date of discovery of a particular tort was necessary to bring the claim. News articles on TV and the Internet concerning Liar Loans, Robo-Signers, Mortgage Back Securities, Bank of America and Countrywide being fined millions of dollars for fraud were numerous in 2010 and continue today. After such news in 2010 and the past actions of the defendant, a reasonable man could only conclude that the 'Loan Origination Agent' committed the negligence, fraud and other acts of tort'."

> *"The Court's Memorandum states on page 4: "The facts __are__ __undisputed__ that the plaintiff __learned in__ 2005, __and at the latest__ 2006, that the Loan Origination Agent had misrepresented the yearly property tax assessments for 2006 and future years."*

"The above statement is false because, if plaintiff had realized that "the Loan Origination Agent had misrepresented the yearly property tax assessments," it would be only reasonable that plaintiff would have sued the defendant when plaintiff sued the Montgomery Central Appraisal District, which he did NOT do. Six months ago plaintiff did NOT know what a Negligent Misrepresentation was as a cause of action, but plaintiff does now."

"The Court's Memorandum states on page 4: "Finally, he knew that neither Countrywide nor BAC caused or participated in the removal of the variance on his property."

"The above statement is true as plaintiff has never accused or meant to claim or insinuate that Countrywide or BAC caused or participated in the removal of the variance on plaintiff's property. Plaintiff understands that the cause was by the Chief Appraiser of the Montgomery Central Appraisal District and no one else. The evidence presented in plaintiff's Exhibits show that Countrywide and/or BAC conspired with someone in the appraisal district and the third party debt collector law firm Barrett Daffin Frappier Turner & Engel, LLP to steal plaintiff's property by the defendant paying the property tax donations without giving notice to plaintiff, waiting to foreclose until plaintiff equity of $25,000 was used up, then by auctioning off plaintiff's home the defendant is NOT required to give full disclosure to the unexpected buyer of the damage to the property. The new owner would NOT know why he and his family were getting sick in the new home until he traced the information back to the previous owner. Then the new owner would have a piece of property that he could NOT sell, as the law requires the owner to fully disclose the property and the cycle would continue by foreclosure. Plaintiff would NOT have purchase the property if the property tax variance would had been removed before closing."

"The Court's Memorandum states on page 4: "However, __assuming__ that the discovery rule __would__ __fix another date__, that date __came no later than__ January of 2006 when the 2005 taxes were due. __Hence__, the plaintiff knew in 2006 that the statement made by the Loan Origination Agent __would not hold true__."

"The above statement is false as the case cites referenced in Plaintiff's Motion To Amend or Supplement Plaintiff's Complaint that the discovery of a past act of fraud is as vital as the time it was dealt. Plaintiff bares a continuing injury whereby a past wound is open each year, then plaintiff recognized in 2010 that the cause of the wound was by an intentional act of fraud instead of an accident, the time of the realization of the act as intentional begins the statutes of Fraud clock, NOT the time the act was commenced."

"The Court's Memorandum states on page 5: "Therefore, the Court __is of the opinion__ and holds that the plaintiff's __common-law and statutory claims for fraud are barred by limitations__ and, should have been brought on or before June 29, 2008, and no later than 2009, the next year. These claims are dismissed as a result."

"Here the Court ignores claims brought forth in Plaintiff's First Amended Complaint concerning the claim of fraud by the plaintiff. On page 3 of Plaintiff's First Amended Complaint, plaintiff complains that the defendant has committed fraud as to the ability to foreclose. The law states under U.C.C. 3.203 & 3.405 that the defendant must produce the original Note showing the indorsement by the previous owner of the Note and that the indorsement was NOT fraudulent. Defendant's Exhibit A indicates that the indorsement (if there is an indorsement) on the original Note is fraudulent as U.C.C. 3.405 states:

UCC 3.405

Sec. 3.405. Employer's Responsibility for Fraudulent Indorsement byEmployee

(a) In this section:

(1) "Employee" includes an independent contractor and employee of an independent contractor retained by the employer.

*(2) "**Fraudulent indorsement**" means:*

(A) in the case of an instrument payable to the employer, a forged indorsement purporting to be that of the employer; or

(B) in the case of an instrument with respect to which the employer is the issuer, a forged indorsement purporting to be that of the person identified as payee."

"The Court's Memorandum states on page 5: "Section 4 requires the borrower to promptly pay any lien that has the potential or ability to attain priority over BAC's lien" and states "Because the plaintiff failed to pay the 2006 assessed taxes timely, a lien attached to the property and BAC was free to proceed under the provisions of the deed of trust, including section 4, to protect its lien position."

"The above statement is false as Section 4 of the Deed of Trust gives plaintiff choices other than "promptly pay any lien that has the potential or ability to attain priority over BAC's lien". Plaintiff took the option under Section 4 of the Deed of Trust to contest the lien, as there was only a current threat of proceedings and no need to defend against enforcement of the lien. The defendant did NOT give plaintiff "a notice identifying the lien" as per the Deed of Trust. Plaintiff was never given the opportunity to defend against the enforcement of the lien that was pending. (See Plaintiff's Exhibit L & M) The defendant did NOT dispute that it was the policy of the defendant to give a '30 day notice' to a Borrower, before paying any amount concerning the Escrow Account. The defendant Breached the Contract by paying the tax donations without giving plaintiff notice of its intention thereby harming plaintiff and creating a situation that devalued plaintiff's property and made plaintiff's property un-sellable, other than by auction."

*"The Court's Memorandum states on page 5: "Therefore, it is **undisputed** that a priority lien existed against the plaintiff's property, placing the plaintiff in default under the terms of the note and deed of trust. Hence, the plaintiff's breach of contract claim is **unmeritorious** in that **it fails** to state a cause of action."*

"The above statement is false because, the existence of a priority lien against the plaintiff's property does NOT place the plaintiff in default under the terms of the note and deed of trust. Plaintiff was allowed many choices to deal with a priority lien against plaintiff's property as Section 4 in the Deed of Trust confirms. The defendant breached the contract by removing plaintiff's choices available to him by failing to give him notice identifying the lien, then paying the tax donation without his consent thereby removing his option of contesting the lien or defending against the enforcement of the lien if proceeding were commenced. The Court fails to address the other breach of the contract issues that the defendant provided the evidence of the breach. Plaintiff's Exhibit AX shows many torts by the defendant by failing to apply plaintiff's monthly promissory Note payments as required by the Deed of Trust. Plaintiff Affidavit In Support of Plaintiff's Motion For Reconsideration show in detail the many separate torts committed by the defendant while acting as Mortgage Servicer.

Point 1: The defendant defaulted by NOT filing its response to Plaintiff's First Amended Complaint in a timely manner. As a matter of justice, the case should have been in favor of plaintiff.

Point 2: The Deed of Trust confirms that plaintiff has a right to contest and defend against any lien that may connect to plaintiff's property. The defendant violated plaintiff's rights according to the Deed of Trust by ignoring specific provisions within the contract.

Point 3: The Deed of Trust confirms that the defendant acting as a Mortgage Servicer violated provisions in the Deed of Trust which specifically stated that the monthly Note payment would be applied to the interest, then to the principle and then to any escrow account if established. The defendant violated this provision in the Deed of Trust multiple times.

Point 4: The documents submitted to the court indicating that the defendant was assigned the Note and Deed of Trust is fraudulent. The same people that signed the notary logbook did NOT create the signatures on the documents filed in Montgomery County by the defendant. The Court should NOT allow fraud on the court by the defendant.

Point 5: The defendant violated the Truth in Lending Act. That was proven in Plaintiff's Response To Defendant's Motion To Dismiss Plaintiff's First Amended Complaint For Failure To State A Claim.

Point 6: Plaintiff has the right to supplement or amend his complaint as to prosecute any affirmative defense claim by the defendant by use of the discovery rule. Fraud is conditioned by the term 'accrue'. Cause of action "accrues" on the date that damage is sustained and NOT date when causes are set in motion which ultimately produce an injury.

Point 7: Defendant's argument concerning plaintiff's Fair Debt and Collections Act violation claim is moot due to 15 U.S.C. § 1692 statute having been changed in 1986 to include the defendant and its contractors as a debt collector."

Please keep in mind, the attorneys for BAC never entered any affidavit, or other sworn testimony, of any of their claims.

> "**Where there are no** depositions, admissions, or affidavits **the court has no facts to rely on for a summary determination**."
> *Trinsey v. Pagliaro, D.C. Pa. 1964, 229 F. Supp. 647.*

Even though Judge Hoyt had, "no facts to rely on for a summary determination," Judge Hoyt also changed the rules, when convenient, as to make it harder for me to respond, to Judge Hoyt's Orders; and make it impossible for me to win by default.

*Townsend's pleading - [Dkt#47] "On February 7, 2010, plaintiff filed his first amended complaint (Docket # 26) and it was served on the defendant on February 9, 2010 (See Plaintiff's Affidavit In Support of Clerk's Entry of Default filed on April 4, 2010). Per Rule 15(a)(3) of the FRCP, defendant had 14 days to answer after service of the amended complaint. The defendant did not answer, but instead filed a Motion to Dismiss (Docket # 34) **that was eight days late** according to Rule 15(a)(3) of the FRCP. The answer to Plaintiff's First Amended Complaint required the defendant to admit or deny the allegations of plaintiff as per Rule 8(b) of the FRCP. For the Court **to appear to be impartial** toward the plaintiff and the defendant, **the rules say** that the defendant defaulted as to answer plaintiff's first amended complaint in a timely manner and that judgment for plaintiff is in order. Plaintiff filed Plaintiff's Motion For Default Judgment (Docket # 35) on March 14, 2010 concerning the late filing of the defendant Motion to Dismiss (Docket # 34). The record shows that **plaintiff's Motion for Default Judgment was ignore by the***

Court *violating plaintiff right to due process. The record shows that* **Plaintiff's Motion for Default Judgment is unopposed** *as no response to said motion was filed.* **The Court does not have discretion** *to wave the rules for the defendant, after the fact.* **It is an abuse of discretion by the Court's own motion, declaring that defendant's Motion to Dismiss was timely filed, when it was not.***"*

Remember, Judge Hoyt <u>never</u> gave me an open hearing, to argue anything concerning my case. Notice above, Judge Hoyt only gave me seven (7) days, to amend my Original Petition. Rule 15 gives the attorneys twice the time (14 days) to respond, of which they, without any reason to worry, took <u>22 days</u> to respond. Did I mention, the law firm I was fighting was really BIG? One Hundred Fifty-Plus attorneys, against little Ol' Me, and they get twice as much time to respond. No bias here. **It Shocks the Conscience**.

FRCP
Rule 15. Amended and Supplemental Pleadings
(a) AMENDMENTS BEFORE TRIAL.
(1) Amending as a Matter of Course. A party may amend its pleading once as a matter of course within:
(A) 21 days after serving it, or
(B) if the pleading is one to which a responsive pleading is required, 21 days after service of a responsive pleading or 21 days after service of a motion under Rule 12(b), (e), or (f), whichever is earlier.
(2) Other Amendments. In all other cases, a party may amend its pleading only with the opposing party's written consent or the court's leave. **The court should freely give leave when justice so requires***.*
(3) Time to Respond. Unless the court orders otherwise, any required response to an amended pleading must be made within the time remaining to respond to the original pleading or **within 14 days after service of the amended pleading***, whichever is later.*

Judge Hoyt gave the attorneys, for BAC, eleven (11) days to respond, to my Dkt#47. Judge Hoyt's explanation [Dkt#50], for the errors I found in his M&O, was, "plaintiffs motion for reconsideration (#45) is DENIED." The Great and Powerful OZ has spoken. Off to the United States Court of Appeals For the Fifth Circuit. Surely I will get justice, in one of the highest courts in the land. Don't call me Shirley.

Fifth Circuit
IN THE UNITED STATES DISTRICT COURT
FOR THE SOUTHERN DISTRICT OF TEXAS
HOUSTON DIVISION

Bobie Kenneth Townsend §
§
§ *CASE NUMBER: 4:10cv3751*
v. § *District Judge: Kenneth M Hoyt*
§ *Court Reporter(s):*
BAC Home Loans Servicing, LP§

NOTICE OF THE FILING OF AN APPEAL
In connection with this appeal, instrument # 51, filed by Bobie Kenneth Townsend, a copy of the notice of appeal, the order being appealed and the docket sheet are attached.
In regard to this appeal:
*• The Court of Appeal **$455.00 filing and docketing fees have been paid** or a motion for in forma pauperis has been granted.*
*• **This case was decided without a hearing - no transcripts**.*
David Bradley, Clerk

Notice, "no transcript." As I stated before, I was NOT allowed an open hearing—as the law firm was in the Dallas, Texas area, and we would NOT want to inconvenience one of the largest law firms in the country.

180

FIFTH CIRCUIT
OFFICE OF THE CLERK
LYLE W. CAYCE
CLERK

TEL. 504-310-7700
600 S. MAESTRI PLACE
NEW ORLEANS, LA 70130

May 05, 2011
Mr. Bobie Kenneth Townsend
1504 Memorial Lane
Conroe, TX 77304

No. 11-20319, Bobie Townsend v. BAC Home Loans Servicing, L.P.
USDC No. 4:10-CV-3751

We have docketed the appeal as shown above, and ask you to use the case number above in future inquiries.

Filings in this court are governed strictly by the Federal Rules of Appellate Procedure. **We cannot accept motions submitted under the Federal Rules of Civil Procedure. We can address only those documents the court directs you to file, or proper motions filed in support of the appeal.** See FED. R. App. P. and 5TH Cir. R. 27 for guidance. Documents not authorized by these rules will not be acknowledged or acted upon.

To receive the record for preparing your brief, counsel, including CJA attorneys, must provide the appropriate district court with a United Parcel Service, or similar commercial delivery service, account number. If you wish to receive exhibits, you must specifically request them. The district court will charge your account for shipping you the record on appeal. In the alternative, you may contact a local courier or attorney support services firm to pick up the record and ship it to you. CJA counsel may add these shipping fees to their vouchers.

Sincerely,
LYLE W. CAYCE, Clerk
By: Steve A. Totora, Deputy Clerk

The appellate court gives you a warning, straight off the press. If you file something NOT specifically dictated to be done by the appellate rules, the court will act as though it was never filed. This is a typical warning, to *pro ses*. They hate dealing with those guys, so they have to put their foot down at the beginning, or you never know what they could be capable of doing. But, the rest of the notice is directed, to attorneys with an account number. They don't advise what a *pro se* would do, without an account number. Notice the Clerk is too busy to sign their own documents, and the Deputy Clerk can't do anything on their own, without getting spanked. Or at least, that was what I was informed, by the Clerk.

On June 20th, 2011, I have my Appellate Brief and the Record Excerpts ready, and file it into the court; and I send a copy to the Akerman Law Firm. Record Excerpts are like an appendix, attached at the end of the brief; and you cite such documents, in your brief. The defendant's Appellee Brief is due, on or about August 15th, 2011, so they call the judge up and ask for an extension—to August 24, 2011, which is granted. As to be expected, the attorneys for BAC file another motion, to have another extension of time, to file their Appellee Brief. Remember again, there are over a hundred attorneys, in this law firm. They ask for an extra month, but the court lets them have until September 9th, 2011. The clerk, I mean the judge, is really mean to the attorneys, and only gives them an extra three weeks to file their brief. The attorneys get it filed, under the wire, on September 9th, 2011. I file my Reply Brief For Appellant, on or about September 19th, 2011. I file my "Appellant's Motion To Introduce New Evidence," on or about September 20th, 2011, which was granted. I then filed my, "Supplemental Reply Brief For Appellant," on or about October 8th, 2011. Now we wait, until the Fifth Circuit gets around, to kicking my feet out from under me.

On December 5th, 2011, my case was before King, Jolly, and Graves—Circuit Judges of the Fifth Circuit. What other last names of judges could I expect? The King has spoken, with Jolly vagueness, as he Orders the Graves to be dug. After all the hundreds of pages of pleadings in the record, it only took seven pages in their Memorandum Opinion (MO), to affirm Judge Hoyt's dismissal. Let's look at what IS printed in the case law books, forever.

What is the most important issue to Justices, about this case?

5th Circuit Memorandum Opinion
*"In July 2007, a law firm representing the taxing authorities sent Townsend a letter demanding payment of the 2006 taxes. Townsend responded by letter, demanding, among other things, the attorney's Texas Bar Association card number and **a copy of her license to practice law**, as well as documentation that the property is located in Texas."*

Do you think attorneys feel threatened, when you ask for their authority, to claim to be member a privileged club? Here is the actual statement, in the letter, referenced by the court:

Townsend's Exhibit M
*"Next: Please provide me with any documentation that would indicate that you are qualified to represent J. R. Moore, Jr. Tax Assessor/ Collector by providing your Texas Bar Association's Bar Card number and **a copy of your license to practice law** in the State of Texas."*

The Justices start off, by citing my first causes of action, correctly.

5th Circuit Memorandum Opinion
"Townsend **timely filed** an amended complaint, asserting claims for common law fraud, statutory fraud, conspiracy to commit fraud, breach of contract, negligent misrepresentation, and violation of the Truth in Lending Act ("TILA")."

Then, the Justices do a little *Pro Se* bashing. Note: Before you think of suing without an attorney, first take five years of legal writing. The attorneys will appreciate it, or NOT.

5th Circuit Memorandum Opinion
"Townsend's brief **is poorly organized, repetitive, and difficult to comprehend**. The statement of facts **consists primarily of arguments that the district court was biased and violated his due process rights, and that the district court clerk's staff was incompetent**. In his statement of issues, he lists eight issues, but the argument section of his brief discusses ten arguments, which do not correspond to the issues listed in his statement of issues."

As you see, the Justices—or rather the Briefing Attorneys of the Justices—caught onto the fact I was observant the staff of the trial judge could NOT follow local rules. As the MO shows, the Justices did NOT rebut my claim, of the staff being "incompetent," but instead changed the subject.

5th Circuit Memorandum Opinion
"**As best we can understand them**, Townsend's arguments on appeal appear to be:
(1) BAC defaulted by not answering the First Amended Complaint;
(2) the district court erred by allowing BAC to file a motion to dismiss in the same document as a motion for a more definite statement;
(3) the district court erred by dismissing the claims in the original petition;

(4) the district court erred by not giving reasons for the dismissal;

(5) BAC lacks authority to foreclose because it is not a holder in due course;

(6) the assignment of the deed of trust to BAC was fraudulent and, therefore, BAC lacks standing to foreclose;

(7) BAC breached the deed of trust by paying the property taxes without prior notice to Townsend;

(8) BAC breached its fiduciary duty to Townsend by misapplying his monthly note payments to the escrow account that it established without Townsend's consent, instead of applying the note payments to interest and then to principal;

(9) the district court erred by ignoring Townsend's request for leave to amend the complaint to invoke the discovery rule; and

(10) the district court erred by not remanding the case to state court."

Actually, there were more issues I could have brought up in my Brief, but due to page and word restrictions, I decided the ones listed above were more evident.

5th Circuit Memorandum Opinion
*"Throughout his brief, **Townsend complains that the district court judge was biased against him and in favor of BAC, and that BAC has committed "fraud upon the court."** In his prayer for relief, he asserts that the district court judge should recuse himself and the case should be assigned to a different judge."*

Courts have repeatedly held that positive proof of the partiality of a judge is not a requirement, only the appearance of partiality. *Liljeberg v. Health Services Acquisition Corp., 486 U.S. 847, 108 S.Ct. 2194 (1988) (**what matters is not the reality of bias or prejudice but its appearance**); United States v. Balistrieri, 779 F.2d 1191 (7th Cir. 1985) (Section 455(a) "is directed against the appearance of partiality, whether or not the judge is actually biased.") ("Section 455(a) of the Judicial Code, 28 U.S.C. §455(a), is not intended to protect litigants from actual bias in their judge **but rather to promote public confidence in the impartiality of the judicial process**.").*

As we go through, paragraph-by-paragraph of the MO, you will see that the Justices never comment, whether the attorneys committed "fraud upon the court," or whether Judge Hoyt should have recused himself. The Justices let the dead dog lie.

5th Circuit Memorandum Opinion
*"In a supplemental reply brief and appendix, **Townsend presents new evidence and arguments** that were not presented to the district court."*

5th Circuit Memorandum Opinion
*"... **we do not consider the new arguments and evidence** that Townsend presents for the first time on appeal, in his supplemental reply brief and appendix."*

I filed my, "Supplemental Reply Brief For Appellant," showing multiple new evidence that supported my claims. Let's NOT address anything that would cloud the reason, to affirm the trial court judge.

5th Circuit Memorandum Opinion
*"We review a dismissal "for failure to state a claim de novo, accepting all well-pleaded facts as true and viewing those facts in the light most favorable to the plaintiff." Brown v. Continental Airlines, Inc., 647 F.3d 221,225·26 (5th Cir. 2011) (internal quotation marks and citations omitted). "A plaintiff fails to state a claim **when the complaint does not contain 'enough facts** to state a claim to relief that is plausible on its face.'" Del-Ray Battery Co. v. Douglas Battery Co., 635 F.3d 725, 728-29 (5th Cir. 2011) (quoting Bell Atl. Corp. v. Twombly, 550 U.S. 544, 570 (2007». **Viewing the complaints in the light most favorable to Townsend**, we find no reversible error in the district court's dismissal of his claims."*

Again, the 5th Circuit cites their own case law; but then, rarely is a U.S. Supreme Court case being quoted, partially, by the 5th Circuit. Notice the buzz words, "well-pleaded facts." If one is without a source, to determine if the facts stated are "well-pleaded," then the creation of a closed shop has appeared—and the wind determines if something is "well-pleaded." Makes you wonder, if laws created, by the Texas Legislature, are "well-pleaded"?

5th Circuit Memorandum Opinion
*"**BAC was not in default, because it filed a motion to dismiss**. See FED.R.CIV.P. 12, 55."*

The statement, above, is deceptive, because I had filed one original and one amended petition; and the attorneys filed only one Motion to Dismiss concerning the original petition, in a timely manner. The attorneys defaulted, concerning the amended petition. The Justices also show a typo, since Rule 12 is associated with Rule 56, and NOT Rule 55, as shown above.

5th Circuit Memorandum Opinion
*"**Townsend failed** to adequately brief his contention **that the district court erred** by dismissing the claims in his original petition **and failed to explain how** the cases he cites entitle him to any relief on appeal. **The district court was not required to explain its reasons for dismissal**. See FED.R. CN. P. 52(a)(3)."*

The above statement can be said, of any brief that is submitted. The Justices give No explanation or an example, of any one statement found in my Appellant Brief that the Justices would consider "inadequate." Also, look above where I am being spanked, for NOT saying the magical term, "erred."

FRCP
Rule 52. Findings and Conclusions by the Court; Judgment on Partial Findings
(a) FINDINGS AND CONCLUSIONS.
(3) For a Motion. **The court is not required to state findings or conclusions when ruling on a motion under Rule 12 or 56 or, unless these rules provide otherwise, on any other motion.**

What is meant, by the comment that Judge Hoyt is NOT required to reply, to a Motion For Reconsideration, other than "Motion Dismissed"? Our system of justice made a Rule, where Judge Hoyt is NOT required to explain why he lied; in his Memorandum Opinion [Dkt#47]—concerning the reason Judge Hoyt dismissed my case. Previously, I have shown the reader, where Judge Hoyt made several statements in his Memorandum, where the record evidenced the statements were false. The system is designed to cover the judges' asses. The judges can lie all they need, make sh_t up and never have to explain the lies. Is this a Great Country or what?

5th Circuit Memorandum Opinion
*"**There is no authority for Townsend's claim that BAC lacks authority to foreclose** because it is not a "holder in due course.""*

What could the above statement, "There is no authority...," mean? I make a claim, in discovery I ask for documentation, in their possession that would support BAC was holder in due course concerning the subject property. O' Yeah, That's Right, Judge Hoyt denied my right to discovery to ask the question. Apparently the Texas Government Code, the Texas Local Government Code and the Texas Business and Commerce Code are NO type of authority, in United States District Courts.

Appellant's Brief, Pages 4-5
*"**Appellant's case is unique** as it involves a foreclosure, **whereby the appellant was current on his promissory note payments at the time of the accelerated maturity of the debt by the appellee**, when the appellee was not Holder in Due Course and the Public Notaries of*

appellee's Exhibits violated the Texas Government Code Sec. 406.014 (Dkt#44), creating fraudulent documents (Dkt#13-1, appellee Exhibit A) (Dkt#22, Pgs. 23-24, Exhibit G) filed in the Montgomery County Clerk's office, by the appellee."

Appellant's Brief, Pages 15-16
"**There is nothing entered into evidence that BAC has a lien associated with appellant's property**. Appellee has not provided evidence that appellee is Holder in Due Course. Appellee's Exhibit A (Dkt#13-1) is fraudulent on its face (See appellant's affidavit Dkt#44). Appellant has a right to offer proof in open court. Appellant incorporates the entire pleading (Dkt#45) of appellant's motion for reconsideration as to the detailed information that rebuts Judge Hoyt's memorandum (Dkt#42). Appellant filed an affidavit (Dkt#47) in support of appellant's motion for reconsideration that was apparently ignored as well by Judge Hoyt. Judge Hoyt's memorandum appears to be written by the appellee's attorneys as it only regurgitates the appellee's pleadings without reference to any appellant rebuttal in previous pleadings. **Judge Hoyt's memorandum makes statements (Dkt#42, Pg. 5, Last Paragraph) that could have only been formulated by reading pleadings of the appraisal district's attorneys from the state court cases currently under appeal. Judge Hoyt displayed bias against appellant** by ignoring all of appellant's Exhibits, just like Judge Hoyt ignored most pleadings by appellant."

Next, the Justices of the 5th Circuit parrot the attorneys' pleading, claiming MERS is "the original beneficiary," where multiple court cases have proved MERS could NOT be a beneficiary of anything—and keep their bankruptcy remote status. Go back to Chapter 25, "MERS 1 & 2," for review, if you do not recall.

5th Circuit Memorandum Opinion
"Townsend's argument that the assignment of the deed of trust to BAC from the original beneficiary, Mortgage Electronic Registration Systems, Inc. ("MERS"), is fraudulent because it contains no corporate seal, as required by Section 16.033 of the Texas Civil Practices and Remedies Code, **is meritless. Section 16.033 applies to**

*instruments that convey real property, and the assignment of the deed of trust is not such an instrument. **Townsend's contention that MERS ceased to do business in Texas is unsupported and irrelevant to the validity of the assignment from MERS to BAC.***"

I know NOT where the justices are coming from; stating an assignment of the Note and Deed of Trust does NOT "convey real property." Then how, pray tell, would an Entity think it has the right to sell the subject property, if the Entity does NOT think it has been conveyed the real property? Is it possible to sell someone's property and NOT believe you have been conveyed ownership, to sell such property? Are we talking semantics, only? Can it be possible a defect in a Deed of Trust or Assignment conveying rights to property be irrelevant to the actions of another document? And, how is it a certified document, from the Texas Secretary of State, confirms an Entity, called, "Mortgage Electronic Registration Systems, Inc.," has changed its name to Altech Properties, yet can be considered being "unsupported" where MERS ceased to do business in Texas? The Justices do NOT say. How is it irrelevant someone claiming to be an employee of MERS, working in Texas, alleges an assignment has been done, "after" a substitute trustee is appointed, by the Entity that has NOT been assigned the Note and Deed of Trust, before the act? The Justices will NOT say.

5th Circuit Memorandum Opinion
*"BAC did not breach the deed of trust by paying the delinquent property taxes, because Townsend did not contest the property tax lien in good faith through a legal proceeding. **Townsend was not entitled to notice of payment of the property taxes because the deed of trust provides that the Lender "may" give such notice.***"

How do they sleep at night? It is hard to hold your composure when, supposedly-impartial Justices pick a magical term out of a paragraph, like "may," as an excuse for the behavior of the defendant. Stating in their Opinion, above, I was NOT "entitled" to notice—because the justices found the magic term of "may" in a sentence, is blatant incompetence, at the very least. Read for yourself, below, what is stated in the Deed of Trust, concerning the magical term, "may." First, the Lender has to know about a lien, or it canNOT give notice to the Borrower, to satisfy the lien. Even if the Lender knows about a lien, it 'may' ignore the lien, by simply NOT informing the Borrower of the lien. That is where the "magical term," "may," comes from. If the Lender would like the lien to be satisfied, then, the Lender is required give notice, to the Borrower of the lien; and within 10 days of that notice, the Borrower is required to do something about the lien, like defend it.

> *Townsend's Deed of Trust*
> *"4. Charges; Liens.*
> ***If*** *Lender determines that any part of the Property is subject to a lien which can attain priority over this Security Instrument,* ***Lender may give Borrower a notice identifying the lien. Within 10 days of the date on which that notice is given, Borrower shall satisfy the lien or take one or more of the actions set forth above in this Section 4.****"*

How do you contest a lien, in "good faith," if you are NOT allowed to defend the lien? Doesn't the Deed of Trust allow for the option, to defend the lien? The Justices turned a blind eye to my lawful option, my right to defend. How would a defendant start a court case and be the defendant? I do NOT have a clue. How I defended the lien was to send a letter, to the law firm that threatened to take my property; and told them when and where I would be available, to be served with a complaint. What more could I do?

> *Townsend's Deed of Trust*
> *4. Charges; Liens.*
> *Borrower shall promptly discharge any lien which has priority over this Security Instrument* ***unless Borrower****: (a) agrees in writing to the payment of the obligation secured by the lien in a manner acceptable to Lender, but only so long as Borrower is performing such agreement;* ***(b) contests the lien in good faith by, or defends***

against enforcement of the lien in, legal proceedings which in Lender's opinion operate to prevent the enforcement of the lien while those proceedings are pending, but only until such proceedings are concluded; or (c) secures from the holder of the lien an agreement satisfactory to Lender subordinating the lien to this Security Instrument."

There is NO other option available, in the Deed of Trust, where the Lender can just pay the lien, without giving notice to the borrower it plans to pay the lien. This is one more example, why I do NOT trust any court opinion I read, anymore.

5th Circuit Memorandum Opinion
*"There is no fiduciary relationship between BAC and Townsend and, **even if there were**, BAC did not breach it by paying the delinquent property taxes and establishing an escrow account."*

Here above, the court is NOT sure of its decision, other than BAC could NOT have done anything wrong, whether or NOT BAC did or did NOT do something.

5th Circuit Memorandum Opinion
*"**It would have been futile** for Townsend to amend his complaint to invoke the discovery rule because **his own pleadings show that he knew or should have known the basis for his fraud**, negligent misrepresentation, and TILA claims **more than four years before he filed suit**. See TEX. CIV.PRAC.& REM.CODE§ 16.004(a)(4) (**four-year limitations period for fraud claims**); Exxon Corp. v. Emerald Oil & Gas Co., L.C., 348 S.W.3d 194, 202 (Tex. 2011) (two-year limitations period for negligent misrepresentation claims); 15 U.S.C. § 1640(e) (one-year limitations period for TILA)."*

Here again, the Justices parrot the attorney's pleading, which contains nothing to support their opinion. First, BAC was NOT the original Lender. They only claimed interest in the subject property, less than a year ago, from when I filed suit. I was claiming the actions, against BAC, and NOT Countrywide. The Justices knew this, but instead just parroted the attorney's pleadings.

5th Circuit Memorandum Opinion
The district court did not err *by not remanding the case to state court. See 28 U.S.C. 1332(a), 1447.*

United States Code
TITLE 28 - JUDICIARY AND JUDICIAL PROCEDURE
PART IV - JURISDICTION AND VENUE
CHAPTER 85 - DISTRICT COURTS; JURISDICTION
Sec. 1332. Diversity of citizenship; amount in controversy; costs
(a) The district courts shall have original jurisdiction of all civil actions **where the matter in controversy exceeds the sum or value of $75,000**, *exclusive of interest and costs, and is between*

> *(1) **citizens** of different States;*
>
> *(2) **citizens** of a State and citizens or subjects of a foreign state;*
>
> *(3) **citizens** of different States and in which citizens or subjects of a foreign state are additional parties; and*
>
> *(4) **a foreign state**, defined in section 1603(a) of this title, as plaintiff and citizens of a State or of different States.*

For the purposes of this section, section 1335, and section 1441, an alien admitted to the United States for permanent residence **shall be deemed a citizen of the State** *in which such alien is domiciled.*

United States Code
TITLE 28 - JUDICIARY AND JUDICIAL PROCEDURE
PART IV - JURISDICTION AND VENUE
CHAPTER 89 - DISTRICT COURTS; REMOVAL OF CASES FROM STATE COURTS
Sec. 1447. Procedure after removal generally
(a) In any case removed from a State court, the district court may issue all necessary orders and process to bring before it all proper parties whether served by process issued by the State court or otherwise.
(b) It may require the removing party to file with its clerk copies of **all records and proceedings** *in such State court or may cause*

the same to be brought before it by writ of certiorari issued to such State court.

*(c) A motion to remand the case on the basis of any defect **other than lack of subject matter jurisdiction** must be made within 30 days after the filing of the notice of removal under section 1446(a). If at any time before final judgment it appears that the district court lacks subject matter jurisdiction, the case shall be remanded. An order remanding the case may require payment of just costs and any actual expenses, including attorney fees, incurred as a result of the removal. A certified copy of the order of remand shall be mailed by the clerk to the clerk of the State court. The State court may thereupon proceed with such case.*

*(d) An order remanding a case to the State court from which it was removed is not reviewable on appeal or otherwise, **except** that an order remanding a case to the State court from which it was removed pursuant to section 1443 of this title shall be reviewable by appeal or otherwise.*

*(e) If after removal the plaintiff seeks to join additional defendants **whose joinder would destroy subject matter jurisdiction, the court may deny joinder,** or permit joinder and remand the action to the State court.*

This is where the BS hits the fan. In my case, we are talking about a corporation, and NOT a citizen. A corporation does NOT breathe, does NOT eat, does NOT go to the bathroom and does NOT think on its own. It is simply a piece of paper. It has no rights and can only have privileges. Privileges are granted by another thing, a body of people acting as a thing, like a corporation. The courts act unconstitutionally, when it comes to corporations. Let's review the preamble of the Constitution, for the United States of America:

Preamble

*"We **the People** of the United States, in Order to form a more perfect Union, establish Justice, insure domestic Tranquility, provide for the common defence, promote the general Welfare, and secure the Blessings of Liberty to ourselves and our Posterity, do ordain and establish this Constitution for the United States of America."*

I can only assume the term, "People," found in the Constitution, was meaning someone alive at that time—who was thinking, eating, going to the outhouse, among other things people did at that time. It was people creating a thing that could NOT and does NOT act upon its own, called a constitution. We will see later, the mentality of the people who sit on benches of courts, when it comes to things. When you look again, at the above 28 U.S.C. §1332(a) and 28 U.S.C. §1447, you will notice it talks of "citizens," in various status. It does NOT talk about the parent's citizenship concerning their children, but instead the direction to the courts is just to the "citizen." Also above, you will see the term, "permanent residence," concerning a "citizen." Logically, I think when a corporation buys or rents a building, in a location within a State; it has the intent to do business in that State. Such action, by the corporation, should be abundantly clear to all, it is the intent of that corporation, to have a "permanent residence" in that State.

Federal Courts claim to obtain jurisdiction over a corporation, with "permanent residence," in the State—where the Federal Court has located its "permanent residence," in the same State. Without constitutional authority, the Federal Judges created their own law, where they can make a determination the "permanent residence" of the parent, of that corporation, is the controlling factor—whether or NOT the Federal Court has jurisdiction. Now realize, there is no law created by Congress or the Texas Legislature that made this bizarre idea of federal Judges, a fact. They made it up, themselves. This ridiculous idea a Federal Court can obtain jurisdiction, because one corporation is doing business in a different State, matters NOT the corporation you are suing has a "permanent residence," in the same State, where you are domiciled and the injury occurred. It only matters where the parent, of that other corporation, has a "permanent residence." So, if you live in a State where the parent of a corporation you want to sue has a "permanent residence," you can sue that corporation in a State Court; otherwise, the corporation attorneys moved the State-filed case to Federal Court, so it can be dismissed and NOT be resolved. **It Shocks the Conscience**.

> *5th Circuit Memorandum Opinion*
> *"**The grounds for recusal asserted by Townsend-the district judge has a line of credit from Bank of America and the judge did not read or acknowledge his pleadings or exhibits-are baseless.**"*

Here, we see Judge Hoyt has a line of credit, with Bank of America, at the same time Judge Hoyt will have ignored the fact Judge Hoyt's line of credit could be canceled, by BOA—if he ruled against BOA. Why should Judge Hoyt have a problem with BOA canceling his line of credit, if he ruled in my favor? "Baseless." Also, there is no mandate that Judge Hoyt has to read a *pro se*'s pleadings. So what, if Judge Hoyt did NOT read plaintiff's pleadings? There is no <u>ground</u> for recusal, say the Justices of the 5th Circuit. Did you know electricians want a <u>ground</u> in their circuits, as well? Coffee lovers want their coffee beans ground, but they throw out the grounds when they are through. Judges throw out the grounds before they are through. Damn Rabbit Trails.

The Justices never addressed my causes of action, of "Negligent Hiring" or "Theft." What does this say about due process?

> **Judgment is a void judgment** if court that rendered judgment **lacked jurisdiction of the subject matter, or of the parties, or acted in a manner inconsistent with due process**, *Fed Rules Civ. Proc., Rule 60(b)(4), 28 U.S.C.A.; U.S.C.A. Const Amend. 5. Klugh v. U.S., 620 F.Supp. 892 (D.S.C. 1985)*

196

History and the Election of Attorney Causation

On or about September 24, 1789, Congress established a Supreme Court, 13 district courts, 3 circuit courts, and the position of Attorney General. Look how the Federal system has grown today. Attorneys have learned an easy way to get a case dismissed, by moving a State case to Federal Court, where jurisdiction is lacking to hear the case. There is no reason for a Federal Circuit Court to go by the mandates of the Supreme Court (SC) of the United States of America, because nothing will happen if they ignore the SC. Congress failed to provide you with remedy. There is no need for a Pro Se to appeal to the SC. Congress determined a few years back, the SC was NOT required to address all appeals filed with the SC; rather, the SC is now allowed to pick and choose the cases SC Justices want to hear.

It Shocks the Conscience.

LAWYER JOKE

HOW MANY LAWYER JOKES ARE THERE?
ONLY THREE. THE REST ARE TRUE STORIES.

CHAPTER 29
MY FOURTH LAWSUIT

In this time frame, my wife still has her Black Toxic Mold Dream House, and I get to protest the property tax—once again. I am still doing research to see where the authority lies, for the central appraisal district to do the things they do to us.

I am now going to get into, "Powers of Appointment." I learned about, "Release of Powers of Appointment," back in the late 1990s. You will find the information you need, for confirmation of the facts I state, at Texas Property Code Sections 181.001 – 181.058.

Texas Property Code
Sec. 181.002. APPLICATION. (a) Except as provided by Subsection (b), this chapter applies:
*(1) to a power or **a release of a power**, regardless of the date the power is created;*
(2) to a vested, contingent, or conditional power; and
(3) to a power classified as a power in gross, a power appurtenant, a power appendant, a collateral power, a general, limited, or special power, an exclusive or nonexclusive power, or any other power.
(b) This chapter applies regardless of the time or manner a power is created or reserved or the release is made and regardless of the time, manner, or in whose favor a power may be exercised.
(c) This chapter does not apply to a power in trust that is imperative.

I sent the Chief Appraiser Castleschouldt, a "Release of Powers of Appointment." The purpose of this "Release" document is to inform the powers-that-be, **if**, by some known or unknown act on my part, there is an assumption I have given or consented to allow another to act in my behalf on any manner; then, such assumption of authority has been withdrawn—or, in a word, released.

I have a video of the protest meeting, where Castleschouldt admits that he never read the document I sent him. Yes, I would like to get him fired. Castleschouldt did NOT want to be at my protest meeting, but I found in the Texas Tax Code, where all chief appraisers are required to be at every protest meeting, with the ARB.

Texas Tax Code
Sec. 41.45. HEARING ON PROTEST.
*(c) The chief appraiser **shall appear at each protest hearing** before the appraisal review board to represent the appraisal office.*

Also, you have the right to be given any and all evidence the appraisal district has and/or intends to use, as support of their position at the protest hearing.

Texas Tax Code
Sec. 41.461. NOTICE OF CERTAIN MATTERS BEFORE HEARING.
*(a) **At least 14 days before** a hearing on a protest, **the chief appraiser shall**:*
*(1) **deliver** a copy of the pamphlet prepared by the comptroller under Section 5.06(a) to the property owner initiating the protest if the owner is representing himself, or to an agent representing the owner if requested by the agent;*
*(2) **inform** the property owner that the owner or the agent of the owner may inspect and may obtain a copy of the data, schedules, formulas, and all other information the chief appraiser plans to introduce at the hearing to establish any matter at issue; and*
*(3) **deliver** a copy of the hearing procedures established by the appraisal review board under Section 41.66 to the property owner.*
(b) The charge for copies provided to an owner or agent under this section may not exceed the charge for copies of public information as provided under Subchapter F, Chapter 552, Government Code, except:
(1) the total charge for copies provided in connection with a protest of the appraisal of residential property may not exceed $15 for each residence; and

(2) the total charge for copies provided in connection with a protest of the appraisal of a single unit of property subject to appraisal, other than residential property, may not exceed $25.

When I sent in my protest form, to the appraisal district, there were only three (3) issues to be decided, by the ARB.
1.   *Property should not be taxed in Montgomery County.*
2.   *Exemption was denied, modified or canceled.*
3.   *Property should not be taxed in this appraisal district or in one or more taxing units.*

I did NOT protest the appraisal amount. I protested the Taxable Situs of my property.

Texas Tax Code
*Sec. 41.42. PROTEST OF SITUS. A protest against the inclusion of property on the appraisal records for an appraisal district **on the ground that the property does not have taxable situs in that district** shall be determined in favor of the protesting party if he establishes that the property is subject to appraisal by another district **or that the property is not taxable in this state**. The chief appraiser of a district in which the property owner prevails in a protest of situs shall notify the appraisal office of the district in which the property owner has established situs.*

My research led me to the fact property, NOT owned by a firm, company or corporation or used for commercial purposes, **had to be** rendered for taxation—by the property owner, to be placed on the appraisal roll. I understood going down this avenue would be an uphill battle. I will attempt to make my case—and you are the judge and jury.

First, let's review a few things found in the Texas Tax Code, and other sources, associating "taxable" and "used for business purposes."

CHAPTER 21. TAXABLE SITUS
*Sec. 21.021. VESSELS AND OTHER WATERCRAFT. (a) A vessel or other watercraft **used as an instrumentality of commerce** (as*

defined in Section 21.031(b) of this code) **is taxable** *pursuant to Section 21.02 of this code.*

*Sec. 21.06. INTANGIBLE PROPERTY GENERALLY. (a) Except as provided by Sections 21.07 through 21.09 of this code, intangible property is taxable by a taxing unit if the owner of the property resides in the unit on January 1, unless the property normally **is used in this state for business purposes outside the unit**. In that event, the intangible property **is taxable** by each taxing unit in which the property normally is used for business purposes.*

Above is just a short example of conditions that must be used for property to be considered as "taxable property." Even the 1st Court of Appeals in Houston, Texas have slipped and let the cat out of that bag. In *City of Houston v. Morgan Guaranty*, **666 S.W.2d 524 (Tex.App. 1st Dist. 1983),** the 1st Court of Appeals determined the term, "...**located in this state**, ..." found in the Texas Tax Code, "...means both **doing business** in this state and domiciled here."

More evidence surfaces, when you look at the rules the Chief Appraiser is mandated to go by.

Texas Tax Code
Sec. 23.01. APPRAISALS GENERALLY.
*(b) The market value of property shall be determined **by the application of generally accepted appraisal methods and techniques**. If the appraisal district determines the appraised value of a property using mass appraisal standards, **the mass appraisal standards must comply with the Uniform Standards of Professional Appraisal Practice**.*

All licensed appraisers have to go by the **Uniform Standards of Professional Appraisal Practice**, or the appraisers could lose their license(s). The Chief Appraiser has specific instructions, when it comes to appraisals, where the market value is determined by the interior of the structure.

UNIFORM STANDARDS OF PROFESSIONAL APPRAISAL PRACTICE
USPAP 2008–2009
Standards Rule 6-5
In developing a mass appraisal, when necessary for credible assignment results, an appraiser must:
(d) identify the need for and extent of any physical inspection.70

70 See Advisory Opinion 2, Inspection of Subject Property

Advisory Opinion 2, Inspection of the Subject Property advises that if adequate information about __the relevant characteristics of the subject property, such as an interior inspection, is not possible__ by personal inspection or from sources the appraiser believes are reliable, __an appraiser must withdraw from the assignment unless__ the appraiser can:
modify the assignment conditions to expand the scope of work to include gathering the necessary information; or
use an extraordinary assumption about such information, if credible assignment results can still be developed....

When the Tax Code allows a chief appraiser to enter businesses, but restricts the entry to non-businesses, a reasonable person should assume the Chief Appraiser has no authority to appraise a non-business—since he has no authority to enter the structure, unless the property has been rendered for taxation— and even then, permission from the property owners, for entry, is mandated.

Texas Tax Code
Sec. 22.07. INSPECTION OF PROPERTY. (a) The chief appraiser or his authorized representative __may enter the premises of a business, trade, or profession and inspect the property to determine the existence and market value of tangible personal property used for the production of income and having a taxable situs in the district__.

Rendering property for taxation has never been mandatory, for property NOT used for commercial purposes.

Texas Tax Code
Sec. 22.01. RENDITION GENERALLY.
*(c) A person **may render** for taxation any property that he owns or that he manages and controls as a fiduciary on January 1, although he is not required to render it by Subsection (a) or (b) of this section.*

Texas Tax Code
*Sec. 22.22. METHOD FOR REQUIRING RENDITION OR REPORT. The chief appraiser **may require a rendition statement or property report he is authorized to require** by this chapter by delivering written notice that the statement or report is required to the person responsible for filing it. He shall attach to the notice a copy of the appropriate form.*

*Vernon's...and city laws restricting suffrage in bond elections to **persons who have made available for taxation some item of real...property**...were not necessary to further state's interests in limiting the electorate to those who could pay the financial obligation created by the bonds or to maintain a penalty **that would encourage voluntary rendering of property for taxation which would enrich the state and city treasuries**... Stone v. Stovall (D.C. 1974) 377 F.Supp. 1016, affirmed 95 S.Ct. 1637, 421 U.S. 289, 44 L. Ed.2nd 172, rehearing denied 95 S.Ct. 2617, 422 U.S. 1029, 45 L.Ed.2nd 686.*

*Each person, partnership, and corporation owning property within the limits of the corporation **shall**, between January first and April first **of each year**, hand to the city assessor and collector a full and complete sworn inventory of the property possessed or controlled by him, her, or them, within said limits on the first day of January of the current year. If the fiscal year of a municipal corporation runs **otherwise than the calendar year**, **such corporation** may by ordinance require said inventory to be made as of the first day of the fiscal year, in which case the inventory shall be handed to the city assessor and collector within the first three months of the fiscal year. (As amended Acts 1934, 43rd Leg., 3rd C.S., p. 50, ch.27, Sec.*

1.) Pocket Part Vol. 2, Vernon's Annotated Statutes, art. 1043.

The time fixed for rendition of property *to city for taxation by statute, providing that owner "shall" hand city assessor and collector complete sworn inventory of property within first three months of each calendar or fiscal year,* **is not mandatory, but directory**... *MARKOWSKY et al. v. NEWMAN et al., 136 S.W.2d, 808(1940)*

The above paragraphs should be an eye opener to you. You see, rendering property is NOT mandatory. In fact, the Justices in **Stone v. Stovall** confirm rendering is encouraged by the judges, to increase funds in the state and city treasuries; but at the same time, indicating such rendition is voluntary, by the property owner.

If you do not recall Chapter 12, "Can You Really Own Property?," you need the review to remember about the history documents recorded in the Montgomery County Clerk's Office that are certified that the term "person" that you find in the Texas Tax Code today concerning assessment and collection of property taxes is only a "firm," "company," or "corporation".

If you go to the Montgomery County Clerk's Office, at 210 West Davis, Conroe, Texas 77305, or write, at P.O. Box 959, Conroe, Texas 77301; then, ask for a certified copy of the following documents:

Document   PI145-2012092268-10 is "Chapter 157 (CIVII), Pages 275 through 281, of the General Laws of the State of Texas, Passed at the Session of the Fifteenth legislature."

Document   PI145-2012092269-05 is "Article 7149, Pages 2068 and 2069, Volume II of the Revised Civil Statutes of the State of Texas, Adopted at the Regular Session of the Thirty-Ninth Legislature, 1925".

Document PI145-2012092270-4 is *"Article 7149, Page 934, Volume 2 of West's Texas Statutes and Codes, published by West Publishing Co."*

At your leisure just call them and for about Thirty dollars, you too can have for yourself—to share with others, over One Hundred (100) years, of documents proving the intent of the Texas Legislature—concerning the assessment and collection of taxes. This issue will NOT go away, simply because the judges and administrative bodies refuse to read the pleadings of a *Pro Se.*

Back to the Protest Hearing....

At the protest hearing, the Chairman of the ARB refused to hear my protest, concerning the Property Situs of the subject property. The ARB simply went into standard, status-quo custom-and-policy mode; and just changed the assessed market value, of the subject property, back to the amount I paid for the property—back in 2004.

ORDER DETERMINING PROTEST
On 11/15/2011 the Appraisal Review Board of Montgomery County, Texas, heard the above protest concerning the appraisal record for tax year 2011.
The taxpayer and chief appraiser appeared. *A summary of the chief appraiser's testimony, a list of witnesses and **a list of evidence submitted** appear as part of the records of this case,*
*The taxpayer's notice of protest **was flied in time**. The Appraisal Review Board **found that it had jurisdiction over the case**. The Appraisal Review Board delivered written notice of the hearing in the manner required by law.*
VALUE IS OVER MARKET VALUE
Having heard the evidence and arguments from both sides, the Appraisal Review Board with quorum present determined that:
The appraisal records are incorrect *and should be changed.*
The Appraisal Review Board therefore ORDERS that:
The 2011 value is $124,900
Terry F Bowie, Chairman
Appraisal Review Board

You will notice above, nothing is mentioned about the property situs, which the protest was only about. But they did send it certified mail—so, they had a record when I received it, this time.

On or About January 13th, 2012, I filed suit, case number 12-01-00485 CV, in the State District County in Montgomery County, Texas: *Bobie Kenneth Townsend vs. Montgomery Central Appraisal District; Montgomery Central Appraisal District, Chief Appraiser Mark Castleschouldt In His Official & Individual Capacity; Appraisal Review Board of Montgomery County, Texas; Appraisal Review Board of Montgomery County, Texas Chairman Terry Bowie In His Official & Individual Capacity.* (Yes, all them, at once.)

The causes of action claimed in my petition were: The appraisal district and the ARB are NOT a republican form of government; lack of jurisdiction of the MCAD and the ARB; Failure to adhere to the Uniform Standards of Professional Appraisal Practice; Violation of plaintiff's vested right to property; The removal of Castleschouldt from the office of Chief Appraiser; Appraisal NOT consistent with records of MCAD; Final Order of ARB NOT consistent with intent of Texas Legislature.

The case was assigned to the 359th District Court, the Honorable Judge Kathleen A. Hamilton presiding, again. Drawing Judge Hamilton again led me to believe that this was NOT a coincidence—Not a random draw.

The law firm contracted to defend such actions, against the MCAD, was Perdue, Brandon, Fielder, Collins & Mott, L.L.P., 1235 North Loop West, Suit 600, Houston, Texas 77008. The attorneys representing the defendants were Robert Mott SBN: 14596450 and Joseph T. Longoria SBN: 12544860.

The attorneys did the standard, "Defendants' Original Answer, Plea to the Jurisdiction, Special Exceptions, Special Denials and Affirmative Defenses"; "Defendant's Motion to Dismiss For Want of Jurisdiction"; and "Defendants' First Supplemental Original Answer, Plea to the Jurisdiction, Special Exceptions, Special Denials and Affirmative Defenses."

Most of the attorneys' pleadings were BS. But, the documents had me hopping, from research to research, to understand their response to my petition. I responded with my, "Plaintiff's Response to Defendants' Motion To Dismiss For Want Of Jurisdiction," and my "Plaintiff's Response to Defendants' Original Answer." For some unexplained reason, Judge Hamilton denied the attorneys' Motion to Dismiss For Lack of Jurisdiction, on or about March 2nd, 2012. We will get to the other details, as we go along.

The fist thing I want to do is recuse Judge Hamilton. I file my, "Plaintiff's Motion For Recusal," on or about February 27th, 2012. Remember, I had Judge Hamilton in two (2) prior cases: No. 09-12-12429-CV and No. 10-08-09020-CV. Below are just some of the grounds I submitted, for Judge Hamilton's recusal:

Plaintiff's Motion For Recusal
"Judge Kathleen Hamilton of the 359th District Court __violated__ Canon 2(A), Canon 3(B)(1) & Canon 3(B)(8) __by refusing__ to give plaintiff an open hearing throughout the entire case even though plaintiff filed motions and requested an open hearing (as shown in attached "Clerk Notes" & "All Notes"). Canon 2(A), Canon 3(B)(1), Canon 3(B)(5) & Canon 3 (C)(1) were __violated__ by Judge Hamilton for __failing to read plaintiffs pleadings or even adjudicate plaintiffs motions__. Apparently because defense attorney Joseph T. Longoria did not know whom Mr. Longoria client's name was, Mr. Longoria answered for an entity that plaintiff had not sued nor was Mr. Longoria' law firm contracted to represent."

There are no impartial courts that I know of, anywhere, when it comes to *pro ses*, but at least the system should allow you a different Hanging Judge, if one is available. This would NOT be the case, for me.

My Motion For Recusal was sent to Judge Olen Underwood, presiding Judge, Second Administrative Judicial Region of Texas, 301 North Thompson, Suite 102, Conroe, Texas 77301. Judge Underwood denied my demand for recusal, of Judge Hamilton, claiming what I accused Judge Hamilton of doing, in my previous cases, was NOT, "extra-judicial conduct on the part of the trial judge that would constitute a basis for a recusal." No wonder the judges do what they do, to *pro ses*. The bad judge has a ringer judge in their corner, to claim the particular wrong-doing was NOT in the class of wrong doings that would warrant the recusal of this BAD judge.

Speaking of things that Judge Underwood does, I have pasted, below, part of an Order—by Judge Underwood.

THE STATE OF TEXAS
SECOND ADMINISTRATIVE JUDICIAL REGION
ORDER OF ASSIGNMENT BY THE PRESIDING JUDGE
*Pursuant to Section 74.056, Texas Government Code, **I hereby**
assign the Honorable Olen U. **Underwood**, Senior Judge of the 284th Judicial District Court, to the 359th Judicial District Court of Montgomery County, Texas.*

This assignment begins the 4th day of April, 2012 and is for the primary purpose of hearing cases and disposing of any accumulated business requested by the court.

***Ordered** this 4th of April 2012.*
*Olen **Underwood, Presiding Judge***
Second Administrative Judicial Region

Does anyone have a problem with Judge Underwood assigning himself to a different court? NOT much oversight in the

208

judicial branch. Isn't it interesting a judge can just step in on a case, and "dispose of any accumulated business requested by the court"—and know nothing what has actually transpired in the case.

I have no crystal ball, but I can clearly see where this case is going. Next, I file a Motion to Show Authority, concerning the attorneys that claim to represent each and every defendant. This motion comes from Texas Rules of Civil Procedure Rule 12.

Texas Rules of Civil Procedure
RULE 12. ATTORNEY TO SHOW AUTHORITY
*"**A party** in a suit or proceeding pending in a court of this state **may, by sworn written motion** stating that he believes the suit or proceeding is being prosecuted or defended without authority, **cause the attorney to be cited to appear before the court and show his authority to act.** The notice of the motion shall be served upon the challenged attorney at least ten days before the hearing on the motion. At the hearing on the motion, **the burden of proof shall be upon the challenged attorney** to show sufficient authority to prosecute or defend the suit on behalf of the other party. **Upon his failure to show such authority,** the court shall refuse to permit the attorney to appear in the cause, and shall strike the pleadings if no person who is authorized to prosecute or defend appears. The motion may be heard and determined at any time before the parties have announced ready for trial, but the trial shall not be unnecessarily continued or delayed for the hearing."*

The Rule 12 has little room for confusion or interpretation, of what has to be done, when a Motion For Showing Authority is filed in Court. Again, Judge Hamilton never allowed an open hearing concerning my Rule 12 motion. But, unexpectedly, one of the attorneys voluntarily submitted the contract the law firm was relying upon, to represent all the defendants. The contract specifically stated the law firm could represent all employees of MCAD. But, the contract only allowed the law firm to give legal advice to the employees of the ARB; and no where was the authority for the law firm to represent any employee of the ARB, or any employee sued in their individual capacity. So, by the rules of procedure, Judge Hamilton was required to strike all pleadings that could be considered as done in behalf of the ARB, Terry F Bowie (Bowie) in his official and individual capacity and all pleadings done in the behalf of Castleschouldt in his individual capacity. As I stated before, I never got an open hearing in front of Judge Hamilton, even though I asked for a hearing, more than once. So, instead I went through the "Plaintiff's Motion for Default Judgment," according to Rule 239 & Rule 240 of the Texas Rules of Civil Procedure. I did everything necessary by the rules to obtain a default judgment against the ARB, and against Castleschouldt in his individual capacity and Bowie in his official and individual capacity. The clerk of the court was supposed to serve the parties, of the default judgment, for NOT being represented in a case where they were served with process. But, the clerk of the court failed her duty. Apparently there is no default judgment <u>for</u> a *pro se*, only against a *pro se*. **It Shocks the Conscience**.

I noticed the court I had paid a jury fee, and I demanded a trial by jury. Remember, I reviewed Article 1, Section 15 of the Texas Constitution, where it states: "The right of trial by jury shall remain inviolate." Apparently, A-1, S-15 does NOT apply to a State District Judge. I never got my trial by jury.

I filed my, "Plaintiff's Motion For First Declaratory Judgment," showing the court had jurisdiction, under Texas Tax Code Section 42.24(3), to grant me relief.

Texas Tax Code
Sec. 42.24. ACTION BY COURT. In determining an appeal, the district court may:
*(3) enter other orders necessary **to preserve rights protected by and impose duties required by the law**.*

No, Judge Hamilton does NOT give open hearings to *pro ses*—or even submission hearings—to decide on motions filed, by pro ses. Why should she, since Judge Underwood has declared such actions, by Judge Hamilton, are NOT to be considered as extra-judicial conduct that would cause a recusal. Anything a judge wants to do will be declared just fine on review.

Judge Hamilton did dismiss all my causes of action, for lack of jurisdiction, except for the part that concerned the final Order, of the ARB. In the same Order, Judge Hamilton Ordered the parties to file a Brief supporting their position, as to the jurisdiction, or lack thereof, concerning the appeal of the 2011 protest. I filed mine; the attorneys did NOT file theirs. I had already filed three separate Notices of Submission, to hear my pending motions, to no avail. I filed my, "Motion For A Open Hearing," naming the pleadings that needed to be heard.

Preliminary Matters	*Filed On or About*
Plaintiffs Motion For Showing Authority	February 27, 2012
Plaintiffs Motion For Default Judgment	February 27, 2012
Plaintiffs Motion For First Declaratory Judgment	April 30, 2012
Plaintiff's Memorandum Of Law In Support Of Plaintiffs Original Petition	May 7, 2012
Plaintiff's Motion To Compel Discovery	May 22, 2012
Plaintiff's Motion For This Court To Take Judicial Notice	October 19, 2012
Plaintiffs Motion For Continuance	November 5, 2012
Plaintiffs Judgment By Default	January 18, 2013
Order of Partial Dismissal For Lack Of Subject Matter Jurisdiction	January 22, 2013
Plaintiff's Motion For Clarification	January 28, 2013
Scheduling Order-Civil-Jury	February 28, 2013
Plaintiffs Motion For Summary Judgment	August 5, 2013

The attorneys filed their; "Defendant's "No Evidence" Motion For Summary Judgment and Traditional Motion For Summary Judgment." The attorneys made outlandish claims I provided no evidence concerning my claims, even though my Original Petition contained twenty-four (exhibits), which were supported by an affidavit of foundation. The attorneys did NOT address any of my exhibits as being no evidence, other than just making the claim the record was lacking any exhibits that could be considered evidence. Just making such a claim is good enough for Judge Hamilton. Judge Hamilton signed the attorneys' proposed Order, even though Judge Hamilton was supposed to have picked one of the alternatives of the Order; and didn't select either, indicating both alternatives applied, at the same time. **It Shocks the Conscience.**

I filed a Motion for a Void Judgment, because my due process was violated. Judge Hamilton did NOT waste her time by denying the motion. I filed a Request For Findings of Fact and Conclusions of Law, which Judge Hamilton ignored. I am to guess why Judge Hamilton did what she did. I filed my Notice of Appeal, on or about December 6th, 2013.

"If you are made aware of a lie & you do nothing to expose the lie, then you become part of the lie. There can be a million lies, but there is only one truth". - David Riddell

CHAPTER 30
BACK TO THE NINTH COURT OF APPEALS, IN BEAUMONT, TEXAS, I THOUGHT

I paid $651, to get the Clerk's Record, of 651 pages, sent to the Ninth Court of Appeals, Case Number 09-13-00565-CV. Please keep in mind, the case was dismissed on a No Evidence Summary Judgment that contained 651 pages, which allegedly lacked any Evidence. Well, the clerk doesn't really send a stack of papers, she just takes the scanned documents and copies the files to a computer disk; and mails it to the Clerk of the Court, of the Ninth Court of Appeals. I consider myself lucky, if the clerk gets me a copy of the disk sent to the court of appeals. I pay the unjust-enrichment appeal filing fee, of $195.00. What a racket.

If it is NOT apparent by now, after reading this far, I had multiple court cases going, at the same time. I am attempting to go chronologically, according to the filing dates of the lawsuits, as each separate case may have taken longer or shorter than another case. One of my cases may have started before another, yet taken longer to be disposed of than a case started, afterwards. If you are confused, so was I—at the time.

When another of my District Court cases is appealed, again to the Ninth Court of Appeals, I found it necessary to file a Motion For Recusal. I really thought my recusal Motion had worked, as I received notice my case had been transferred, to the Fourteenth Court of Appeals, in Houston, Texas. I received a letter, dated January 31st, 2014, from the Clerk of the Court of the Ninth Court of Appeals that stated:

Clerk of the Court Letter dated Friday, January 31, 2014
*"The Supreme Court of Texas **has ordered the equalization of the dockets across the state**; therefore the above cause is TRANSFERRED to the Court of Appeals for the 14th District. The complete file has been forwarded to the 14th Court of Appeals in Houston."*

I was feeling pretty good, about the transfer to the 14th District, but it was still a hell of a coincidence. My youngest son researched the 14th Court of Appeals and found, more than average, their opinions held up the rights of people. I asked for an Oral Hearing. I will get into why I wanted to recuse the Justices, of the Ninth Court of Appeals, later on in the story. And I use the term,. "Justices," loosely.

Rabbit Trail: You see, above, I asked for an Oral Hearing. By now, I felt confident I could argue my case, before the neighbor Justices. What I did NOT know, until much later, is NO Texas Appellate Court has ever had a *pro se* argue, in front of any Appellate Court Justices, since the creation of the Texas appellate courts. I got it straight from the Clerk of the Court, of the Ninth Court of Appeals. I am pretty sure I have her stating so, on audio. How I found this out was, I received a notice from the clerk that I had requested NO Oral argument, when in fact I had. I called her up to correct the error, and that is when she told me what was up—with Oral Arguments in front of appellate court justices. I am fairly certain NO *pro se* has been in front of the Texas Supreme Court, as well. At this time-frame, I had my doubts the Texas Supreme Court had ever granted a Petition For Review, from a *pro se*. We can No longer have faith and confidence, in the Judiciary Branch of our governments. The evidence is overwhelming. A fair hearing canNOT be obtained by someone, without an attorney. I have doubts having an attorney will allow a fair hearing. We The Poor People, need to clean the peoples' house of the Bar Card vermin.

(Jumping off that rabbit trail.)

Well, as with the Ninth Court of Appeals, it is evident the Fourteenth Court of Appeals, or at least the Justices and their Briefing Attorneys, do NOT read *pro se* pleadings, either.

The appeal was heard by Chief Justice Frost and Justices Christopher and Busby. The nineteen (19) page opinion was by Justice Tracy Christopher, on March 3rd, 2015.

14th District Memorandum Opinion March 3rd, 2015
*"In this case concerning a homeowner's tax protest, **the trial court dismissed most of the homeowner's claims for lack of subject-matter jurisdiction and granted summary judgment to the appraisal district on the homeowner's remaining claim** regarding his 2011 property taxes. The homeowner challenges these rulings, and additionally argues that **the trial court erred** in failing to set other matters for submission or for an oral hearing. **Finding no reversible error, we affirm**."*

I found later that Chief Justice Frost was highlighted, as one of the worse judges in Texas, on one of the websites. Did you notice, it took four (4) years from the appraisal protest hearing, to find out that I am wasting my time, just pay the tax?

The court starts off, by mentioning my first attempt to appeal an ARB decision, as the opinion calls the attempt, *"Townsend I,"* associated with case number 2011 WL 3207955 that was heard by the Ninth Court of Appeals. I find it interesting: the admission by the 14th found in #1 foot note, found on page 2.

14th District Memorandum Opinion March 3rd, 2015-#1 foot note
*"**We must** decide this case **in accordance with the precedent of the Ninth Court of Appeals under principles of stare decisis** if our decision **otherwise** would have been inconsistent with **our sister court's precedent**. See TEX. R. APP. P. 41.3."*

I take the above admission, as: 'since the 9th was wrong before, we must go along with what our sister has done in the past, or she will talk bad about us on Facebook.' You will see later, how wrong the 9th was; then remember the above statement. They all pee in their Bed with each other, and they don't change the sheets.

The 14th then talks of my second attempt, to appeal a decision of the ARB, of which the 14th labels as, *"Townsend II,"* associated with case number 2011 WL 3847430 that was also heard by the 9th.

14th District Memorandum Opinion March 3rd, 2015
*"On appeal, Townsend argued that the Board's final order did not sufficiently explain how he was required to serve the pleading he filed in the district court to obtain judicial review. Id. at *3. **The appellate court explained that this information is not required** by section 41.47(e) of the Tax Code, which specifies what must be included in an appraisal review board's final order. See id. Rather, information on serving the pleading is found in section 42.21(b) of the Tax Code. See id."*

The 14th confirms it is too bad for me and other *pro ses*, who want to appeal a decision of the ARB, because the ARB can do what it wants—and there is nothing you or anyone else can do about it. Then the 14th feels sorry for me, and lets me know what section of the Tax Code tells me who to serve process on—to be able to appeal.

The 14th then explains I do NOT have standing, to have Castleschoultd fired.

14th District Memorandum Opinion March 3rd, 2015
*"Our legislature has enacted statutes identifying those empowered to remove a person from a position as a district's chief appraiser or as a member of an appraisal review board. See TEX. TAX. CODE ANN. § 6.05(c) (West Supp. 2014) (providing that **the chief appraiser "serves at the pleasure of the appraisal district board of directors"**); id. § 6.41 (identifying the means and grounds for removing a member of an appraisal review board). **Townsend does not contend that he is among those with a statutory right to have either defendant removed from his respective position."***

The 14th admits a Texas District Judge canNOT Order any public servant fired. Sounds like a rogue agency has it made, if a Texas District Judge canNOT remove someone from office, fails to do his duty. What is to be done about this flaw in the system?

14th District Memorandum Opinion March 3rd, 2015
*"**Townsend also is not a person empowered to initiate a quo warranto proceeding.** See TEX. CIV. PRAC. & REM. CODE ANN. § 66.002 (West 2008) (**providing that a quo warranto proceeding is initiated by "the attorney general or the county or district attorney of the proper county"**); see also Bute v. League City, 390 S.W.2d 811, 815 (Tex. Civ. App.—Houston 1965, no writ) ("**Quo warranto is***

not available to a private citizen in his private capacity, *although it may be brought upon facts related and verified by him.").*"

I made the mistake in my Original Petition, and titled one of my causes of action, "Quo Warranto." I understand that *Quo Warranto* is a Latin term that means, "By What Authority." No where in the body of the cause of action do I mention *Quo Warranto* again, but because of a subtitle name, I get the above paragraph, from the 14th. I find it interesting a "private citizen" does NOT have the access, to an extraordinary Writ of Quo Warranto, but that a "public citizen" may have access to the writ.

14th District Memorandum Opinion March 3rd, 2015
*"The Property Tax Code **authorizes a property owner** to protest the actions listed in Tax Code section 41.41(a), including: the property's appraised value, its unequal appraisal, its inclusion on the appraisal records, the whole or partial denial of an exemption, "identification of the taxing units in which the owner's property is taxable," **or "any other action of the chief appraiser, appraisal district, or appraisal review board that applies to and adversely affects the property owner."** Id. § 41.41(a)."*

I hate the term, "Property Tax Code." When the Texas Legislature codified the Revised Civil Statutes, they created a "Tax Code" and they also created a "Property Code." I have NO idea why they named "Title 1" in the Tax Code, as "Property Tax Code." The one and only place in the Tax Code, where you find the term "Property Tax Code," is in Sec. 1.01. The term is **never** used in any other place in the Tax Code or Property Code. **However,** it is well established in case law, Titles of statutes have no ability to sway the actual intent of the statute created.

TAX CODE
TITLE 1. PROPERTY TAX CODE
SUBTITLE A. GENERAL PROVISIONS
CHAPTER 1. GENERAL PROVISIONS
Sec. 1.01. SHORT TITLE. This title may be cited as the Property Tax Code.

Did you notice, above, the admission of the 14th of my right to jurisdiction, by them stating: "or "any other action of the chief appraiser, appraisal district, or appraisal review board **that applies to and <u>adversely affects the property owner</u>**""? When an appellate court needs to find a reason, to throw a *pro se*'s case out, the last thing an appellate court would like to explain is the intent of the Texas Legislature concerning that statement.

14th District Memorandum Opinion March 3rd, 2015
*"A trial court lacks subject-matter jurisdiction to hear <u>**an untimely petition for review**</u>. See id. § 42.21(a); **Townsend I**, 2011 WL 3207955, at *3. And although a property owner may protest and appeal tax decisions based on any action of the chief appraiser or the Board, the Property Tax Code's exclusive procedures authorize a petition for review to be filed only against the District, not against the chief appraiser, the Board, or the Board's members. See TEX. TAX CODE ANN. § 42.21(b); see also **Townsend I**, 2011 WL 3207955, at *5 (affirming the trial court's dismissal of Townsend's claims against Castleschoultd <u>**for lack of jurisdiction**</u>). Thus, to the extent that Townsend's remaining claims raise a ground of protest authorized under the Property Tax Code, <u>**the trial court has subject matter jurisdiction over the part of the complaint that is both timely and is brought against the proper party.**</u>"*

Things like this, is what I hate about BAD case law. The 14th is lying to the public, about what the Tax Code really says concerning the time-frame, when the case was filed. The appellate court was required to use the Tax Code that was current, at the time the case was filed.

Texas Tax Code (2011)
"Sec. 42.21. PETITION FOR REVIEW.
(b) … Any other petition for review under this chapter must be brought against the appraisal district. A petition for review is not required to be brought against the appraisal review board, but may be brought against the appraisal review board in addition to any other required party, if appropriate."

You are the judge. Did I bring my suit against the proper party? My protest started in May, of 2011. The 14th says that the ARB could NOT be a party, when the case was filed. Were they wrong? The Texas Legislature changed the law, about ARBs, in September of 2011. Yes, they were wrong. Now concerning Castleschoultd and Bowie, by what direction would a *pro se* know, if a potential party is required and appropriate for the case? I'll go out on a limb and say it would be the decision of the Plaintiff that is bringing the case. This calls for another rabbit trail.

Rabbit Trail: The 14th has only one place in its opinion where it mentions *"ultra vires* conduct."

14th District Memorandum Opinion March 3rd, 2015
*"The court also held that because Townsend's claims against Castleschoultd concerned the chief appraiser's statutory duties of determining a home's market value for the District's records, **they were not claims of ultra vires conduct over which the trial court could exercise jurisdiction**."*

The above statement, by the 14th, is referencing the "*Townsend I*" case that was in front of the 9th. The 14th never mentions the term "*ultra vires,*" again, in its opinion—even though it was part of my claim, in front of the 14th.

> **_A state official's illegal or unauthorized actions are not acts of the State._** Accordingly, an action to determine or protect a private party's rights against a state official **_who has acted without legal or statutory authority is not a suit against the State that sovereign immunity bars._** In other words, **_we distinguish suits_** to determine a party's rights against the State from suits seeking damages. **_A party can maintain a suit to determine its rights without legislative permission._**
> Fed. Sign v. Tex. S. Univ, 951 S.W.2d at 404 (citations omitted)

> TEX. GOV'T CODE § 2001.038(a), (c) ("The validity or applicability of a rule . . . may be determined in an action for declaratory judgment **_if it is alleged that the rule or its threatened application interferes with or impairs . . . a legal right or privilege of the plaintiff._** . . . The state agency must be made a party to the action.").

> "However, governmental immunity does not preclude prospective injunctive remedies in official capacity suits against **_government employees who violate statutory or constitutional provisions._**"
> City of El Paso v. Heinrich, 284 S.W.3d 366,368-69 (Tex. 2009)

Case precedent means something, if it is in the direction the court is willing to go. Otherwise, case precedent is irrelevant, and readily ignored, by inferior courts making BAD case law. Court policy & expedience will always override the Legislature's intent of the written statute, creating BAD case law.

As you have reason to believe, after reading thus far, the central appraisal districts are a "for profit corporation;" and it and certain employees of it are subject to the *ultra vires* doctrine, for unlawful acts against property owners. It is obvious what the *"objects clause"* is, of each and every central appraisal district (CAD). It is to service its customers, which are the "taxing units," within the local district. The property owners are the "cash flow," of the "taxing units." To increase cash flow, every possible way to increase revenue to its customers ensures a steady increase, in cash flow to the CAD. But, any time the CAD, or its employees, acts unlawfully while doing business it is considered an *ultra vires* act. Neither the CAD, nor the taxing units, can justify or authorize the CAD's custom and policy, which is NOT authorized by law. Such unlawful acts have no force and effect, on the property owners; and such acts should remain null and void—unless a court, like the 9th and the 14th, creates BAD case law.

To sue, under the *ultra vires* doctrine, there must rest upon the existence of a contract, express or implied in fact. (See, *United States v. North American Co.*, 253 U. S. 330, 335, 40 Sup. Ct. 518, 64 L. Ed. 935) Under the *ultra vires* doctrine, you have a right to challenge the legality of a power exercised. When, as a result of an *ultra vires* contract, one of the parties is enriched at the expense of the other, the law creates an obligation, to repay *ex aequo et bono*, to the extent of the enrichment. (See, *Portsmouth Harbor Land & Hotel Co. v. United States*, 260 U.S. 327 (1922))

*"It goes without saying that in all dealings with the government contractors and agents alike are under an obligation to deal strictly within the limits of the statutes and with absolute honesty. Criminal sanctions enforce this rule. Similarly, the doctrines of fraud, unconscionable dealing and unjust enrichment **are to be strictly applied to insure fair and honest dealing between the government***

and its citizens."
Muschany v. U.S., 324 U.S. 49 (1945) Mr. Justice BLACK, dissenting

The 14th NOT only ignored my *ultra vires* challenge, they never reviewed the challenge.

(Jumping off that rabbit trail.)

The 14th continues addressing my causes of action stating most are held jurisdictional, under the Tax Code. Then it comes to my claim, of Entrapment concerning the denial of the variance concerning the Black Toxic Mold still present in the structure—until the property is torn down to the slab.

14th District Memorandum Opinion March 3rd, 2015
*Townsend is contesting the District's denial of his request to extend the variance and the resulting increase in the appraised value of his property. These complaints concern the denial of a variance in appraised value, which is a ground of protest within section 41.41's scope; **however, Townsend complains of actions taken many years ago**. Because the complaint is untimely, the trial court properly dismissed it. See Townsend I, 2011 WL 3207955, at *3 (holding that Townsend's judicial challenges to the tax decisions of 2005, 2006, 2008, and 2009 were time-barred, and thus, appropriately dismissed for lack of subject-matter jurisdiction).*

This is BAD case law. The court knew, or should have known, each year has nothing whatsoever to do, with the year previously concerning the same property. The appraiser should NOT take it for granted, since the roof was perfect last year, it may NOT be—the following year.

Tax Code
CHAPTER 23. APPRAISAL METHODS AND PROCEDURES
SUBCHAPTER A. APPRAISALS GENERALLY
*Sec. 23.01. APPRAISALS GENERALLY. (a) Except as otherwise provided by this chapter, **all taxable property is appraised at its market value as of January 1**.*

Even, rendering property must be done, each and every year, or the system must consider the property is no longer taxable. Notice that the statute above does NOT say "all property", but rather "all taxable property".

Tax Code
CHAPTER 22. RENDITIONS AND OTHER REPORTS
SUBCHAPTER A. INFORMATION FROM TAXPAYER
*Sec. 22.01. RENDITION GENERALLY. (a) Except as provided by Chapter 24, a person shall render for taxation all tangible personal property **used for the production of income** that the person owns or that the person manages and controls as a fiduciary on January 1.*
*(b) When required by the chief appraiser, **a person shall render** for taxation any other taxable property that he owns or that he manages and controls as a fiduciary on January 1.*
*(c) **A person may render** for taxation any property that he owns or that he manages and controls as a fiduciary on January 1, although he is not required to render it by Subsection (a) or (b) of this section.*

Tax Code
*Sec. 22.05. RENDITION BY RAILROAD. (a) In addition to other reports required by Chapter 24 of this code, a railroad corporation **shall render** the property the railroad corporation owns or possesses as of January 1.*

Tax Code
Sec. 22.23. FILING DATE. (a) **Rendition statements** *and property reports must be delivered to the chief appraiser after January 1 and* **not later than** *April 15, except as provided by Section 22.02.*

As I confirmed previously, the 14th created BAD case law when it stated my claim was untimely, when the claim was actually associated with a different year than alleged by the 14th.

14th District Memorandum Opinion March 3rd, 2015
Finally, **Townsend raised a seventh cause of action**, *which he refers to as "change the final order format." In this section of the petition, he asks the trial court to order the Board to change the format of its final order, primarily to explain that the Board and the District are separate and to explain how to perfect service of an appeal from a tax protest;* **however**, *the state legislature already has determined what information must be included in an appraisal review board's order. See TEX. TAX CODE ANN. § 41.47 (West Supp. 2014).*

Let's review Tax Code Section 41.47(e).

Tax Code
Sec. 41.47. DETERMINATION OF PROTEST. (a) The appraisal review board hearing a protest **shall determine the protest and make its decision by written order**.
(e) The notice of the issuance of the order **must contain** *a prominently printed statement* **in upper-case bold lettering** *informing the property owner* **in clear and concise language** *of the property owner's right to appeal the board's decision to district court. The statement* **must describe** *the deadline* **prescribed by Section 42.06(a)** *of this code for filing a written notice of appeal, and the deadline prescribed by Section*

225

42.21(a) of this code for filing the petition for review with the district court.

When you really read Sec. 41.47(e), do you notice the mention of Tax Code Section 42.06(a)?

Tax Code
*Sec. 42.06. NOTICE OF APPEAL. (a) To exercise the party's right to appeal an order of an appraisal review board, **a party <u>other than</u> a property owner** must file written notice of appeal within 15 days after the date the party receives the notice required by Section 41.47 or, in the case of a taxing unit, by Section 41.07 that the order appealed has been issued. To exercise the right to appeal an order of the comptroller, **a party <u>other than</u> a property owner** must file written notice of appeal within 15 days after the date the party receives the comptroller's order. <u>**A property owner is not required to file a notice of appeal under this section**</u>.*

Do you see the last sentence of Tax Code 42.06(a)? Did the 14th? Really? Do you see the deadline time-frame, for a property owner to file his "Notice of Appeal"? Me neither. Did the Texas Legislature intend for the property owner to get notice of the deadline?

So apparently, the property owners do NOT have a Deadline, to file a Notice of Appeal. Let's look at Tax Code Section 42.21(a).

Tax Code
*Sec. 42.21. PETITION FOR REVIEW. (a) A party who appeals **<u>as provided by this chapter</u>** must file a petition for review with the district court within 60 days after the party received notice that a final order has been entered from which an appeal may be had or at*

any time after the hearing but before the 60-day deadline. Failure to timely file a petition bars any appeal under this chapter.

First, the ARB Final Notice may or NOT be sent to you, by certified mail, so how does the ARB or MCAD know exactly when I received the ARB Final Notice? Ever had mail lost in the mail, and hear the party got it, a month later? I have. I have even had certified mail get lost, and show up a month later—after I had to send another document, certified mail again, because of it. My point is, the rule states the time starts **after** you receive the Final Order.

Page back and look at the 14th pointing to Tax Code Sec. 41.47. Now look at Sec. 41.47 and see that the section mentions Sections 42.06(a) and 42.21(a). Look at the final Order. See if either of those Sections is mentioned? No!—you do NOT. What Section of the Texas Code does the Final Order mention? It mentions Section 42.08(D) of the Tax Code. I have stated this before, to many judges, during these multiple court cases. Section 42.08(D) does NOT exist in the Texas Tax Code. The ARB refuses to correct the typo. The MCAD refuses to correct the typo. All Judges and Justices that have reviewed any case that concerns property tax have refused to Order the ARB to amend their form. **It Shocks the Conscience.**

Let's go back and look at Tax Code Section 41.47(e) (just a few pages back). See the part about: "**in upper-case bold lettering**" and "**in clear and concise language of the property owner's right to appeal**"?

"YOU HAVE THE RIGHT TO APPEAL TO DISTRICT COURT"

Go back to the ARB Final Order. Do you see the above statement, "**in upper-case bold lettering**," anywhere in the ARB Final Order? Neither do I. But, is the above statement really the intent of the Texas Legislature, for "clear and concise language"? If it is their intent, then the joke is on us.

14th District Memorandum Opinion March 3rd, 2015
*"Information about perfecting service is not required to be included; as Townsend acknowledges elsewhere in his complaint, information about perfecting service **is located in section 42.21** of the Property Tax Code. See id. § 42.21; also **Townsend II**, 2011 WL 3847430, at *3 (**pointing out** both statutes in the first case in which Townsend raised this complaint). Moreover, the only injury that Townsend alleges from the formatting of the Board's order is that "[l]ast year, Plaintiff was damaged by [the Board] not giving plaintiff clear and concise language of whom to serve process to." Townsend's **untimely complaint** regarding his 2010 tax protest was adjudicated in **Townsend II**, and **our sister court** already has affirmed the trial court's dismissal of the claim for want of subject-matter jurisdiction."*

The paragraph above is real sad. The 14th says I canNOT bitch about NOT being noticed how to appeal, since I was informed by their "sister court," about Section 42.21. Their sister court is a real bitch. A sister supporting a bitch of a sister creates BAD case law. If I had been noticed properly, how to appeal by the ARB Final Order, then my first 2 cases in front of a District Court would NOT have been dismissed, for NOT following the rules. I was just trying to find a court judge that would correct the ARB Final Order; so others that come after me would be able to get their case in front of a judge the first time, because of procedures lost in the Tax Code.

The 14th follows-up the reason to support the Summary Judgment against me.

> 14th District Memorandum Opinion March 3rd, 2015
> "We begin our review with the motion that the trial court granted. The District sought summary judgment on **both traditional and no-evidence grounds**, and the trial court stated in its order that **it granted the motion on both types of grounds**."

This shows neither Justice of the 14th looked at the proposed Order signed by Judge Hamilton. The Order provided by the attorney was conditional between traditional **and** no-evidence grounds. The proposed Order has "Alternative 1:" and "Alternative 2:". The judge was supposed to have picked one over the other, and the 14th doesn't care. The 14th justifies the error.

> 14th District Memorandum Opinion March 3rd, 2015
> Because **the way in which the claim is characterized** determines **who** bears **the burden of proof**, the District moved for traditional summary judgment on the issue on which **it bore the burden** of proof, and sought no-evidence summary judgment on the issue for which **Townsend bore the burden**.

I like where there is a distinction, between the different types of summary judgments; but I will show the U.S. Supreme Court has found summary judgments should rarely, if ever, be granted—if there is just one issue a jury should decide. But, I will get into that.

14th District Memorandum Opinion March 3rd, 2015
*"Townsend **did not** file anything **styled as a response** to the District's summary-judgment motion."*

14th District Memorandum Opinion March 3rd, 2015
***Townsend also filed** a document **styled as** "Plaintiff's Notice of Objection to Defendant's 'No Evidence' Motion for Summary Judgment and Traditional Motion for Summary Judgment." To the extent that its contents **can be construed** as actual objections, complaints regarding them are waived **because Townsend failed to obtain a ruling** on them. See TEX. R. APP. P. 33.1(a).*

The 14th is correct. I did NOT file a document that had the term "Response," associated with the Defendants' Motion for Summary Judgment. The 14th does mention the name of the document, where I objected to the Summary Judgment, but that will NOT be considered as a "response," because my objections "failed to obtain a ruling on them;" and it is irrelevant Judge Hamilton forbid ever hearing or ruling on any of my motions, in the past as well. Notice how the court pointed to their Rule 33.1(a).

R. APP. P.
Rule 33. Preservation of Appellate Complaints
33.1. Preservation; How Shown
*(a) In General. As a prerequisite to presenting a complaint for appellate review, **the record must show that**:*
(1) the complaint was made to the trial court by a timely request, objection, or motion that:
(A) stated the grounds for the ruling that the complaining party sought from the trial court with sufficient specificity to make the

trial court aware of the complaint, unless the specific grounds were apparent from the context; and

(B) complied with the requirements of the Texas Rules of Civil or Criminal Evidence or the Texas Rules of Civil or Appellate Procedure; and

(2) the trial court:

*(A) **ruled on the** request, **objection**, or motion, either expressly or implicitly; **or***

*(B) **refused to rule** on the request, objection, or motion, and the complaining party **objected to the refusal**.*

Notice it is irrelevant, to the 14th, that there was no "Notice of Submission," concerning the Defendant's Motion for Summary Judgment that should noticed the Plaintiff when the motion would be heard by the Judge. It must be a hindrance, to the 14th, when the attorneys and judges don't follow the rules, when dealing with a *pro se*. They must turn a blind eye, to make it work. Doing so makes BAD case law. Does the record show, the Defendants' attorneys followed the above rule concerning the Motion for Summary Judgment? No, it does NOT, except to a blind eye. **It Shocks the Conscience.**

14th District Memorandum Opinion March 3rd, 2015
*"Townsend still **has failed** to raise a genuine issue of material fact. **He instead** argued that his real property in Montgomery County is not taxable **unless** the District proves either that Townsend has rendered the property for taxation, or that (a) Townsend **is a** "taxpayer" as defined in the Multistate Tax Compact, and (b) **he is a** "person" as that term is used in the Tax Code. He contends that because the District has not proved any of these things, his property is not taxable. But **the District was not required to prove that any of these things are true**, nor could Townsend avoid summary judgment **by proving that any of these things were false**. As **we***

have explained, the District was required to prove **only** that the property is real property located within Montgomery County. **Townsend admitted** in his summary-judgment objections "that the physical boundaries of the subject property are within the physical boundaries of Montgomery County, **thereby claiming a trap effect** which **gives some** taxing units **an interest** in Plaintiff's property." The District therefore **met its burden** to prove that the real property is taxable in Montgomery County."

This is really BAD case law, on purpose, by the 14th. Ignore the evidence, and everything else will fall into place. The matter is cut-and-dried. No matter what history shows, today the State claims interest in your property, simply where it lies within some borders. Doesn't it make you all warm inside, when they show us, above, who's boss, by stating "**As we have explained,...**".

14th District Memorandum Opinion March 3rd, 2015-Footnote #9
*"**Townsend insists** that as used in the Tax Code, **the term "person" excludes human beings and applies only to organizations.** He **does not explain why** the definition of "person" **is relevant**, given that it is "property" that is taxed, **not the owner**. See TEX. TAX CODE ANN. § 11.01. In **any event, he is mistaken**; though **the word "person" is not defined in the Tax Code**, human beings fall within the ordinary meaning of this term. **Furthermore,** "person" is used to mean a natural person many times in the Tax Code, as can be seen by the statutory references to "a disabled person," "a person's lifetime," "a person's spouse," etc. See also TEX. TAX CODE ANN. § 1.03 (West 2008) (providing that the Code Construction Act applies to the Texas Tax Code); TEX. GOV'T CODE ANN. § 311.005(2) (West 2013) ("**'Person' includes a corporation, organization . . . and any other legal entity.**") (emphasis added); id. § 311.005(13) ("**'Includes' and 'including' are terms of enlargement** and not of limitation or exclusive enumeration, and use of the terms does not create a*

presumption that components not expressed are excluded.")."

Do you see above where the Justices claim the government code applies to the tax code? Do you see where the Justices point to a definition of the term "person" where it claims that the term includes "any other **legal** entity"? Do you consider yourself as a **legal** entity? I don't.

I don't think you will find a pleading of mine that has the term "human being(s)" or "organization(s)" in it. Judges stating in their opinions <u>what they think</u> occurred in pleadings, of the parties, may NOT be what actually occurred; since these judges parrot attorney pleadings, and ignore *pro se* pleadings.

*<u>**Townsend's Appellant Brief**</u>, Page 31.*
*"Townsend's "Plaintiff's Memorandum Of Law In Support Of Plaintiff's Original Petition" (CRV1-P283-339) <u>**lays out the Texas legislative intent**</u> and Texas Court findings that leave no doubt that Townsend's private property has no taxable situs without Townsend volunteering to render the subject property for taxation, which was not done by Townsend."*

The 14th never mentions my, "Plaintiff's Memorandum Of Law In Support Of Plaintiff's Original Petition," because it is NOT mentioned in the Defendants' Appellee Brief. Since it is obvious the courts only parrot the attorneys' pleading against a *pro se*, what else could anyone expect, from a State court protecting the State's cash flow? Those in power presume the ability and obligation to raise revenue, which may lead to a pay increase or larger retirement.

As shown in footnote #9 above, the 14th attempts to clarify **the magical-term "person"** in the tax code. But they focus upon someone living on the property, and NOT the one that actually owns the property. They reach into another code, to pull a definition of the term, "person," where it contains the term, "includes." There is no mention of my evidence, of three (3) double-certified documents, in the record of over one-hundred years; where the term, "person," contains the term "include" and NOT the term "includes"—concerning the assessment and collection of taxes.

> PI 145-2012092268-10, document recorded in the Montgomery County Clerk's Office: "The term person, whenever used in this act **or any other act** regulating the assessment and collection of taxes, shall be construed **to include** firm, company or corporation."

> PI 145-2012092269-5, document recorded in the Montgomery County Clerk's Office: "The term "Person" shall be construed **to include** firm, company or corporation. (Source)[Acts 1876, 275; G.L. Vol. 8, p. 1111]"

> PI 145-2012092270-4, document recorded in the Montgomery County Clerk's Office: ""Person."-The term, "person," shall be construed **to include** firm, company or corporation. (Source)[Acts 1925, S.B. 41]"

I really thought the 14th was more credible than the 9th court of appeals, but I was wrong. They create BAD case law, when there is a preference for it. **It Shocks the Conscience.**

14th District Memorandum Opinion March 3rd, 2015
*"In Townsend's remaining issues, he asserts that **the trial court erred or abused its discretion** in **failing** to set a variety of motions*

*on the submission docket **or in failing** to see that the trial court's staff did so; **however**, the **record does not reflect** that the trial court refused to allow any motion to be set for submission."*

The Justices of the 14th claim the record does NOT "reflect" this or that. The only reason the Justices' record appears NOT to reflect the refusal of the trial judge to look at the pro se's pleading, is that the Justices of the 14th would need to look at the actual record for the record to reflex the trial judge's apathy.

Why there is no record, other than multiple Notices of Submission that were ignored by Judge Hamilton, is because there is no transcript of the courts refusal. I was never allowed to have an Open Hearing, in **all** the cases I have been privileged to have Judge Hamilton as a trial judge. What possibly would the appellate court justice expect to find, in the record where everything a *pro se* attempts to do, by pleadings, is ignored by the trial judge and her staff? The record shows three notices for hearings, by me, that were simply ignored by Judge Hamilton. How else would a *pro se* "reflect that the trial court refused" the hearings?

14th District Memorandum Opinion March 3rd, 2015
*Townsend also contends that **the trial court erred** in granting the District's motion for summary judgment before conducting an oral hearing on certain matters. **He filed a** "Motion for An Open Hearing" in which he noted that the trial court's scheduling order provided that the case would be dismissed for want of prosecution at the pretrial conference on October 24, 2013 "if there is no announcement of ready with all preliminary matters addresse[d]." **He asked for an open hearing** to be scheduled "as soon as possible" **on a dozen matters** that he described as "preliminary matters pending to be resolved before trial as per the Scheduling Order."*

After Townsend filed this request, the District filed its motion for summary judgment, and the record does not show that the matters identified by Townsend were set for an oral hearing before the trial court granted the District's summary-judgment motion.

We cannot conclude that the trial court reversibly erred in failing to set these matters for an oral hearing before the date on which the District's summary judgment motion was heard by submission. Townsend's request for a hearing shows that he sought to have the twelve matters he listed heard "as soon as possible," but before the pretrial conference on October 24, 2013, whereas the District set its summary-judgment motion to be heard by submission on September 16, 2013. We cannot tell from record before us that the trial court could have held an oral hearing addressing a dozen matters before the date on which the District's summary-judgment motion was set for submission. Moreover, Townsend neither specified that he sought an oral hearing before September 16, 2013, nor requested a continuance of the hearing on the District's summary-judgment motion.

Here you have it. The 14th, or at least one briefing attorney, read the docket to see that I had twelve (12) different motions, to be heard before the Motion for Summary Judgment was filed and set for hearing; and Judge Hamilton ignored them all. But, it is the *pro se*'s fault, because I "neither specified that he sought an oral hearing before September 16, 2013, nor requested a continuance of the hearing on the District's summary-judgment motion." My bad. I should have known better. How could the justices conclude a request for an "Open Hearing" could possibly mean I "sought an oral hearing"? And by the numerous requests to hear my motions, surely, if I had just motioned the court for a continuance, that one and only motion would have been heard by Judge Hamilton.

It Shocks the Conscience.

By this time, I knew the Supreme Court of Texas would NOT read my writ, so why throw away the money?

Here is where you go back to Chapter 12 and review who can own property.

The greater the number of laws and enactments, the more thieves and robbers there will be. - Lao-tzu

Laws are spider webs through which the big flies pass and the little ones get caught. - *Honoré de Balzac*

Just because the power is out doesn't mean we unplug the constitution. - *Law and Order*, "Darkness"

We don't seem to be able to check crime, so why not legalize it and then tax it out of business? - Will Rogers

A lawyer is a gentleman who rescues your estate from your enemies and keeps it for himself. - Lord Brougham

The United States is a nation of laws: badly written and randomly enforced. - *Frank Zappa*

Thieves for their robbery have authority
When judges steal themselves.
-    *William Shakespeare, Measure for Measure*

CHAPTER 31
MY FIFTH LAWSUIT

Here I am, in 2012, and Bank of America is now trying to foreclose on my wife's Black Toxic Mold Dream House. Again, I file suit, with the intent of stopping it.

On or About March 30th, 2012, I file my "Plaintiff's Original Petition & Application For Temporary Restraining Order." Case Number 2-03-3493-cv, styled: *Bobie Kenneth Townsend v. Barrett Daffin Frappier Turner & Engel, LLP; Shelley Luan Douglass; Kelly Jimenez, Substitute Trustee; and Any and All Known or Unknown Doe Entities 1·10.* --In the Ninth (9th) District Court, 301 N. Main, Suite 110, Conroe, Texas 77301, the Honorable Judge Fred Edwards presiding. You notice that I label the judges Honorable, at first, giving them a benefit of a doubt only to find out, in a short period of time, they deserve no such respect at all.

This is a very interesting case, where I learned a lot of very interesting things. Barrett Daffin Frappier Turner & Engel, LLP (BDFTE) is a very large law firm that deals with many, many foreclosures in Texas. They are what the system calls, "a third party debt collector." The law firm has a few branches of companies that do various functions, concerning foreclosures. They have over a hundred Notaries employed, in their various companies. I made one of them (Donna Workman) quit being a clairvoyant Notary. Donna showed she could predict the future in her Notary Log Book. There is NOT much telling, of how many attorneys and paralegals that works on different projects, for BDFTE.

Shelley Luan Douglass (Douglass) is an attorney that works, or worked, for BDFTE. Douglass claims to be an attorney-in-fact, for Chase and Fannie Mae. Part of her job with BDFTE is <u>to pretend</u> she is also employed with MERS, as an assistant secretary, even though NO ONE works for MERS as an assistant secretary. If Douglass works for MERS, she does it for free. Douglass has no records in her possession, lacks the ability to obtain records, and even lacks the knowledge of for whom she pretends to be an assistant secretary for. If Douglass really has a boss that works for MERS, Douglass has no clue of the name of her boss at MERS. The record shows that Douglass has screwed a lot more people than she ever has with her husband. If this is NOT a fact, then her husband could never leave her side, to be able to keep up, with the amounting numbers of the people being screwed by Douglass on the side.

Rabbit Trail: NOT long before filing this suit, I filed a complaint with the Montgomery County District Attorney's Office, against Douglass. I claimed that Douglass filed fraudulent documents, in the Montgomery County Clerk's Office. I asked that the District Attorney's Office investigate Douglass. I have reason to believe, and do believe, Douglass pretended to be an assistant secretary for MERS, and had no authority to assignment the Note and Deed of Trust of the Black Toxic Mold Dream House to anyone, for anyone.

An Assistant District Attorney got back with me, and stated it appears there are over 10,000 attorneys, doing the same thing Douglass is doing, all over the U.S.; so a precedent has been set. This type of criminal behavior will NOT go to the Grand Jury. The Assistant District Attorney suggested I sue her in District Court. Attorneys are protecting attorneys like cops protect cops, like unions protect their bosses, like politicians protect themselves: in spite of the harm that may occur to their own relatives, neighbors and general population. Remember the attorney's required Oath, to be a member of the BAR? They must protect their brethren, or be subject to losing their Bar Card. **IT SHOCKS THE CONSCIENCE!!!!**
(Jumping off that rabbit trail.)

Kelly Jimenez (Jimenez) is the person that claims to be the appointed Substitute Trustee, to the original Deed of Trust, concerning the Black Toxic Mold Dream House. Jimenez is a mystery woman. I have found little about Jimenez. I have come to the conclusion the name Jimenez uses is really just an alias. I found Jimenez has never owned property in Texas. Every effort to obtain her real identity has been stonewalled, by every public servant from whom I attempted to get verification.

I added, "Any and All Known or Unknown Doe Entities 1-10," to the list of Defendants, as there is no concrete proof, anywhere, of anyone having interest in the Black Toxic Mold Dream House—other than the original Lender, Countrywide Home Loans, Inc. I had initially planned to add Bank of America (BOA) and Federal National Mortgage Association (Fannie Mae) to the lawsuit, as soon as possible, but it did NOT work out as I had planned.

Judge Fred Edwards was having problems with the Republican Primary, during my case with him. Judge Edwards lost his job, during the primary election. I can only assume he was attempting to get his case load down, before having to leave his office, as an excuse of why he did what he did—but I digress he had no concern with due process or the pleadings of a *pro se*.

First thing Judge Edwards did was to deny my Temporary Restraining Order that would have postponed the selling of my property, by Jimenez. Judge Edwards' reason was: "You need to hire an attorney to write the TRO." That was the day before the auction of my property. There was no time to hire an attorney. I got a process server to serve Jimenez at the auction, but she called someone, at BDFTE, and the someone there told her to sell the property.

Rabbit Trail: No one at the auction placed a bid for the property—probably because of the flyers posted, around the room, stating the property had "Black Toxic Mold," in the structure.

NOTICE OF [SUBSTITUTE] TRUSTEE'S SALE

1. Date, Time, and Place of Sale.
Date: April 03. 2012
Time: The sale will begin al 1:00PM or not later than three hours after that time.
Place: 301 N. THOMPSON, ROOM 208, CONROE, TX OR THE LOCATION DESIGNATED BY THE COUNTY COMMISSIONERS' COURT or as designated by the county commissioners.

*2. Terms of Sale. **Cash***

*3. Instrument to be Foreclosed. The Instrument to be foreclosed is the Deed of Trust or Contract Lien dated June 29. 2004 and recorded in Document CLERK'S FILE NO. 2004·073208 real property records of MONTGOMERY County. Texas, with B. KENNETH TOWNSEND AND CAROLYN TOWNSEND, grantor(s} and MORTGAGE ELECTRONIC REGISTRATION SYSTEMS. INC. ("**MERS**") AS NOMINEE, **mortgagee**.*

*4. Obligations Secured. Deed of Trust or Contract Lien executed by B. KENNETH TOWNSEND AND CAROLYN TOWNSEND, securing the payment of the indebtednesses in the original principal amount of $99,900.00, and obligations therein described including but not limited to the promissory note and all modifications, renewals and extensions of the promissory note. BANK OF AMERICA, N.A., SUCCESSOR BY MERGER TO BAC HOME LOANS SERVICING. LP, FK1\ COUNTRYWIDE HOME LOANS SERVICING LP **is the current mortgagee of the note and Deed of Trust or Contract Lien**.*

Kelly Jimenez
Substitute Trustee

Keep in mind, Jimenez states, in her Notice of Substitute Trustee's Sale document fixed to the court house wall, Bank of America N.A. was the current mortgagee. Since there were no Bids for the Toxic Mold Dream House, Jimenez awarded the property to Fannie Mae. What????? Where did Jimenez get that idea? There is nothing in the "NOTICE OF [SUBSTITUTE] TRUSTEE'S SALE" document, about Fannie Mae. Let's review the Deed of Trust, for whom could be awarded the property, at the auction.

> *Deed of Trust, Section 22*
> *"If Lender invokes the power of sale, Lender or Trustee **shall give notice** of the time, place and terms of sale **by** posting and filing the notice at least 21 days prior to sale as provided by Applicable Law. Lender **shall mail** a copy of the notice to Borrower in the manner prescribed by Applicable Law. Sale **shall** be made at public vendue. The sale **must begin** at the time stated in the notice of sale or **not later** than three hours after that time and between the hours of 10 a.m. and 4 p.m. on the first Tuesday of the month. Borrower authorizes Trustee to sell the Property **to the highest bidder for cash** in one or more parcels **and** in any order Trustee determines. **Lender or its designee** may purchase the Property at any sale.*

The "Lender **or** its designee may purchase the Property at any sale." This sentence, in the Deed of Trust, does NOT need interpretation. A reasonable person should determine if you are at an auction, and there are no Bids from the public, the "Lender" could have another auction, at some other time in the future, or have someone representing the "Lender" tell the Substitute Trustee, to award the property to the "Lender," and create a Substitute Trustee's Deed of the subject property in its name. But, to award the subject property to a quasi-governmental agency, which has no previous documented interest in the subject property, smells fishy and bears investigating.

Double Rabbit Trail: Here is the initial problem. Fannie Mae is a created entity by the Federal Government which is in receivership by the Federal Government where the Federal Government is taking on the debt of Fannie Mae backed by tax payer money. In other words, when Fannie Mae allegedly bought my home, it was actually the Federal Government which bought my home. Article 1, Section 8, Clause 17 states land purchased by the Federal Government in the several states must be by "the Consent of the Legislature of the State in which the Same shall be". This restriction keeps the Federal Government from buying up all the land within the several states with their counterfeit money that they print out of thin air. So, the question remains, where is the authority of the Federal Government to allow its agency, Fannie Mae, to purchase my property when there is no established interest in the same property?

Jimenez creates a Substitute Trustee's Deed (STD), and Fannie Mae recorded the STD, in Montgomery County Clerk's Office, document #LT1-1-2012035611-1. The STD states Fannie Mae, 14221 Dallas Parkway, #100, Dallas, TX 75254, was the buyer of the subject property, and paid $122,999.02 for it. (Looks like Fannie Mae is doing business in Texas.) The STD states MERS was the original mortgagee. Makes you wonder who Countrywide really was. Accompanying the STD is an affidavit created by an attorney with BDFTE, by the name of Will Benson (Benson). Mr. Benson states in his affidavit, Bank of America N.A. is merely the mortgage servicer, and never mentions who the current mortgagee was, at the time of foreclosure. Instead of the STD going to Fannie Mae, after recording, it is directed to be returned to the BDFTE law firm.

(Jumping off those rabbit trails.)

Judge Edwards seemed to me to be a cold-hearted SOB. My one and only Open Hearing with him, I got to see him first sentence a poor fellow who had been found guilty of having less than an ounce of Meth, and allegedly having the intent to sell some or all of it. Judge Edwards gave the guy seventy (70) years in prison. That's right, it is NOT a typo, 7-Zero years. For that harsh of a sentence, I must imagine the Meth distributor held a gun to his customers' head, before he could get them to buy his product. No wonder Judge Edwards lost his bid to be re-elected. May he got what he deserves?

Rabbit Trail: Ever read a comic book concerning "Superman Bizarro's World"? Bizarro is a mirror world of Superman's world, but where everything happens in the reverse. This court case with Judge Edwards was like being in this Bizarro World.

Judge Edwards stated he would do things he never did. The attorney for BDFTE and the other defendants stated he would file documents he never filed. Judge Edwards stated he would allow my discovery, after he read a pleading from the attorney that never filed the pleading, and Judge Edwards could NOT have ever read. Judge Edwards dismissed my case, based upon the document the attorney never filed. When I appealed to the Ninth Court of Appeals, the Justices of the 9th affirmed what Judge Edwards did, citing three (3) times, in their opinion, the name of the document never filed in their court, because the District Court Clerk never sent the document to appellant court, because the attorney never filed the document in District Court. BIZARRO!!! **IT SHOCKS THE CONSCIENCE!!!!**
(Jumping off that rabbit trail.)

The law firm that claimed to represent all of the defendants was Leyh & Payne, L.L.P., 9545 Katy Freeway, Suite 200, Houston, Texas 77024. The attorney of record was Steven A. Leyh, Texas Bar No. 12318300.

Concerning my causes of action claimed against the defendants: "Plaintiff claims negligent hiring, by defendant BDFTE. Plaintiff claims breach of fiduciary duty by the defendant Jimenez.

Plaintiff claims Libel against defendant Jimenez. Plaintiff, claims Negligent Misrepresentation by the defendant BDFTE & defendant Douglass. Plaintiff claims violation of the Texas Debt Collection Act by the defendant BDFTE."

The attorney of record filed a general denial of my claims against the defendants. I sent the attorney my request for discovery. In response, the attorney filed his "Defendants' Motion for Protection from Discovery," on or about May 8th, 2012, and noticed the court, for a request for an open hearing concerning his proposed Order, for protection from discovery, on May 25th, 2012, of which Judge Edwards Granted the request.

On May 25th, 2012, Mr. Michael C. Maus, SB NO. 24008803 with LEYH & PAYNE, LLP showed up, to represent all defendants. **THIS IS WHERE BIZARRO STARTS**.

> *REPORTER'S RECORD, May 25th, 2012*
> **THE COURT:**   *So what is this?*
>
> **MR. MAUS:**   *Your Honor, plaintiff has filed a petition against the defendants here, who is the law firm of the trustees, who operated on behalf of the bank to perform a foreclosure activity on Mr. Townsend's property. In response to that, Mr. Townsend has filed a petition with various causes of action that we see as groundless; and **we filed a motion for special exceptions** that was on the docket for this morning for submission. Also, he has filed numerous requests for production, interrogatories, admissions against each of the named defendants which are irrelevant to the matters at hand, especially in light of the fact that the claims brought are -- as I said a few moments ago -- are groundless to these defendants, Your Honor. And from responding to this discovery until -- either it's a motion for special exceptions considered or the Court orders it.*

At this point, Judge Edwards and I, as well as the attorney himself, did NOT know the "motion for special exceptions" had never been filed with the court clerk.

REPORTER'S RECORD, May 25th, 2012
THE COURT: *Okay. So I'm not too sure. **So this is your motion on special exceptions on the submission docket?***

MR. MAUS: Yes, Your Honor.

THE COURT: For today?

MS. SANCHEZ: Yes.

Here the court coordinator, Ms. Sanchez, confirms to Judge Edwards, the non-filed document was actually on submission docket, to be ruled on, that day.

REPORTER'S RECORD, May 25th, 2012
THE COURT: *Okay. I'll give you an answer then in a week. Okay. But **your motion for light discovery?***

MR. TOWNSEND: *Yes, Your Honor.*

THE COURT: *That's your motion for —*

Here Judge Edwards is asking me, about "Plaintiff's Motion for Light Discovery and Response to Defendant's Motion For Protection From Discovery," but the attorney butts in.

REPORTER'S RECORD, May 25th, 2012
MR. MAUS: *Well, that was in response to our motion for -- **we also filed a motion for protection from discovery.** He filed **numerous** discovery requests on April 30th to these defendants that are irrelevant to the causes of action. They are **outside the scope** of any perceived discovery that would take place in regard to these causes of action. Again, we feel the causes of action themselves are groundless. We're going to subject ourselves to answering I think **well over a hundred.***

THE COURT: **Did you file an objection to the request?**

246

MR. MAUS: Well, Your Honor, *I can file an objection to the request.* The answer date isn't until next week. But what we're trying to do is get some guidance from the Court on either *the motion for special* -- I don't want to object to his discovery request in whole. It's just out of hand. If there would be some way that, like I said, to limit this discovery in light of the motion for special exceptions.

Here Judge Edwards is prosecuting from the Bench, reminding the attorney he needs to file an objection, so Judge Edwards can rule the way the attorney wants. Judge Edwards never lets me bring up my Motion for Light Discovery, again.

REPORTER'S RECORD, May 25th, 2012
THE COURT: Let me -- *I rule within a week* on the docket -- on the submission docket. But *we're usually running about a week behind.* But it's not really behind because we don't really get to it until it's actually due. So we have to wait for all the answers to come in and responses.

MR. MAUS: Right.

THE COURT: So *I'll rule in about a week on the special exceptions* which might help clarify things. But *I'll release you* from having to answer any interrogatories or requests for production *until* I have made that *ruling on special exceptions,* and *he has re-pled.*

Here Judge Edwards has clarified everything, by stating **"and he has re-pled."** Judge Edwards hasn't read the attorney's motion and he never will, because it was never filed with the court clerk.

REPORTER'S RECORD, May 25th, 2012
MR. MAUS: Okay. I just want to make sure we're not going to totally waive objections in the meantime.

247

THE COURT: You're not waiving objections. I'm just suspending you from having to respond **until I rule on special exceptions**, and **he has an opportunity to re-plead**, then **we start over**.

That was the first, and last, hearing I had, with Judge Edwards. I filed my, "Plaintiffs Notice of Objection And Notice for Submission," concerning my objection—of the local rules being ignored, by the court staff. I objected the attorneys were NOT following the rules of procedure. I objected to losing a day of work, to attend the Open Hearing, on matters that could have been done by submission. I objected to the attorney that appeared at the Open hearing, was NOT the attorney of record, and did NOT know the matters of which he was trying to argue. I requested again, for my Motion to Show Authority be placed on the submission docket. In a Bizarro ruling, instead of creating an Order dealing with my pleading, Judge Edwards made a copy of my pleading, and just stamped "DENIED," across each page of the pleading, dated and signed under my signature, and then filed it. BIZARRO.

> CLERK NOTES
> Cause No. 12-03-03493
> 05.29.12 PLTF'S NOTICE OF OBJECTION AND NOTICE FOR SUBMISSION
> FILED BY BOBIE TOWNSEND
> 06.08.12 DC COPY OF LETTER TO BOBIE TOWNSEND DATED 06.05.12 – RE CASE REMOVED FROM E-FILING
> FILED BY ATTY MICHAEL MAUS EB
> 06.15.12 **PLTF'S NOTICE OF OBJECTION AND NOTICE FOR SUBMISSION**
> **DENIED/ SIGNED** JUDGE FRED EDWARDS 9TH CL/9TH
> (44844549)

Judge Edwards signed the defendants' proposed Order, on October 1st, 2012. I requested to amend my complaint, with no response from Judge Edwards. I filed my standard motion for reconsideration, request for findings of fact, but they fell on deaf ears and blind eyes. Judge Edwards, apparently by telepathic means, read the non-existing motion the attorney never filed in court; and ruled against my case. **It Shocks the Conscience.**

I appealed to the Ninth Court of Appeals in Beaumont, Texas; case number 09-12-00564-CV. The case was before Justices Gaultney, Kreger, and Horton. The twenty-two (22) page opinion was given, by Justice David Gaultney, on October 31, 2013.

Below, are four (4) different places, in the Ninth Court of Appeals' Opinion, where it mentions a document, "**special exceptions**," that was NOT part of the court record the District Clerk of the Court sent the Justices to review.

Ninth Court of Appeals Opinion NO. 12-00564-CV
*"In issue three, Townsend argues the trial court erred in granting summary judgment when the appellees failed to file timely responses to his discovery requests. The trial court granted protection from Townsend's discovery requests on May 25, 2012, when it excused the appellees from responding to Townsend's discovery requests until the trial court **ruled on their special exceptions**. See Tex. R. Civ. P. 192.6. Townsend **failed to establish** an abuse of discovery. See Tex. R. Civ. P. 215. We overrule issue three."*

Ninth Court of Appeals Opinion NO. 12-00564-CV
*Townsend sent discovery requests to the appellees in April 2012. Before their responses were due, the appellees filed a motion for protection on the ground that the **voluminous** requests were "**purely harassing** in nature in light of the fact that Plaintiff's claims are **groundless, baseless and frivolous**." Townsend responded with a motion for "light discovery." This response agreed that Townsend's discovery should be stayed pending a response to his "light discovery," and stated that a motion to compel would be filed in the event of non-compliance. On May 25, 2012, the trial court excused the appellees from responding to the discovery requests until after the trial court **ruled on the appellees' special exceptions** to*

Townsend's pleadings. The appellees moved for summary judgment in August 2012.

Notice that over four month went by while I waited for answers to my requested discovery before the defendant's motion for summary judgment had occurred.

Ninth Court of Appeals Opinion NO. 12-00564-CV
Townsend alleged Jimenez hurt his reputation in the community by posting an invalid notice of foreclosure. Under Townsend's theory, Jimenez tried to sell the property without verifying her authority to do so. This allegedly false statement does not pertain to Townsend. See McLemore, 978 S.W.2d at 571. **In his response to special exceptions**, *Townsend explained that he was never in default on his monthly installments that were agreed upon between him and Countrywide, and that when he executed the deed of trust he did not intend to become a tax collector for the Montgomery County Central Appraisal District. But Townsend* **did not allege** *in his pleadings that he was not in default of his obligation to pay the taxes on the property. See also Townsend, 783 F. Supp. 2d at 971 (BAC paid the tax assessment that Townsend failed to pay.). Townsend's pleadings* **demonstrate** *the lack of a libel claim.*

Here the Justices **admit** that I responded to the **special exceptions** document the Justices could **NOT** have read. The Justices simply parroted the defendants' attorney's pleadings without reading the pro se's pleadings. I did state in my pleadings that I was **NOT** in default, but the Justices must read the pro se's pleading to know this.

Ninth Court of Appeals Opinion NO. 12-00564-CV
A mortgage servicer administering the foreclosure **must disclose** *the representation* **and provide** *the name of the mortgagee and the address of either the mortgagee or the mortgage servicer in the notice of sale. See Tex. Prop. Code Ann. § 51.0025. The notice of substitute trustee's sale signed by Jimenez* **provided** *the name and address of the mortgage servicer,* **and stated** *that the mortgage servicer was authorized to represent the mortgagee,* **but does not**

clearly state whether Bank of America is the current mortgagee. Townsend alleged the omission invalidated the sale, but **he did not allege** a **causal connection** between that omission and the sale price obtained for the property. **In his response to special exceptions**, Townsend suggested that Jimenez **committed an irregularity** by accepting a bid from FNMA, but **he alleged no causal connection** between a defect in the notice and the acceptance of the bid.

Here again the Justices talk about my response to the 'special exceptions,' but canNOT talk about the actual 'special exceptions' themselves, since they do NOT exist in the record. Let's look at part of the District Clerk of the Court's Docket Record sent to the 9th.

Clerk's Record, Volume I Index	Page
CAPTION	4
DOCKET 5HEET	5
03.30.12 PLAINTIFF'S ORIGINAL PETITION AND APPLICATION FOR TEMPORARY RESTRAINING ORDER	6
04.18.12 BARRED DAFFIN FRAPPIER TURNER AND ENGEL, LLP'S SHELLY LUAN DOUGLASS AND KELLY JIMENEZ'S ORIGINAL ANSWER AND REQUEST FOR DISCLOSURE	79
04.23.12 PLAINTIFF'S DEMAND FOR TRIAL BY JURY	83
04.23.12 PLAINTIFF'S FIRST SUPPLEMENTAL PETITION	85
04.30.12 PLAINTIFF'S CERTIFICATEOF DISCOVERY	118
04.30.12 PLAINTIFF'S RESPONSETO DEFENDANT'S ORIGINAL ANSWER	120

Now let's look at the certificate of service found, on "Barrett Daffin Frappier Turner And Engel, LLP's, Shelly Luan Douglass and Kelly Jimenez's Motion To Dismiss And Special Exceptions" document sent to Plaintiff.

CERTIFICATE OF SERVICE

I hereby certify that a true and correct copy of the foregoing instrument was forwarded to all interested parties in accordance with the Texas Rules of Civil Procedure **on this the 8th day of May 2012,** as follows:

Bobie Kenneth Townsend   Via CMRRR
1504 Memorial Ln.   Via US Mail
Conroe, Texas 77304-1647

Steven A. Leyh

Looking back at the Clerk's Record Volume I Index, do you see anything that resembles "special exceptions," filed at or about May 8th, 2012? Neither do I. When I was appealing, I was going through the Clerk's Record, and I noticed that the "special exceptions" document was missing from the index. I met up with the Clerk of the Court, to ask about the missing document. The clerk went back to the file, and verified there was no such document, in the record. The clerk said, even if the attorney would have filed an electronic version of the document, a physical paper copy had to be filed in the record, for it to appear in the record, to be sent to the appellate court; and there was no such document to send.

I could take up multiple pages in this book, to tell you of the multiple errors I found with the 9th's Opinion; But, what could be the point of the thought process of the Bizarro 9th's reasoning, to affirm a trial court judge had no document to review that could aid in Judge Edwards' predetermined-decision to dismiss my case? Now you see, where I previously mentioned I had filed a "Motion For Recusal" of the 9th to hear this case; and for some unexplained reason that case was transferred to the Fourteenth Court of Appeals—which acted as irrational and unprofessional as the 9th is shown to be, here.

I thought this was a good opportunity, to go to the Supreme Court of Texas, so appealed the 9th's decision. The Court Case Number is: No. 14-0022 and the Petition For Review was filed, on or about January 7th, 2014. In all the other cases, the attorneys were NOT worried about a *pro se* filing an appeal with the Supreme Court of Texas. This was NOT one of those cases. The attorney filed a response, on or about February 6th, 2014.

Attorney Response to Townsend's Petition for Review to the Texas Supreme Court
*Issue 4: The Lower Courts Did Not Rely on **Unfiled Pleadings***

*Townsend does not expand on this issue in his Argument, but there is a mention of **a Special Exceptions pleading** that **was not** made part of the record on appeal. **It is important to note** that Townsend does not state that such a motion never existed or that he was never served with **the Special Exceptions** because he knows that it existed and that he was served. The Reporters Record clearly establishes that there was such a pleading, **that it was discussed** with Judge Edwards and that his decision to postpone Respondent's time for responding to Townsend's Requests for Admissions was based on those Special Exceptions. See (RR 1-9). The Ninth Court of Appeals reviewed the Reporter's Record and determined that Respondents were not required to respond to the Requests for Admissions, which therefore did not become deemed admissions creating a fact issue precluding summary judgment. Therefore, **there is no error of law of such importance** to the state's jurisprudence that it should be corrected.*

See, "what difference does it make?," as Hillary Clinton would say. So what, if the main pleading the trial judge claimed to use—to decide whether discovery would be given to me or NOT—wasn't filed for the judge to read. How could discovery ever help a *pro se* in his case? How could discovery ever help a *pro se* in his case? Does saying it twice give the statement more credibility, more merit, more reasonableness? I wonder if the attorney, Steven A. Leyh, Texas Bar No: 12318300, really believes merely stating the name of a document—in front of the trial judge—and it never being filed in the record, is good enough reason, for a judge to make a judicial decision upon? Are judges that clairvoyant? We will see later, some judges claim they are.

Well, we will never know if the Supreme Court agrees with Mr. Leyh, because:

RE: Case No. 14-0022   DATE: 3/14/2014
COA #: 09-12-00564-CV TC#: 12-03-03493-CV
STYLE: BOBIE KENNETH TOWNSEND v. BARRETT DAFFIN FRAPPIER TURNER & ENGEL, LLP, SHELLEY LUAN DOUGLASS, KELLY JIMENEZ, SUBSTITUTE TRUSTEE, ANY AND ALL KNOWN OR UNKNOWN DOE 1-

10
*Today the Supreme Court of Texas **denied the petition for review** in the above-referenced case.*

> MS. BARBARA GLADDEN-ADAMICK
> MONTGOMERY COUNTY DISTRICT CLERK
> P. O. BOX 2985
> CONROE, TX 77305-2985

The Great and Powerful OZ has spoken.   **It Shocks The Conscience !!!**

Just look at us. Everything is backwards; everything is upside down. Doctors destroy health, lawyers destroy justice, universities destroy knowledge, governments destroy freedom, the major media destroy information and religions destroy spirituality"
....Michael Ellner in: The News Report, Issue 641 "During times of universal deceit, telling the truth becomes a revolutionary act"

You may legislate against nature, but human nature will always get the best of legislation.
- James Lendall Basford (1845-1915), Sparks From The Philosopher's Stone, 1882

Our government... teaches the whole people by its example. If the government becomes the lawbreaker, it breeds contempt for law; it invites every man to become a law unto himself; it invites anarchy.
- Louis Brandeis

Corn can't expect justice from a court composed of chickens.
- African Proverb

CHAPTER 32
THEIR FIRST ATTEMPT FOR EVICTION

On or about May 17th, 2012, my wife was served with a Petition For Forcible Detainer. It was the BDFTE law firm that filed the eviction paperwork. The attorney who initiated the action was Lauren Christoffel, State Bar No. 24065045, 15000 Surveyor Boulevard, Suite 100, Addison, Texas 75001. The case was filed in the Justice of the Peace Court, Precinct Two, 2241 North 1st Street, Conroe, Texas 77301—the Honorable Judge G. Trey Spikes presiding, Case No. 108943EV. On or about May 22nd, 2012, I filed my "Defendants' Answer and Affirmative Defense to Plaintiff's Original Petition For Forcible Detainer (Defendants' Answer)." My arguments, against the forcible detainer, were:

Defendants' Answer
*"This court has jurisdiction to determine the right of possession, **but not** who has title to the property. TEX. PROP. CODE ANN. § 24.004 (Vernon Supp.1995); Haith v. Drake, 596 S.W.2d 194, 196 (Tex. Civ. App. — Houston [1st Dist.] 1980, writ ref'd n.r.e.)."*

Defendants' Answer
*"The only issue in a forcible detainer suit is the right to actual possession; **the merits of the title shall not be adjudicated**. TEX. R. CIV. P. 746; Gentry v. Marburger, 596 S.W.2d 201, 203 (Tex. Civ. App. —Houston [1st Dist.] 1980, writ ref'd n.r.e.); Haith, 596 S.W.2d at 196."*

Defendants' Answer
*"**If it becomes apparent that a genuine issue regarding title exists in a forcible detainer suit, the court does not have jurisdiction over the matter.** Haith, 596 S.W.2d at 197; American Spiritualist Assn. v. Ravkind, 313 S.W.2d 121, 124 (Tex. Civ. App. —Dallas 1958, writ ref'd n.r.e.)"*

It turns out no one from BDFTE showed up, for the hearing in front of Judge Spikes. Some attorney claiming to be, with Rex L. Kesler, State Bar No. 11357500, 2311 Canal Street, Suite 304 Houston, Texas 77003, claimed to represent Fannie Mae.

Judge Spikes called someone on the phone about my argument; and then came back and said he was granting the forcible detainer, and I had thirty days to vacate the premises—or file a bond in the amount of $1,200, and put in a Notice of Appeal within five days.

I filed my Notice of Appeal, my Memorandum in Support of the Appeal Bond, and my Appeal Bond that showed the appeal would be a trial de novo, so no money was required—as no money was required for the hearing in the JP court. The appeal went through.

I had ample time to get serious about defending my rights. The appeal was assigned to County Court at Law #2, 210 West Davis, Conroe, Texas 77301—The Honorable Judge Claudia Laird presiding, Case No. I2-26,346-CV. The County Court hearing was set for July 20th, 2012.

On or about June 25th, 2012, I filed my "Defendant's Demand For Trial By Jury," my "Defendant's Motion For Showing Authority," my "Defendant's First Notice Of Objections," my "Defendant's First Judicial Notice," my "Defendant's Motion For Sanctions," and my "Defendant's Plea To The Jurisdiction and Motion To Dismiss."

On or about July 9th, 2012, that attorney, Rex L. Kesler, filed his, "Notice of Appearance of Local Counsel For Plaintiff, Notice of Intent and Notice of Trial Setting," his "Business Record Affidavit," and his "Notice To Vacate."

At the July 20th, 2012, court hearing, a couple of attorneys showed up claiming to represent Fannie Mae, who pleaded their case in front of Judge Laird. I laid out my case Fannie Mae was NOT represented at the hearing; because I had filed my motion for the attorneys, to show their authority to represent Fannie Mae—and they had NOT done so, which requires Judge Laid to strike their pleadings and dismiss the case. I then brought my plea to the jurisdiction of the court, arguing:

Defendant's Plea To The Jurisdiction
*"The Plaintiff's claim in the instant cause **is necessarily dependent upon** the determination of a valid title to the Property, that being real property 'located in this state', an issue for which **exclusive jurisdiction lies** in District Courts pursuant to Article 5, Section 8 of the Texas Constitution and Section 27.031 of the Texas Government Code."*

Defendant's Plea To The Jurisdiction
*"Townsend respectfully suggest that this Honorable Court **does not have jurisdiction to hear this matter** under Rule 746 of the Texas Rules of Civil Procedure because there is currently a dispute over title to the Property and this Court would be required **to weigh the evidence** concerning title to the Property (**which it may not do**) before determining the right of possession."*
*"The county court's appellate jurisdiction is limited **to the original jurisdiction** of the justice court. Black v. Washington Mut. Bank, 318 S.W.3d 414, 416-17 (Tex.App.-Houston [1st Dist.] 2010, pet. dism'd w.o.j.)"*

Defendant's Plea To The Jurisdiction
*"This Court has jurisdiction to determine the right of possession, but **not who has a valid title to the property**. TEX. PROP. CODE ANN. § 24.004 (Vernon Supp.1995); Haith v. Drake, 596 S.W.2d 194, 196 (Tex. Civ. App. — Houston [1st Dist.] 1980, writ ref'd n.r.e.)."*

*"**By common law, no** charter, sale, or gift will be good, **if** the donor at the time of the contract **is not seised of two rights**, viz., **the right of possession and the right of property.** Of a man has only in him the right of either possession or property, **he cannot convey it to**

any other. (See 2 Blackstone's Commentary 290) To a stranger he must intend; for one by a mere release may convey his right of property to one that is in possession of the lands or tenements, because the occupancy of the release is matter of sufficient notoriety already. (See 2 Blackstone's Commentary 325)"

Defendant's Plea To The Jurisdiction
"**The only issue** in a forcible detainer suit is the right to actual possession; **the merits of the title shall not be adjudicated**. TEX. R. CIV. P. 746; Gentry v. Marburger, 596 S.W.2d 201, 203 (Tex. Civ. App. —Houston [1st Dist.] 1980, writ ref'd n.r.e.); Haith, 596 S.W.2d at 196."

Defendant's Plea To The Jurisdiction
"**If it becomes apparent that a genuine issue regarding title exists in a forcible detainer suit, this Court does not have jurisdiction over this matter.** Haith, 596 S.W.2d at 197; American Spiritualist Assn. v. Ravkind, 313 S.W.2d 121, 124 (Tex. Civ. App. —Dallas 1958, writ ref'd n.r.e.)"

Defendant's Plea To The Jurisdiction
"Mr. Townsend did not include Fannie Mae by name on Cause 12-03-03493-CV, because Fannie Mae **was not listed** on any public document filed in the Montgomery County Clerk's Office prior to the sale showing any interest in Mr. Townsend's Property. But, **for all practical purposes** Fannie Mae is a party to the District Court action **by extension of its counsel and the substitute trustee** as it relates to the Wrongful Foreclosure and Action to Quiet Title. Mr. Townsend **intends** to add Fannie Mae to the Wrongful Foreclosure and to the Action to Quiet Title as a defendant as Mr. Townsend would with any other John Doe that would **claim interest** in Mr. Townsend's Property."

Defendant's Plea To The Jurisdiction
"Defendant's Exhibit 03 **shows** that Countrywide Home Loans, Inc. is the Lender in 2004. There are **no** public documents filed in the Montgomery County Clerk's Office stating otherwise other than documents created by Plaintiff's attorney's law firm BDFTE."

Defendant's Plea To The Jurisdiction
*"Defendant's Exhibit 04 & 05 shows an attorney, Mr. Michael P. Trainer with the Blank Rome LLP law firm, purporting to represent Bank of America **indicating** that Fannie Mae **has always been the holder of the note and deed of trust from day of closing in 2004 through April 13, 2012, but not Holder in Due Course with right to foreclose.**"*

Defendant's Plea To The Jurisdiction
*"Defendant's Exhibit 06 **shows** BDFTE employee Douglass **purporting** to assign the note and deed of trust to an entity of Bank of America in 2010 and again **indicating** holder and **not** Holder in Due Course with right to foreclose."*

Defendant's Plea To The Jurisdiction
*"Defendant Townsend has **offered evidence showing** three entities claiming holder of the note **on the same day in 2010** indicating a genuine issue regarding title that will be resolved by the 9th District Court or Ninth Court of Appeals."*

*"Legal acumen /liygal akyliwman/. The doctrine of legal acumen is that if a defect in, or invalidity of, a claim to land is such as to require legal acumen to discover it, whether it appears upon the face of the record or proceedings, **or** is to be proved aliunde, then the powers or jurisdiction of a court of equity **may be invoked to remove the cloud created by such defect or invalidity**."*

*"**Aliunde** /eyliyondiy/. Lat. From another source; from elsewhere; from outside.*
*Evidence aliunde. Evidence from outside, **from another source**. In certain cases a written instrument may be explained by evidence aliunde, that is, by evidence drawn **from sources exterior** to the instrument itself, e.g., the testimony of a witness to conversations, admissions, or preliminary negotiations. Evidence aliunde (i.e., from outside the will) **may be received to explain** an ambiguity in a will. See Parol evidence."*

*"**Parol evidence**. Oral or verbal evidence; that which is given **by word of mouth**; the ordinary kind of evidence given by witnesses in court. In a particular sense, and with reference to contracts, deeds, wills, and other writings, parol evidence **is the same as extraneous evidence or evidence aliunde**. See also Aliunde; Extraneous evidence; Oral evidence."*

I thought it was strange, when I objected—and Judge Laird overruled my objection; and I stated, "I take exception"—Judge Laird stated she had never heard that phrase before, and seemed to take offense from me using it.

Rabbit Trail: That phrase, "I take exception", is well known in the legal system. As I understand, the phrase, "I take exception," is part of reserving all rights under the objection—and NOT merely accepting the decision of the Judge concerning your objection. You can hear this phrase being used in the 1982 movie, "The Verdict," with Paul Newman.
(Jumping off that rabbit trail.)

During the hearing, I argued my Rule 12 Motion, stating the law firm has had plenty of time to produce their authority to represent Fannie Mae. To my pleasant surprise, Judge Laird told the attorneys they had until the end of the day, to produce their authority to represent Fannie Mae and then show their chain of title—giving her jurisdiction over the matter. Later that day, Judge Laird signed my proposed Order to dismiss.

ORDER FOR DISMISSAL

THIS CAUSE came to be heard upon Defendant's Motion To Dismiss; and

IT APPEARING to the Court for reasons stated in Defendant's Plea To The Jurisdiction and Motion To Dismiss **that there is a genuine issue of title**.

ORDERED that Defendant's Motion to Dismiss is GRANTED.

THIS CAUSE IS FINAL.
SIGNED on this the 20th day of 2012.
HON. JUDGE CLAUDIA LAIRD

The attorneys never appealed Judge Laird's decision. I still have possession of the Black Toxic Dream House.

A judge, new to her bench, did NOT get the word that it was mandatory that the Judiciary will screw Pro Ses.

I had won a battle, but the war continues.....

CHAPTER 33
MY SIXTH LAWSUIT
THE QUIET TITLE ACTION

As I stated, in "My Fifth Lawsuit," I had a plan, to add Bank of America N.A. (BANA) and Federal National Mortgage Association (Fannie Mae) as parties to the fifth lawsuit. But since Judge Edwards was going out of office, he got rid of any *pro se* suit, ASAP he could, to clear his docket. Judge Edwards proved you could get rid of a case, by ruling on a document that was NOT even filed in court, as justification for his decision. The 9th affirmed you could do that, with no problem, when dealing with a *pro se*. As the English people would say "We must bugger on."

Rabbit Trail: This next case is a Quiet Title Action. I learned a lot, from a fellow by the name of John Stuart, who was domiciled in Arizona. You can find many of his videos, on [Link:] YouTube.com. I usually check out and verify everything anyone tells me, concerning legal stuff. I find, a lot of things people try to sell or promote is BS, but the stuff John was saying was verifiable—and it made legal sense, to me. John encouraged people to NOT just jump into a law suit concerning a quiet title; until you give the party, you intended to sue, a chance to sign over any claimed interest they may have in the property by Quick Claim Deed. You send them a notice of your intent to sue, send them a $10 (or more) money order, with a blank Quick Claim Deed that contained the legal description of the subject property— where the party could sign their interest in the property over to you, and NOT be sued. Sounded reasonable, so that was what I was doing, when Judge Edwards got rid of my case—and before I could add those parties that refused to sign the Quick Claim Deed.

John also said, a Quiet Title Action was different than other civil actions, as there could NOT be any presumptions some party owned the subject property. John said it was necessary the court see all the evidence, of all who claimed interest in the subject property; and then the Judge would sign an Order removing any clouds found on the title, which would clean the title to the property: creating a quiet title. John has a workbook, for those that need to quiet the title of their property; and I encourage people in purchasing the workbook, for themselves.

Also, I found out Williamson County Clerk's Office contracted *DK Consultants LLC, San Antonio, Texas,* to do an Audit on their records. On January 29, 2013, the report was issued, to Williamson County Clerk's Office [Link: www.wilco.org]. This audit is a must see, for anyone concerned with foreclosures. It gives sources concerning MERS. On page 10, it states:

> *It is recommended by the audit team that this report be turned over to the Williamson County District Attorney for further consideration in potential prosecution of those responsible, if in fact any "takings" of property using fraudulent documents were found to be "wrongful" or illegal.*

The attorneys referenced Texas Penal Code § 37.01(2) and Texas Civil Practice and Remedies Code § 12, *et seq.,* as a means to deal with the fraudulent documents. This is where I learned about:

Audit Markers are relative indicators that would be utilized to demonstrate suspect issues within the chain of title to any given property. Under the Texas Local Government Code at § 192.007, all documents affecting the chain of title to the property, including all liens and encumbrances, Must be recorded once the claim of lien process to any chain of title has begun.

It would take many pages, here, to give justice to the work *DK Consultants LLC* has made available to the public, concerning foreclosures that are invalid. You should download your own copy, from the Williamson County's website.
(Jumping off that rabbit trail.)

BANA screwed-up, and deposited the Money Order associated with the Quick Claim Deed. Some way, they recovered the instrument from the banking system, and sent it back to me—with all these ink stamps showing the money order had gone places, throughout the banking system. Fannie Mae declined doing anything, and sent back the Money Order, unchanged.

On or About October 29th, 2012, I filed suit in the 284th State District Court, Case No. 12-10-11409-CV—The Honorable Judge Cara Wood presiding. The case was cited: *Bobie Kenneth Townsend v. Bank of America N.A., Successor By Merger to BAC Home Loans Servicing, LP FKA Countrywide Home Loans Servicing LP....* I wasn't in Judge Wood's court long enough to have an opinion, about her dealings with a *pro se*.

If I would have been able to add BANA and Fannie Mae to my fifth lawsuit, it could NOT have been moved to Federal Court.
The case was moved to Federal Court, on or about December 7th, 2012. The case was assigned, to The Honorable United States District Judge Nancy F. Atlas, of the Southern District of Texas, Houston Division; Case Number 4:12-cv-3568. The law firm representing BANA and Fannie Mae was McGlinchey Stafford, PLLC, 1001 McKinney St., Suite 1500, Houston, Texas 77002-6420. The attorneys of record were John L. Verner, State Bar No. 20549500; and Matthew A. Knox, State Bar No. 24071102.

I initially liked Judge Atlas. I found out she was a Democrat, and has been the only Federal Judge who allowed me discovery. I was at a couple of Open Hearings, where Judge Atlas took my side, on various issues. To the surprise of the attorneys,

Judge Atlas granted my request for discovery I had previously filed, while in the State Court.

At one of the hearings, I asked Judge Atlas about the Federal Rule associated with Rule 12 in Texas civil procedure, where I moved the court to see the authority of the attorneys to represent the defending parties. Judge Atlas' response to my request was: "They (the attorneys) would NOT lie to me." I started getting concerned, because I did NOT know if Judge Atlas was so naïve, or if Judge Atlas really knew attorneys never have an actual contract—between the parties they were defending. Just think about it; how can two different banking entities pick the same law firm to represent them both, in a case like this? Logically, something stinks, and the judge is NOT concerned— because the attorneys would NOT lie to her. Right!!

Rabbit Trail: When your case is moved to Federal Court, where does your original petition wind up, in the case-file docket sheet? It is hidden behind some Exhibit Letter the attorney for the defendant has filed. Your original petition has to be literally dug out, from behind one of the defendant's pleadings—named as one of the attorney's Exhibits. Neither the judge—nor the briefing attorneys—have any initiative to dig your claims out, from behind some exhibit. They just go by the pleadings of the attorneys, to base the case upon.
(Jumping off that rabbit trail.)

I recovered over 300 documents, from BANA; and literally no documents, from Fannie Mae, through discovery, as it claimed to have none that I asked for. The attorneys held back some documents, claiming attorney/client privilege. I objected, and made them produce the documents, for the judge to see if that was true. Judge Atlas claimed that the documents did NOT show any interest in the subject property, so I let it drop.

I did a non-party subpoena, on Sharon Vaughan (Vaughan); employee of National Default Exchange, L.P. at 15000 Surveyor Blvd., Addison, Texas 75001-4417. Default Exchange, L.P., is just another company run by the BDFTE law firm. Ms. Vaughan signed a "Business Records Affidavit," filed as an Exhibit by Fannie Mae, stating that Vaughan, and she alone, had "care, custody and control of all records concerning the non-judicial foreclosure and forcible entry and detainer proceeding against Bobie Kenneth Townsend and all other occupants of 1504 Memorial Lane, Conroe, Texas 77304." Vaughan produced 74 pages that were under the control and care of Vaughan, at the time, and she designated such pages as LPM from Vaughan's file—identified as the 'foreclosure file.' Interestingly, Vaughan failed to produce the first document used to appoint the Substitute Trustee, on August 24th, 2010, in behalf of BAC; but I already had the document of the second appointment, of the same Substitute Trustee, in behalf of BANA, dated February 28th, 2012. Just a reminder, the only so-called assignment was to BAC, and NOT BANA.

I did a non-party subpoena, on Shelley Luan Douglass (Douglass), employee of Barrett Daffin Frappier Turner & Engel. LLP; 15000 Surveyor Blvd.. Addison, Texas 75001. I asked Douglass to produce: "Records showing verification of employment with MORTGAGE ELECTRONIC REGISTRATION SYSTEMS. INC. (MERS) from August 12, 2010 through September 24, 2010 and the name and location of your supervisor with MERS during that time."

Remember, Douglass is the one that pretended to be an assistant secretary for MERS and under so-called authority of MERS. Douglass created an Assignment, of the Note and Deed of Trust, to BAC. The so-called "assignment" never indicated any entity, claiming to be the Lender having the Note and Deed of Trust transferred to BAC. Douglass' response to the subpoena was, as follows:

Shelly Luan Douglass Response to Plaintiff's Subpoena
II. Shelley Luan Douglass
3. Plaintiffs subpoena directed to Douglass requested that she produce for inspection the following documents by February 1, 2013:

*"Records showing verification of employment with Mortgage Electronic Registration Systems, Inc., (MERS) from August 12, 2010 through September 24, 2010 and the **name** and **location** of **your supervisor with MERS** during that time."*

*4. Douglass responds that **she has no documents responsive to this request**.*

You would think just the above admission, on the part of Douglass, would quiet the title to me; but that is NOT the reason a case is moved to Federal Court. The goal of an adverse party, moving a case to Federal Court, is to have the case dismissed. It is NOT having a better chance, in defending against an allegation. I have also seen State judges protect the system by such unscrupulous means that **It Shocks the Conscience**. As you will see, it appears Federal Judges have no jurisdiction over State property, when the government does NOT claim interest in the property—even though a quasi-governmental corporation, like Fannie Mae, does claim some interest. Fannie Mae was in receivership, by the Federal Government, during this time frame.

Most Quiet Title Actions in Texas assume (or accept) the fact if you buy property in Texas, at closing all previous liens are extinguished, leaving a single Note and Deed of Trust, as the sole cloud over the property. This act establishes the borrower's (property owner's) Warranty Deed as the starting point judges must use, to determine whether there is a genuine issue of title, when another—other than the borrower and original Lender—claims interest in the borrower's property. The borrower's Warranty Deed is the place where the adverse party must show a chain of title, to their superior interest in the property. If there is a

Deed of Trust involved, then there must be a recorded document, in the County Clerk's Office, showing the parties passing the Deed of Trust—up to the time of the one that claims holder of the Note and Deed of Trust. (See above, Texas Local Government Code Sec. 192.007.) If the record shows a break in chain of title, then the judge must assume the Note and Deed of Trust must have been discharged—and quiet the title back to the borrower.

> "... Rogers, as plaintiff, **need only** demonstrate good title coming from **that common source** to meet its burden of proof." See United States v. Denby, 522 F.2d 1358, 1362 (5th Cir.1975).
> Rogers v. Ricane Enters., Inc., 884 S.W.2d 763, 768 (Tex. 1994)

> "The plaintiff may recover (1) by proving a regular chain of conveyances from the sovereign, (2) by proving **a superior title out of a common source**, (3) by proving title by limitations, **or** (4) by proving **prior possession**, and that the possession has not been abandoned.
> Land v. Turner, 377 S.W.2d 181, 183 (Tex.1964)."

> "Generally, the earlier title emanating from **a common source** is **better title** and **superior** to others." Diversified, Inc. v. Hall, 23 S.W.3d 403, 406 (Tex.App.-Houston [1st Dist.] 2000, pet. denied). Thus, "[w]hen properly recorded and indexed, an abstract of judgment creates a judgment lien that is superior to the rights of subsequent purchasers and lien holders." Wilson v. Dvorak, 228 S.W.3d 228, 233 (Tex.App.-San Antonio 2007, pet. denied).
> Gordon v. West Houston Trees, Ltd., 352 SW 3d 32 - Tex: Court of Appeals 2011

> Fee simple or otherwise **incontestible title** in plaintiff is not necessary for maintenance of suit **to remove cloud**.
> Dalton v. Davis, 1 S.W.2d 571, Commission of Appeals of Texas, Section A (1928)

*Where pleadings and proof show that plaintiff owns a tract of land and that defendant is asserting some right, title, and interest and claim thereto, plaintiff **seeking to remove cloud** from title **is not required to establish an incontestable chain of title** from sovereignty of the soil or from a common source.*
Lee v. Groupe, 223 S.W.2d 548, Court of Civil Appeals of Texas, Texarkana.(1949)

Looks like the Supreme Court of Texas is well-settled, on who had the superior title of a piece of property in Texas, when there was a cloud on the title. It is the party who has the "common source title," and that is me. In the record, I had filed a certified copy, of the Warranty Deed I and my wife received, from the previous owners. I had filed in the record an affidavit of foundation that indicated where the Warranty Deed came from. I entered the response, from Douglass, indicating she had no documents that indicated she had ever worked for MERS—which would authorize Douglass, to assign the Note and Deed of Trust, to anyone or anything. Looks like Judge Atlas had no other choice than to quiet the title, to me. But, what if Judge Atlas had no authority, to quiet a title concerning Texas land, what else could she do?

Judge Atlas Memorandum & Order, October 23rd, 2013
*"The parties also have filed cross-motions for summary judgment. Defendants filed a Motion for Summary Judgment [Doc. # 27], **to which Plaintiff responded** [Doc. # 32].2 **Plaintiff also filed a Motion for Summary Judgment** [Doc. # 36], to which Defendants responded [Doc. # 37] and **Plaintiff replied** [Doc. # 38].*
*The motions **are ripe** for review. **Having considered** the parties' submissions, **all matters** of record, and **applicable** legal authorities, **the Court denies** Plaintiff's Motion for Reconsideration, **denies** Plaintiff's Plea to the Jurisdiction, **grants** Defendants' Motion for Summary Judgment, and **denies** Plaintiff's Motion for Summary Judgment."*

The only issue before the court was to quiet the title of the subject property. I even told the judge to quiet the title to somebody, so the matter could be settled.

Judge Atlas Memorandum & Order, October 23rd, 2013
*"Plaintiff further argues that "this court's **pend[e]nt jurisdiction** concerning state matters . . . **is discretionary** and this court **is not mandated** to quiet the title concerning Texas land **even if** the matter is before this court." Plea, at 2, ¶ 7. **However**, in this case, Plaintiff's state law claim has reached this Court **through removal** from state court based on the **complete diversity** of citizenship between the parties and an **adequate amount** in controversy. See 28 U.S.C. § 1332(a). A defendant that **is not a citizen** of Texas and that has been sued by a Texas citizen on a claim where the matter in controversy **exceeds** $75,000 has **the right to avail itself** of the Court's diversity jurisdiction. Id. The Court **need not and does not** exercise "pendent jurisdiction," **also known as** supplemental jurisdiction, over Plaintiff's claim.*
*Plaintiff has raised **no valid challenge** to the Court's subject matter jurisdiction."*

Notice Judge Atlas does NOT state she has jurisdiction, to quiet a title, concerning Texas land.   Judge Atlas elaborates criteria, to quiet a title.

Judge Atlas Memorandum & Order, October 23rd, 2013
*Plaintiff's **single claim** in this case is **a cause of action to quiet title** to the Property.11 "'**A suit to clear title or quiet title**—also known as **a suit to remove cloud from title**—relies** on the **invalidity** of the defendant's claim to the property.'" Morlock, L.L.C. v. JP Morgan Chase Bank, N.A., No. 12-20623, 2013 WL 2422778, at *1 (5th Cir. June 4, 2013) (**unpublished**) (quoting Essex Crane Rental Corp. v. Carter, 371 S.W.3d 366, 388 (Tex. App.—Houston [1st Dist.] 2012, pet. denied)). **To recover** on a claim **to quiet title**, the plaintiff **must prove** that his title to the property **is superior** to the defendant's title. Id. (citations omitted); **Rogers v. Ricane Enters., Inc.,** 884 S.W.2d 763, 768 (Tex. 1994). A plaintiff **may not simply rely** on the*

weakness of his adversary's title. *See, e.g., Browning v. PHH Mortg. Corp.*, No. H-12-0886, 2013 WL 3244094, at *6 (S.D. Tex. June 26, 2013) (**unpublished**) (quoting *Fricks v. Hancock*, 45 S.W.3d 322, 327 (Tex. App.—Corpus Christi 2001)). **Therefore**, "the plaintiff **has the burden** of supplying the proof necessary to establish **his superior equity and right to relief**." *Morlock*, 2013 WL 2422778, at *1 (quoting *Hahn v. Love*, 321 S.W.3d 517, 531 (Tex. App.—Houston [1st Dist.] 2009, pet. denied) (emphasis added by *Morlock*)).

Judge Atlas quotes from the *"Morlock"* case (Judge Atlas' case), which is irrelevant to my case. Morlock purchased a piece of property that previously contained a note and deed of trust attached to the property, and failed to contest either. Morlock could not have claimed superior title, over a lien that previously existed, at time of purchase by Morlock. Judge Atlas was merely parroting the attorney's pleading.

Notice above, Judge Atlas cited the *"Rogers"* case, indicating I must show my tile is superior to Fannie Mae's title. I never knew about the *"Rogers"* case, before Judge Atlas cited it. If you bookmark this page, and flip back a couple of pages, you will see where I quote the *"Rogers"* case. The Supreme Court of Texas **confirmes** my Warranty Deed is superior, as it **is** the "common source title," of the subject property and where a chain of title must start.

Judge Atlas Memorandum & Order, October 23rd, 2013
*"Plaintiff's action to quiet title **fails because** his briefing and evidence establish **that he no longer holds title** to the Property. Plaintiff admits in his Complaint, and the summary judgment evidence reflects **unequivocally**, that the Property **was sold** at foreclosure on April 3, 2012. See Complaint, at 7, ¶ 49 ("[O]n April 3rd, 2012 at the sale concerning Plaintiff's property, the substitute trustee **fraudulently claimed** in public that Defendant **Fannie Mae was the Lender and awarded the sale of Plaintiff's property to Defendant Fannie Mae**"); Substitute Trustee's Deed (Exhibit V to Complaint). The Substitute Trustee's Deed reflects that on April 3,*

2012, at 1:51 p.m., the Property was sold to Fannie Mae for $122,999.02."

Judge Atlas is just parroting the attorney's pleadings, again. In every quiet title action, at least two parties claim to own the same property. In most-every quiet title case, one party claims to obtain the property before or after the other. Whether there was a sale is irrelevant, if there should NOT have been a sale.

Judge Atlas Memorandum & Order, October 23rd, 2013
*"**Plaintiff has submitted no evidence** that, at the time this suit was filed, **he had any right** to the Property, or had any rights after April 3, 2012, when the foreclosure occurred and Fannie Mae purchased the Property. Plaintiff **therefore has failed to demonstrate a genuine issue of material fact** that his title to the Property **is superior** to that of Defendants. See Morlock, 2013 WL 2422778, at *2."*

Judge Atlas is parroting the attorney's pleadings, again. Anyone can make a statement, in a pleading, someone has "submitted no evidence;" but making such statement does NOT prove anything. If there are Exhibits filed in the record, and an affidavit of foundation of such exhibits is filed in the record, then it is up to a jury, as the fact finder, to determine if there is no evidence. Judge Atlas is NOT the fact finder, since there is a demand for a trial by jury, in this case.

Judge Atlas Memorandum & Order, October 23rd, 2013
*Plaintiff has **filed multiple documents** advancing the argument that **Defendants cannot demonstrate an unbroken chain of title** from 2004 through the present. **However, even assuming that Plaintiff could prove his allegations** regarding a broken chain of title, **such a showing would be insufficient** to defeat Defendants' summary judgment motion. **As held above**, an action to quiet title **requires proof** of Plaintiff's "superior title" to the property in issue. **See Morlock**, 2013 WL 2422778, at *2 (because plaintiff's challenge to the validity of the assignment of the deed of trust "**merely questions**"*

[which entity] has authority" to enforce the deed of trust, and does not assert superior title, the plaintiff *"**fails to advance a plausible quiet-title claim**"); Khan v. Wells Fargo Bank, N.A., No. 4:12-CV-1116, 2013 WL 5323098, at * 7 (S.D. Tex. Sept. 20, 2013) (plaintiff's argument that the assignment of the deed of trust was invalid **is insufficient** to establish a claim for quiet title **without evidence of superiority** of the plaintiff's own title); Browning, 2013 WL 3244094, at *6 (a plaintiff seeking to quiet title **may not simply rely** on the weakness of his adversary's title). Because Plaintiff **has failed to demonstrate a genuine issue of material fact** as to his "superior title" to the Property, summary judgment is granted for Defendants. **Plaintiff's request for summary judgment is denied**.*

The above paragraph tells it all. Judge Atlas violates Texas law, by declaring Townsend's Warranty Deed is <u>NOT</u> proof of superior title, even though the Supreme Court of Texas, at "*Rogers*," says Townsend's Warranty Deed is the "common source title," and the courts must recognize it as such. Judge Atlas uses her own previous rulings on other cases, to justify her reasoning, even though neither of such cases have any resemblance to the case before her. The purpose of a quiet title action is to remove any clouds found, concerning the chain of title to Texas property. Judge Atlas determines it does <u>NOT</u> matter, if I <u>CAN</u> prove there is a broken chain of title, in his quiet title action. Judge Atlas ignores Texas and Federal law, by stating it makes <u>NO</u> difference <u>which entity</u> has the authority to enforce the note and deed of trust. Judge Atlas allows the Defendant to violate Texas law, by stating it does <u>NOT</u> matter, if the assignment of the Note and Deed of Trust was invalid. **IT SHOCKS THE CONSCIENCE!!!!!**

There is little need to review why Judge Atlas granted Fannie Mae's motion for summary judgment, as it was a means to dismiss the case—without having to quiet the title of the subject property, to anyone. Bear in mind, the cloud on the title remains, forever—until quieted.

*A trustee-removal action can also be analogized to a real-property action to remove a cloud on title. **We have held that as long as an injury clouding the title remains, so too does an equitable action to remove the cloud; therefore, a suit to remove the cloud is not time-barred.** (See Tex. Co. v. Davis, 113 Tex. 321, 254 S.W. 304, 309 (1923).)*
Ditta v. Conte, 298 SW 3d 187 - Tex: Supreme Court 2009

Since I was fortunate enough to have the funds to appeal, I did. I must find out how the 5th Circuit can justify what Judge Atlas has done, in this Quiet Title Action.

Plaintiff's Notice of Appeal
I, Bobie Kenneth Townsend, in propria persona, without the benefit of counsel, herein after known as plaintiff, respectfully submit this Notice of Appeal from the Final Judgment of Judge Atlas with the United States District Court, Southern District of Texas, Houston Division to the United States Court of Appeals for the Fifth Circuit.
__Plaintiff claims the right of appeal__ of Orders (See Docket #24, #25, #39, #20, #24, #33 & #50), Memorandum & Order (See Docket #41), the Final Judgment (See Docket #42) filed on October 23, 2013 and Memorandum & Order (See Docket #49) filed on November 26, 2013 concerning Case No. 4:12-cv-3568.

I am very willing to offend any neighbor of mine who attempts to pull the wool over my eyes with false claims of lawful authority when he cannot even tell me WHEN he went from being a mere neighbor to one so vested with the authority to order me about in a way I cannot so order him about. I claim that if they cannot tell me when that was, then it most likely never happened. And if they do give me a date, it will have to be supported by official evidence, as I do not believe trained liars.
FROG FARMER

CHAPTER 34
THE FIFTH CIRCUIT, LEARNED IN LAW

The Federal 5th Circuit accepted my filing fee, and assigned the appeal, to Case No. 13-20762. When I filed my brief, what I did NOT know was, the rules of appellate court had changed concerning form of the brief. The 5th Circuit was gracious in allowing me to amend my appellant brief consistent, with the new (baseball) rules.

5TH Cir. Rules & Federal Rules of Appellate Procedure-2014
28.3 Brief - Order of Contents. The order of the contents of the brief is governed by FED.
*R. App. P. 28 and this rule and **will be as follows**:*
(a) Certificate of interested persons required by 5TH CIR. R. 28.2.1;
(b) Statement regarding oral argument required by 5TH CIR. R. 28.2.3 (See FED. R. APP.
P. 34(a)(1));
(c) A table of contents, with page references (see FED. R. APP. P. 28 (a)(2));
(d) A table of authorities (see FED. R. APP. P. 28(a)(3));
(e) A jurisdictional statement as required by FED. R. APP. P. 28(a)(4)(A) through (D);
(f) A statement of issues presented for review (see FED. R. APP. P. 28 (a)(5));
(g) A concise statement of the case setting out the facts relevant to the issues submitted for
review (see FED. R. APP. P. 28(a)(6));
(h) A summary of the argument (see FED. R. APP. P. 28(a)(7));
(i) The argument (see FED. R. APP. P. 28(a)(8));
(j) A short conclusion stating the precise relief sought (see FED. R. APP. P. 28 (a)(9));
(k) A signature of counsel or a party as required by FED. R. APP. P. 32(d);
(l) A certificate of service in the form required by FED. R. APP. P. 25;
(m) A certificate of compliance if required by FED. R. APP. P. 32(a)(7) and 5TH CIR. R.
32.3. (see FED. R. APP. P. 28(a)(10));

When you're in a baseball game, you must play by baseball rules. I paid to be in the game, so I would assume when I get a ruling from the referee, I would expect the referee to explain his ruling. Wouldn't you? Surely, the Justices of the 5th Circuit realize the wisdom of their rulings will be printed, in volumes of law books—for those who look for their wisdom, for hundreds of years in the future.

Appeal from the United States District Court
for the Southern District of Texas
USDC No. 4:12-CV-3568
No. 13-20762
Before WIE ER, OWEN, and HAYNES', Circuit Judges.
PER CURIAM:"
*Plaintiff-Appellant, Bobie Kenneth Townsend, **proceeding pro se**, appeals the district court's October 23, 2013 Final Judgment that granted Defendants-Appellees' summary judgment motion and **dismissed with prejudice all** of Townsend's claims and related motions, and the court's November 26, 2013 Memorandum and Order that denied Townsend's several post-judgment motions and objections. In its initial Memorandum and Order, the district court **addressed** Townsend's Motion for Reconsideration, Plea to Jurisdiction, and Motion for Summary Judgment, and his Claim to Quiet Title, **as well as** Defendants-Appellees' Cross Motion for Summary Judgment. **In its subsequent** Memorandum and Order, the district court **addressed** Townsend's Objection, Motion to Amend, Motion for New Trial, and Motion to Alter or Amend Judgment. **We affirm the judgments and orders** of the district court **for the reasons set forth in its** Memorandum and Order of October 23, 2013, **and in its additional** Memorandum and Order of November 26, 2013.*
*This appeal **is the culmination of a saga** that began in June 2004 with Townsend's purchase **of residential property** in Conroe, Texas, including his execution of a promissory note secured by a deed of trust. This was followed by Townsend's tax protest in the form of refusing to pay his 2006 and 2007 property taxes on that real estate. That in turn led to this protracted litigation which eventually resulted in the district court's 2013 judgments and orders that*

Townsend appeals here.

*Just as the Defendant-Appellees **patiently addressed** Townsend's **largely baseless** pleadings and assertions, and just as the district court **patiently addressed** his numerous claims and contentions, we have **patiently reviewed** the record on appeal, including the briefs of the parties and both of the district court's memoranda and orders. Our review leads us to conclude that **there is no merit in any** of Townsend's contentions on appeal. **Neither do they warrant further discussion or explanation**. Accordingly, the judgments of the district court are, in all respects,*
AFFIRMED.

Here, I would like to point out, there is no definition of the term "residential" in the Texas Tax Code. That partial, one-page Opinion, of the 5th Circuit, will be found in law books, **forever**. Did the referees explain why they affirmed the trial court? It does NOT look like it to me. But, I am NOT an attorney, thank God. If I was, I may have the same reasoning defects, as the Justices of the 5th Circuit have here.

***merits.** (18c) 1. The elements or grounds of a claim or defense; **the substantive considerations** to be taken into account in deciding a case, **as opposed to extraneous or technical points**, esp. of procedure <trial on the merits>. 2. EQUITY (3) <on questions of euthanasia, the Supreme Court **has begun to concern itself with the merits** as well as the law>.*
Black's Law Dictionary-Edition-9

***brief on the merits.** A brief that sets out **the issues to be decided, the party's position, and the arguments and authorities in support**. Also termed **points and-authorities** brief; merits brief [Cases; Appeal and Error 761]*
Black's Law Dictionary-Edition-9

"...there is no merit **in any** of Townsend's contentions on appeal." If you read it enough times, you have to believe it, right? I mean, does it make you want to go find my brief, and find each and every "contention" Townsend alleged that apparently had no "substantive considerations," to be taken into account in deciding a case"?

> Townsend's-Brief For Appellant, Page 1, Case No. 13-20762
> "...Townsend claims that Judge Atlas **lacks jurisdiction to quiet the title** of the subject property **as the elements of the case** does not adhere to the Quiet Title Act as found in 28 U.S.C. § 2409a. Townsend's case **does not involve a TORT ACTION** where 28 U.S.C. §§ 1441, 1446, and 1332 would apply, **but rather** an **equity of right to clear a title** concerning Texas land **where value is irrelevant** and not to be declared or to be determined by the court.
> Townsend has reason to believe **and does believe** that Judge Atlas **is not mandated by law to quiet titles concerning Texas land and has only the incentive to dismiss a Texas Quiet Title Action**, thereby removing Townsend's remedy to remove clouds from Townsend's title that has no statute of limitations."

The above paragraphs have no merit, according to the Justices of the 5th Circuit, and it does NOT "warrant further discussion or explanation," even though there is no record I can find in Harris County, or Montgomery County, where a Federal Judge has ever quieted a title concerning Texas land.

> Townsend's-Brief For Appellant, Page 2-3, Case No. 13-20762
> **ISSUES PRESENTED FOR REVIEW**
> **Issue 1:** Whether Judge Atlas has jurisdiction to quiet a title concerning Texas land that does not adhere to Quiet Title Act as found in 28 U.S.C. § 2409a and where the value of the subject property is irrelevant and is not requested to be determined by the court in resolving a genuine issue of title.
> **Issue 2:** Whether BANA and Fannie Mae being incapable of producing a chain of title from Townsend's Warranty Deed and there being no defect in Townsend's Warranty Deed and is the common source of this Quiet Title Action; BANA's and Fannie Mae's only option is to convince Judge Atlas to dismiss the case "With Prejudice," thereby bypassing the mandates of the UCC, condemning the subject property to have a genuine issue of title for an undetermined period of time, giving the opportunity for Appellees to sell their so-called interest to an unexpected buyer.

Issue 3:   *Whether Townsend's right of remedy has been denied to Townsend by Judge Atlas dismissing, "With Prejudice," Townsend's solely cause of action, being a Quiet Title Action, which does not involve a tort action or money reparations, but rather a desire of Townsend's to cure a genuine issue of title concerning the subject property that was determined by a Texas County Judge.*

Issue 4: *Whether Judge Atlas abused her discretion and/or erred by failing to grant Townsend's Motion for a New Trial.*

The Justices of the 5th Circuit have agreed, with Judge Atlas, it does NOT matter whether the assignment of the Note and Deed of Trust is invalid, and it does NOT matter which entity has the authority (or lack of authority) to sell the property; and it does NOT matter clouds remain on the subject property, as long as the case is dismissed—where the court does NOT have to deal with the situation. Oh Yes, and my claims do NOT "warrant further discussion or explanation" that could possibly reveal the lack of Federal authority, to quiet titles of Texas land. The Great and Powerful OZ has spoken. **IT SHOCKS THE CONSCIENCE!!!!!**

I did NOT get my money's worth, when I paid the filing fee, to appeal to the 5th Circuit.

"If I had an hour to solve a problem and my life depended on it, I would use the first 55 minutes determining the proper question to ask, for once I knew the proper question, I could solve the problem in less than five minutes."
- Albert Einstein

It is not what a lawyer tells me I may do; but what humanity, reason, and justice tell me I ought to do.
- Edmund Burke, Second Speech on Conciliation, 1775

CHAPTER 35
THEY FINALLY GET
THE BLACK TOXIC MOLD DREAM HOUSE

I received my second notice, to vacate the Black Toxic Mold Dream House, on or about March 24th, 2014. My quiet title action case was still going on. I had reservations the BDFTE law firm was resilient, and would continue to harass me, until I was moved out of my home. On or about April 4th, 2014, my wife was served with a forcible detainer action filed in the same Justice of the Peace Court, as before; and as before, with the same JP, Judge G. Trey Spikes. For some unknown reason, I was given more time to prepare for trial. I received Trial Notice, on or about July 17th, 2014, that the trial, case No. 0110256EV, was set for August 7th, 2014. I was a lot more prepared, than the last time before Judge Spikes.

I also, decided to file suit, against Fannie Mae, at the same time—to attempt to obtain a Temporary Restraining Order, against Fannie Mae, trying to evict me from the Toxic Mold Dream House. See the Fannie Mae Suit, below.

On August 7th, 2014, I had already filed my - "Defendants' Answer and Affirmative Defense and Counterclaim;" "Defendant's Plea to the Jurisdiction and Motion to Dismiss;" "Affidavit Supporting Foundation of Defendants' Exhibits;" and "Defendant's Motion For Sanctions"—where I used Rule 13, of the Texas Rules of Civil Procedure, as grounds to sanction the attorney—for bringing the action. I really did NOT expect a non-attorney, Judge Spikes, to sanction an attorney—but you never know. I would have, if I would have been the judge.

Texas Rules of Civil Procedure
RULE 13. EFFECT OF SIGNING PLEADINGS, MOTIONS AND OTHER PAPERS; SANCTIONS

The **signatures of attorneys or parties** constitute a certificate by them that they have read the pleading, motion, or other paper; that to the best of their knowledge, information, and belief formed **after reasonable inquiry** the instrument **is not groundless and brought in bad faith or groundless and brought for the purpose of harassment.** Attorneys or parties **who shall bring a fictitious suit** as an experiment to get an opinion of the court, or **who shall file any fictitious pleading** in a cause for such a purpose, or **shall make statements** in pleading **which they know to be groundless and false**, for **the purpose of securing a delay** of the trial of the cause, **shall be held guilty of a contempt**. If a pleading, motion or other paper **is signed in violation of this rule**, the court, upon motion **or upon its own initiative**, after notice and hearing, **shall impose an appropriate sanction** available under Rule 215-2b, upon the person who signed it, a represented party, or both.

Courts **shall presume** that pleadings, motions, and other papers **are filed in good faith**. No sanctions under this rule may be imposed except for good cause, the particulars of which must be stated in the sanction order. **"Groundless"** for purposes of this rule **means no basis in law or fact** and not warranted by good faith argument for the extension, modification, or reversal of existing law. A general denial does not constitute a violation of this rule. The amount requested for damages does not constitute a violation of this rule.

Since this was practice court, there was no need to file a Rule 12 Motion. If you can remember back to 2012 actions, where the same attorneys tried to get me evicted, it was appealed to the Montgomery County Court at Law #2—where Judge Laird dismissed the case, for lack of jurisdiction. Since nothing had changed, since the last time before Judge Spikes' court, I expected Judge Spikes would recognize a superior court decision—on the same matter—and dismiss the case, for the same grounds. There still was a genuine issue of title, and Judge Spikes was forbidden to determine the issue of title, i.e., Judge Spikes lacked jurisdiction, to hear the matter before him.

Judge Spikes is NOT an attorney, but he apparently knew, or has been informed, who butters his bread. Judge Spike took no time to inform me it did NOT matter what evidence was before him, because he would always rule against me, concerning an eviction. **IT SHOCKS THE CONSCIENCE!!!!!**

I had plenty of witnesses that heard what Judge Spikes said to me, and he made no bones about it. He admitted to everyone, I had appealed without paying anything the last time, and he would allow the Appeal Bond to be filed—the same as it was before. Bookmark this page. I need you to come back here, later, and see what Judge Spikes said, about paying money to appeal, after a few months.

We appealed, and it was, again, assigned to the Montgomery County Court at Law #2, where Judge Laird was still presiding. I expected the same result, as nothing had changed, concerning the genuine issue of title. Boy, I was wrong.

I paid the filing fee of $235.00, on or before September 11, 2014, to appeal. I received a Docket Control Order, from Judge Laird.

DOCKET CONTROL ORDER

__It is ordered adjudged and decreed__ that the following deadlines shall apply to this case, said deadlines shall continue to be in effect upon any change in the trial date. Any date that falls on a weekend or legal holiday (as determined by Montgomery County Commissioners Court) shall be moved to the next day. Failure to appear as required for any docket will result in dismissal of the case with no further notice.

1. TUESDAY PRIOR TO TRIAL

    CALL IN ANNOUNCEMENT DOCKET

__All parties must__ contact the Court Coordinator Peggy Freeman AT 936.539.7832 to make trial announcements by noon.

2. FRIDAY PRIOR TO TRIAL PRE TRIAL CONFERENCE
ONLY THOSE PARTIES NOTIFIED BY THE COURT AFTER CALL IN DOCKET SHALL APPEAR
*a. **If a jury fee has been paid**, a proposed jury charge must be filed by this date. The jury charge must be provided to the Court in electronic format.*
b. All contested motions for continuance will be heard at this time.
*c. All motions in limine **must be in writing** and will be heard at this time. A separate proposed limine order **must be filed** with the motion.*

12/08/2014 at 9:00 a.m. -TRIAL *(Trials on call for two weeks)*
ONLY THOSE PARTIES NOTIFIED BY THE COURT AT PRE-TRIAL CONFERENCE SHALL APPEAR

Signed on this the 6th day of November, 2014.

Judge Claudia L. Laird

Getting ready for trial, I timely filed my, "Defendant's Demand For Trial By Jury;" "Defendant's Plea to the Jurisdiction and Motion For Dismissal;" "Affidavit Supporting Foundation of Defendants' Exhibits;" Defendant's Motion For Sanctions;" "Defendant's Notice of Hearing;" Defendant's Jury Instructions;" and my proposed, "Order For Dismissal"—similar to that Judge Laird had signed, before, in 2012.

At our first hearing, we soon saw something had changed, with the demeanor of Judge Laird. She was acting in the same manner Judge Spikes had acted, in the JP Court. It seemed Judge Laird was looking to the attorney representing Fannie Mae, for direction of her response to our arguments. I had over six (6) people in the court that came as court watchers which observed the same concern, over Judge Laird's bias, in favor of the attorney. We all saw we would NOT get a fair trial, in Judge Laird's Court, this time. It was apparent she was compromised, or otherwise had been instructed, to do what was necessary—to find in favor of Fannie Mae.

When we left the court room, all the court watchers met at my home; and took turns writing their own affidavit, of what had occurred, at the court hearing. Within a few days, I created a "Venue Change By Affidavit," under Rules 257 & 258, of the Texas Rules of Civil Procedure, and attached nine (9) affidavits to it.

My youngest son, who was a defendant also—since he was living in the Black Toxic Mold Dream House, with my wife and I—filed his, "Defendant's Motion For Showing Authority."

We received another Docket Control Order, from Judge Laird.

DOCKET CONTROL ORDER

It is ordered adjudged and decreed that the following deadlines shall apply to this case, said deadlines shall continue to be in effect upon any change in the trial date. Any date that falls on a weekend or legal holiday (as determined by Montgomery County Commissioners Court) shall be moved to the next day. Failure to appear as required for any docket will result in dismissal of the case with no further notice.

1. TUESDAY PRIOR TO TRIAL
    CALL IN ANNOUNCEMENT DOCKET
All parties must contact the Court Coordinator Peggy Freeman AT 936.539.7832 to make trial announcements by noon.

2. FRIDAY PRIOR TO TRIAL PRE TRIAL CONFERENCE
    ONLY THOSE PARTIES NOTIFIED BY THE COURT AFTER CALL IN DOCKET SHALL APPEAR
a. If a jury fee has been paid, a proposed jury charge must be filed by this date. The jury charge must be provided to the Court in electronic format.
b. All contested motions for continuance will be heard at this time.
c. All motions in limine must be in writing and will be heard at this time.A separate proposed limine order must be filed with the motion.

__2/17/2015 at 9:00 a.m. -TRIAL__ (Trials on call for two weeks)
ONLY THOSE PARTIES NOTIFIED BY THE COURT AT PRE-TRIAL
CONFERENCE SHALL APPEAR

Signed on this the 9th day of December, 2014.

Judge Claudia L. Laird

As we have seen, previously—throughout the book, judges will NOT allow a jury to hear the facts of the case, if there is another avenue to get rid of the case. Juries are unpredictable.

Rule 257 and Rule 258 are associated with Rule 86 and Rule 87, of the Texas Rules of Civil Procedure, where, "each party is entitled to at least 45 days notice of a hearing on the motion to transfer" the case, to another venue.

Judge Laird apparently got with Judge Underwood, and converted the Venue Change, to a motion to recuse.

__ORDER DENYING__ *PLAINTIFF'S VENUE CHANGE By AFFIDAVIT*
MOTION TO RECUSE

The Court has reviewed the motion and determined that it complains of the trial judge's rulings and actions in the case, __but does not allege extra-judicial conduct__ on the part of the trial judge __that would constitute a basis for a recusal__. A party's __remedy for unfair rulings is to assign error__ regarding the adverse rulings. See Grider v. Boston Co" 773 S.W.2d 338, 346 (Tex. App.-Dallas 1989, writ denied). __The Rule unambiguously indicates__ that __a motion to recuse__ "must not be based solely on the judge's rulings in the case." See TEX.R. Civ. P. 18a(a)(3). A judge's conduct during a case __does not constitute a basis for recusal unless__ it indicates __a high degree of favoritism or antagonism__ that __renders fair judgment impossible__. See Sommers v. Concepcion, 20 S.W.3d 27,41 (Tex. App.-Houston [14th Dist.] 2000, pet. denied); L1Ldiow v. DeBerry, 959 S.W.2d 265, 270-72 (Tex.App. - Houston [14th Dist.] 1997, no writ). The motion

does not *meet this standard.*

*The Court **ORDERS** the Clerk of the Court to transmit a certified copy of this order to*

Olen Underwood, *Presiding Judge*
Second Administrative Judicial Region of Texas
301 North Thompson, Suite 102
Conroe, Texas 77301
Fax: (936)538-8167
Date Signed: December 15th, 2014, Judge Olen Underwood, Presiding

Notice that Judge Underwood Orders the court clerk to transmit a certified copy, of this order, to himself. This Order is from the guy who appointed himself to a different court. As shown in the Order above, Rule 18a and Rule 18b of the TRCP deals with Motions to recuse or to disqualify a judge, of which there was no motion for recusal to be found in the record. Notice there is no mention of Rules 86 or Rule 87, or Rule 257 or Rule 258 that are associated with the Venue Change demand, in the Order. This is the typical Bait and Switch, what the system does to make stuff disappear, when they do NOT want to deal with the situation.

I objected to Judge Underwood's Order, and put in a Motion for Reconsideration, which fell on deaf ears of Judge Underwood. Instead on January 2nd, 2015, Judge Laird denied my Motion for Reconsideration, even though the motion was to Judge Underwood. The railroad was going, full-speed ahead.

During this 45-day wait, my son filed his, "Defendant's Motion For Striking Plaintiff's Pleadings." Remember, **if** the attorney canNOT prove up the authority to represent Fannie Mae, it is mandatory the judge strike ALL pleadings from the attorney, in behalf of Fannie Mae.

Texas Rules of Civil Procedure
RULE 12. ATTORNEY TO SHOW AUTHORITY
*... Upon his failure to show such authority, **the court shall
refuse to permit the attorney** to appear in the cause, **and
shall strike the pleadings** if no person who is authorized to
prosecute or defend appears. The motion may be heard and
determined **at any time before** the parties have announced
ready for trial, but the trial shall not be unnecessarily
continued or delayed for the hearing.*

The attorney responded, to my son's Motion to Strike
Pleading; and on January 2nd, 2015, Judge Laird signed an Order
denying the Motion to Strike, before there was a hearing to see
such authority.

Rabbit Trail: Attorney Kesler Takes It Up A Notch

Apparently, I was causing the local Attorney Rex L. Kesler,
Texas Bar No. 11357500, 2311 Canal Street, Suite 304, Houston,
Texas 77003-1565, so many problems, he decided to get Judge
Spikes (of the Justice of the Peace Court, in Precinct 2) involved—
where he didn't belong. But first, Mr. Kesler wrote me a letter,
dated December 24th, 2014, letting me know what he intended to
do.

Dear Mr. Townsend and All Other Occupants:
*__As you are aware__, I am local counsel for Plaintiff's attorneys of
record. __As you are also aware__, you appealed the judgment by the
Justice of the Peace, Pct. 2, Place 1, of Montgomery County, Texas,
in favor of Plaintiff for possession of the real property and
improvements located at 1504 Memorial Lane, Conroe,
Montgomery County, Texas 77304. __You filed an Appeal Bond__ as
part of that appeal on August 7, 2014. A copy of that Appeal Bond is
attached. __That Appeal Bond is defective.__*
*__Your appeal bond is defective__ in several respects, __including but not
limited to__ (a) a failure to either post a cash deposit or provide a*

*bond with sufficient surety or sureties, (b) a failure to make the bond payable to the appellee Federal National Mortgage Association, a/k/a Fannie Mae, (c) a failure to condition the bond on your prosecution of the appeal to effect; and (d) a failure to condition the bond on your payment of any judgment and all costs rendered against you on appeal. **You shall have** through Monday, December 30, 2014, within which **to cure the defects in your appeal bond**.*
Very truly yours,
Rex L. Kesler

Shortly thereafter, I get a letter, on January 12ᵗʰ, 2015 dated January 6ᵗʰ, 2015, from Judge Spikes (from the JP Court). The letter was apparently meant to be received, by me, too late to do anything about it. Think about it. It took 6 days, for mail to go from Conroe, Texas, to Conroe Texas. I don't think so.

Mr. Townsend
*When reviewing your case **it has come to the courts attention** that the required appeal bond has not been deposited into the registry of the court. This letter is to inform you that **you have (7) seven days to perfect your appeal**. If you have any questions **please feel free to contact my office** at (936)538-3788.*
Thank you
Judge G. Trey Spikes
Justice of the Peace, Pct. 2

Go find your Bookmark, where Judge Spikes said I didn't have to pay any money, to appeal. What changed, in five months? Was there an Ex Parte, collusion, conspiracy, getting access to a crystal ball, a fortuneteller, acquiring knowledge by way of a dream?

I got the letter the day before the deadline stated in the letter, i.e., it was mailed the way the Postal Service prohibits (backdating AND pre-dating), except for their own delivery needs.

Let this soak in a while..... The final judgment of Judge Spikes is dated August 7th, 2014. Five months later, Judge Spikes just happens to review my case, and gives me one (1) day to cough up $1,200, while Judge Laird, NOT judge Spikes, has the jurisdiction to question the sufficiency of my appeal bond.

Plenary Power of a judge is the jurisdiction to act, after a final judgment has been issued. This time frame is usually about 30 days after final judgment, but rarely much after that time. On or about August 19th, 2014, I received notice from Mark Turnbull, County Clerk, Montgomery County, Texas, my appeal was assigned to the County Court at Law #2, where Judge Laird was presiding. After I paid the filing fee, Judge Laird acquired jurisdiction over the case, and the issue was no longer a matter for Judge Spikes.

I take off work, on January 13th, 2015, to see if I can resolve this Bond-money matter. My son, Bob, and I, first contacted the Montgomery County Attorney's Office; and spoke to Mr. Ryan L. Morris, Assistant County Attorney, about Judge Spikes' letter—in hopes to resolve the matter, before I was damaged. Mr. Morris stated to us his client was Montgomery County, and he could NOT interfere with Judge Spikes' activities, concerning Montgomery County—but he was obligated to defend any claims, against Montgomery County. Mr. Morris did suggest we contact Judge Laird's court clerk, and ask when the court clerks of the two judges could possibly discuss the jurisdiction conflict, between the two courts. I have no reason to believe that Mr. Morris, or anyone associated with the Montgomery County Attorney's Office, contacted Judge Spikes, concerning this matter.

After leaving the Montgomery County Attorney's Office, Bob and I went to Judge Laird's office, and talked with Ms. Freeman—the court coordinator of County Court at Law #2, about the question of jurisdiction. Ms. Freeman assured Bob and I Judge Laird still claims jurisdiction over the matter. Ms. Freeman alleged

Judge Laird was not aware of Judge Spikes' demand for money concerning the appeal bond. Ms. Freeman suggested I formally inform Judge Laird, of any jurisdictional conflict, by filing whatever I felt appropriate, to give Judge Laird such notice.

Afterwards, Bob & I then went to the Justice of the Peace, Precinct 2 building, located at 2241 North 1st Street, in Conroe, Texas—to see if we could resolve the matter. We talked with the senior court clerk, who identified herself to us, as Anna. We asked Anna if we could speak to Judge Spikes, concerning the matter. Anna left the room; and when she returned, she said Judge Spikes told her he (Judge Spikes) would NOT talk to us about the letter, even though the letter stated: "if you have any questions please feel free to contact my office at (936)538-3788." I told Anna I had several questions.

I asked Anna for a copy of the Order, from Judge Spikes, which demanded some amount of money, before I was allowed to appeal. Anna stated Judge Spikes' final judgment indicated the amount; and I asked Anna to pull up a copy of Judge Spikes' judgment—and show me the amount I owed. Anna went to her desk, and printed out a copy of the judgment. When Anna returned, she gave us the copy of the judgment, and stated even though the judgment did NOT specify an amount, the appeal bond I had filed did state the amount owed. Bob & I had a copy of the appeal bond with us; and Bob pointed out to Anna the conditions of the bond, to be required to pay the amount indicated—and that the conditions of the bond had NOT been violated. Bob asked Anna, if the review of the old case had given discovery, of a violation of the conditions of the appeal bond? Anna stated, the conditions in the appeal bond did NOT matter, because Judge Spikes did NOT sign the bond agreeing to the conditions. Anna belligerently threatened I needed to pay the amount found on the appeal bond, or my appeal would NOT be considered perfected by Judge Spikes. Since neither the letter nor the judgment specified an amount owed to the court, I told Anna I had the funds with me to pay, as long as she would give me a signed letter indicating I was required to pay a fixed amount—for the appeal to be considered perfected by the court. Anna told me she would NOT be giving me anything in writing, other than a receipt for the amount paid. I explained, since I would be paying the funds under duress, I needed something in writing, other than the vaguely-stated letter sent to me, by certified mail. Anna stated she did NOT care, if I paid the amount, or not. Anna refused to inform the judge, of my demand for a written request, requiring a known amount; and my appeal would NOT be considered perfected by the JP court—unless the amount was paid to the court.

I have reason to believe—and do believe—the senior clerk, Anna, and Judge Spikes were conspiring to take my home; if I failed to pay the verbal amount, specified by Anna, by the end of the work day, indicated on Judge' Spikes letter—and/or the senior clerk, Anna, and Judge Spikes were conspiring to have my compliance to pay indicate I had paid the money voluntarily—and NOT under duress.

Since I felt threatened, by Judge Spikes and the senior court clerk, Anna; I decided I needed an official from Montgomery County that had no interest in the matter, to witness me paying the money, under duress. I called the Montgomery County Sheriff's Department and requested a deputy sheriff be dispatched, to the JP court building. The dispatcher took my information, and within 20 minutes, a deputy sheriff, by the name of J. Parker, arrived at the court building. Deputy Parker talked with Constable Bond, before he talked with me. I have reason to believe—and do believe—Constable Bond acts as the bailiff, for Judge Spikes. After talking with Constable Bond, Deputy Parker listened to my problem; and I explained I felt threatened, and I believed money was being extorted, from me. I explained to Deputy Parker the senior clerk, Anna, had verbally demanded $1,200 from me, on the threat Judge Spikes would dismiss my ongoing appeal, but then refused to give me anything in writing, demanding the same. I told the Deputy Sheriff I feared the repercussions could be done by Judge Spikes, if I did NOT pay the amount verbally demanded by the senior clerk, Anna. The deputy was there to see I was paying the cash money, under threat, duress and coercion—because the senior clerk, Anna, stated she would NOT accept any other form of payment that would state on its face it was being paid under duress. Deputy Parker observed me paying a clerk of the court $1,200.00 cash money, under duress, and the clerk giving me a receipt that only indicated cash bond.

I complained to Judge Laird, about the attorney Rex L. Kesler and Judge Spikes conspiring against me; Judge Laird had no comment. **IT SHOCKS THE CONSCIENCE!!!!!**
(Jumping off that rabbit trail.)

My son filed his, "Defendant's Amended Motion For Showing Authority," on or about January 14th, 2015. Instead of just showing his authority to represent Fannie Mae, the attorney complained of a technicality, of which my son closed with the amended motion.

> When a party **_files a motion to show authority_**, the challenged attorney **_must appear before the trial court_** to show his authority to act on behalf of his client.
> In re Guardianship of Benavides (App. 4 Dist. 2013) 403 S.W.3d 370.

> Fact that proposed ward **_was entitled to jury trial_** on issue of his competency in contested guardianship proceedings **_did not preclude trial court from determining fact issues related to motion to show authority_** with respect to proposed ward's counsel.
> In re Guardianship of Benavides (App. 4 Dist. 2013) 403 S.W.3d 370

> **_Rule 12 motion is the exclusive method_** for questioning the authority of an attorney to represent a party in any court proceeding.
> Kindle v. Wood County Elec. Co-op, Inc. (App. 12 Dist. 2004) 151 S.W.3d 206, review denied, rehearing of petition for review denied.

The primary purpose of Rule of Civil Procedure permitting party __to cause opposing party's attorney to show his authority to prosecute or defend suit is to enforce a party's right to know who authorized the suit__.

At hearing on motion to show authority, __the burden of proof is on the challenged attorney to show his authority to prosecute or defend the suit.__

R.H. v. Smith (App. 5 Dist. 2011)339 S.W.3d 756.

__No written answer is necessary__ to a motion that an attorney be required to show his authority; __he may, in answer to the motion, exhibit to the court the evidence of his authority__.

Bridges v. Samuelson (Sup. 1889) II S.W. 539, 73 Tex. 522.

On or about January 20th, 2015, I tried a different approach; and filed my, "Defendant's Affirmative Defense of Adverse Possession."

__The fact that adverse possession will defeat a deed__ even if the adverse possessor has knowledge of the deed is not new. Humbert v Rector, Churchwardens & Vestrymen of Trinity Church, 24 Wend 587, 604 [1840]

"__Adverse possession__, although not a favored method of procuring title, __is a recognized one__. It is a __necessary means of clearing disputed titles__ and the courts adopt it and enforce it, because, when adverse possession is carefully and fully proven, __it is a means of settling disputed titles__ and this is desirable" (Belotti v Bickhardt, 228 NY at 308; see generally Hindley v Manhattan Ry. Co., 185 NY 335, 355-356 [1906]).

Vernon's Tex. Civ. St article 5510: Any person who has the right of action for the recovery of lands, tenements or hereditaments against another having peaceable and adverse possession thereof, cultivating, using or enjoying the same, __shall institute his suit therefor within ten years next after his cause of action shall have accrued__, and not afterward.

I filed my, "Defendant's Affirmative Defense of Homestead Claim."

"__A spouse's homestead right in Texas predates statehood__. See TEX. CONST. art. XVI, § 50 interp. commentary (Vernon 1993). __Spousal homestead rights have been constitutionally guaranteed since the first constitution of the State of Texas__. See TEX. CONST. of 1845, art. VII, § 22. The constitution currently provides that "[a]n owner or claimant of the property claimed as homestead __may not sell or abandon the homestead without the consent of each owner and the spouse of each owner__, given in such manner as may be prescribed by law." TEX. CONST. art. XVI, § 50(b) (emphasis added)"
GELDARD v. WATSON, 214 S.W.3d 202 (2007)

"Whether the homestead is the separate property __of either spouse or community property__, __neither__ spouse may sell, convey, or encumber the homestead without the joinder of the other spouse except as provided in this chapter or by other rules of law." See TEX. FAM.CODE ANN. § 5.001."
GELDARD v. WATSON, 214 S.W.3d 202 (2007)

"__The homestead right constitutes an estate in land__. Laster v. First Huntsville Prop. Co., 826 S.W.2d 125, 129 (Tex.1991). "This estate is analogous to a life tenancy, with the holder of the homestead right possessing __the rights similar to those of a life tenant__ for so long as the property retains its homestead character." Id. The homestead estate is a vested interest. See Morris, 393 S.W.2d at 387. The homestead estate has the effect of reducing the underlying ownership rights to "something akin to remainder interests." Laster, 826 S.W.2d at 129 (quoting United States v. Rodgers, 461 U.S. 677, 686, 103 S.Ct. 2132, 76 L.Ed.2d 236 (1983))."
GELDARD v. WATSON, 214 S.W.3d 202 (2007)

"The determination of Watson's right to possession in her forcible detainer action __necessarily required an adjudication of the merits of title__ between Watson (by conveyance from Wanda) and Geldard (as the claimant of a homestead right under Wanda's separate title). Thus, the justice court adjudicated the merits of title in determining Watson's right to possession in her forcible detainer action. __The__

justice court's judgment, and the county court at law judgment on appeal, are void. See Gentry v. Marburger, 596 S.W.2d 201 (Tex.Civ.App.-Houston [1st Dist.] 1980, writ ref'd n.r.e.)."
GELDARD v. WATSON, 214 S.W.3d 202 (2007)

I filed my, "Defendant's Affirmative Defense Due To Note Being Discharged By Accord and Satisfaction."

Texas Local Government Code
*Sec. 192.007. RECORDS OF RELEASES AND OTHER ACTIONS. (a) To release, transfer, assign, or take another action relating to an instrument that is filed, registered, or recorded in the office of the county clerk, a person must file, register, or record another instrument relating to the action **in the same manner as the original instrument was required to be filed, registered, or recorded**. (b) An entry, including a marginal entry, may not be made on a previously made record or index to indicate the new action.*

*"[I]t is not uncommon for notes and mortgages to be assigned, often more than once. When the role of a servicing agent **acting on behalf of a mortgagee** is thrown into the mix, **it is no wonder that it is often difficult for unsophisticated borrowers to be certain of the identity of their lenders and mortgagees**."*
In re Schwartz, 366 B.R. 265, 266 (Bankr. D. Mass. 2007)

*"**Under Texas law '[a]gency is never to be presumed; it must be shown affirmatively**. The party who asserts the existence of an agency relationship has the burden of proving it.'"*
Allamon v. Acuity Specialty Products, Civil Action No. 1:10-CV-294-TH (USDCt. E.D. Tex. 6-26-20 12)

*The foreclosing party **must be vested with both a valid Deed of Trust and the underlying Note** that Deed of Trust secures in order to foreclose on the property. Scott v. Hewitt, 127 Tex. 31; 90 S.W.2d 816 (1936)*

*"The mortgaged premises are pledged as security for the debt. **In proportion as a remedy is denied the contract is violated, and the***

rights of the assignee are set at naught. In other words, the mortgage ceases to be security for a part or the whole of the debt, its express provisions to the contrary notwithstanding."
Carpenter v. Longan, 83 U.S. 271

"The note and mortgage are inseparable; *the former as essential, the latter as an incident.* **An assignment of the note carries the mortgage with it, while an assignment of the latter alone is a nullity.**"
Carpenter v. Longan, 83 U.S. 271

"The mortgage loan becomes ineffectual when the note holder did not also hold the deed of trust." Bellistri v. Ocwen Loan Servicing, LLC, 284 S.W.3d 619, 623 (Mo. App. 2009)

"Moreover, in the case of original mortgages and promissory notes, **they are not merely exhibits but instruments which must be surrendered prior to the issuance of a judgment**. The judgment takes the place of the promissory note. Surrendering the note is essential so that it cannot thereafter be negotiated. See Perry v. Fairbanks Capital Corp., 888 So. 2d 725, 726 (Fla. 5th DCA 2004). **The judgment cancels the note.** The clerk cannot return these instruments to the parties." See: District Court Of Appeal Of The State Of Florida Fourth District January Term 2010: JAMES F. JOHNSTON and SANDRA JOHNSTON, Appellants, V. JEANNE HUDLETT Appellee. No 4D08-4636 [March 31 2010]

"If an instrument not in the possession of the original holder **lacks a written indorsement and proof of the chain of title, the person in possession does not have the status of a holder."** (citing Jernigan v. Bank One, Tex., N.A., 803 S.W.2d 774, 776 (Tex.App.-Houston [14th Dist.] 1991, no writ) "... Mills relies on his own affidavit testimony and that of Bell and Comstock to establish a chain of title to the Leavings' note and trust deed. Under Texas law, the transfer of a note may be proved by testimony rather than by documentation. Priesmeyer, 917 S.W.2d at 939; Christian v. Univ. Fed. Sav. Ass'n, 792 S.W.2d 533, 534 (Tex.App.-Houston [1st Dist.] 1990, no writ). However, to support summary judgment, affidavit testimony must affirmatively show that it is based on personal knowledge; it must be admissible in evidence; and it is inadequate unless it affirmatively

*shows that the affiant is competent to testify to the matters stated therein. TEX.R. CIV. P. 166a(f). **The mere recitation that an affidavit is based on personal knowledge is inadequate if the affidavit does not positively show a basis for such knowledge.** Priesmeyer, 917 S.W.2d at 939-40; Geiselman, 965 S.W.2d at 537." "... Moreover, the documents Mills testifies to do not show the chain of title of the Leavings' note from "builder" to himself."*
Leavings v. Mills, 175 S.W.3d 301 (TX, 2004)

I more-than proved there was a genuine issue of title. I left no doubt the court lacked jurisdiction to hear the right of possession. Apparently, the fix was in—before it got started.

A hearing was scheduled, for January 30th, 2015, to resolve the Venue Change and for the attorney to show his authority, to represent Fannie Mae.

The attorney Rex L. Kesler finally brought to court the alleged authority he was relying upon, to represent Fannie Mae. It turns out to only be an email, from Vaughan, which is only an employee of BDFTE.

Sharon L. Vaughan SharonV@bdf9roup.com   Wed, Sep 17, 2014 at 10:01 AM
To: rex.kesler@gmail.com
MONTGOMERY COUNTY CCL2/ CAUSE NO. 14-28407
Attached are all of the documents pertaining to the eviction appeal litigation on the above referenced file.

*Please enter an appearance on behalf of FNMA, request a trial setting and seek entry of a judgment for possession of the property and costs of court. Please notify the undersigned of the trial setting. Please obtain any certified copies of title documents needed for the trial. Please include the costs in your invoice to our office. **You are authorized for billing at the rate of $150.00 per hour for a maximum of 5 hours.** Of course, please advise us of any questions or if you need additional information or documentation.*

*I will forward a business records affidavit to you shortly via FEDEX. This file is assigned to Joseph Vacek. **Please advise** if you need any additional information or documentation regarding the same.*
Shari Vaughan*

Lead Legal Assistant to JosephVacek
The BDF Law Group
Barrett Daffin Frappier Turner& Engel, LLP(Texas)
Barrett Daffin Frappier Treder& Weiss, LLP(California/Nevada)
Barrett DaffinFrappier Levine & Block, LLP(Georgia)
15000 Surveyor Blvd., Suite100
Addison,Texas75001
972·340·7967- Direct
972-341-0734- Fax
sharonv@bdfgroup.com
*not licensed to practice law

That's it. That's all the proof the attorney Rex L. Kesler could come up with, having had almost two (2) months to produce something credible showing the authority to represent Fannie Mae. Notice the email is dated four (4) months prior the hearing on January 30, 2015. Is it reasonable that Mr. Kesler spent more than five hours on this case?

My son Bob examined Mr. Kesler under Oath, asking if anyone mentioned in the email was an employee of Fannie Mae. No, there wasn't. Did Mr. Kesler think that email was a contract, between his law firm, or him directly with Fannie Mae? No it wasn't. My son moved the court to strike all pleadings, by Mr. Kesler and Fannie Mae.

Rule 12 of the TRCP does NOT give the court discretion to strike. Rule 12 states: "Upon his failure to show such authority, the court **shall refuse to permit the attorney to appear in the cause, and shall strike the pleadings** if no person who is authorized to prosecute or defend appears." This is NOT a judicial decision, but is an administrative duty, of the court, to follow the rules.

IT SHOCKS THE CONSCIENCE!!!!!

Next, the Venue Change hearing occurred. Judge Laird ordered the people—who had made affidavits stating they did NOT believe we could get a fair trial in Judge Laird's Court—take the stand, where the attorney could question them concerning their affidavits. This behavior was NOT part of the rules concerning Rules 86, 87, 257 & 258, of the TRCP.

Texas Rules of Civil Procedure
RULE 258. SHALL BE GRANTED
Where such motion to transfer venue is duly made, it shall be
***granted, unless** the credibility of those making such application, or*
their means of knowledge or the truth of the facts set out in said
*application **are attacked by the affidavit of a credible person**; when*
thus attacked, the issue thus formed shall be tried by the judge; and
the application either granted or refused. Reasonable discovery in
support of, or in opposition to, the application shall be permitted,
and such discovery as is relevant, including deposition testimony on
file, may be attached to, or incorporated by reference in, the
affidavit of a party, a witness, or an attorney who has knowledge of
such discovery.

It does NOT take a scholar to read the intent of Rule 258, above. It states the motion "shall be granted, unless" a credible person makes an affidavit attacking the affidavits of the other people stating venue needs to be changed. Unless there is an affidavit filed in the record attacking the other affidavits, then the motion to change venue ""shall be granted." No discretion is allowed by the judge, to decide otherwise. AND there was no filed affidavit against those of the court watchers! After hearing the testimony of my affiants, Judge Laird gets up and walks out. We ask the court clerk what happened. The court clerk stated we would be notified.

SUMMARY JUDGMENT

*BE IT REMEMBERED that, on this day, a day of the regular term of this Court, came on for consideration Plaintiff's Motion for Summary Judgment, **any response thereto** of Defendant and **any reply** of Plaintiff, filed in the above entitled and numbered cause pending in this Court, The Court, judicial notice of the case requested by defense, **overrules defense objections** to the evidence, & **having considered** the pleadings, summary judgment evidence and law, **finds** that Plaintiff is entitled to judgment against Defendants Bobie Kenneth Townsend and all other occupants thereof for possession of the real property and improvements located at 1504 Memorial Lane, Conroe, Montgomery County, Texas 77304, which real property is more particularly described as follows:*

Lot 2 of MCDADE ESTATES SUBDIVISION, Section 1, in the W.S. Allen Survey, A-2, according to the map or plat records formerly recorded in Volume 9, Page 23, but now recorded in Plat Cabinet A, Sheet 12, Map Records of Montgomery County, Texas (the "Premises"), and for its costs of Court.

***It is, therefore, ORDERED, ADJUDGED, and DECREED by this Court** that Plaintiff Federal National Mortgage Association, a/k/a Fannie Mae, **is entitled to and shall have judgment against** Defendants Bobie Kenneth Townsend and all other occupants of the Premises **for possession of the Premises** and that, in the event Defendants Bobie Kenneth Townsend and all other occupants of the Premises do NOT vacate the Premises **on or before 2/10 2015**, then a writ of* *possession and such writs and orders __as are necessary to enforce this judgment shall issue__.*

It is, further, ORDERED, ADJUDGED, and DECREED by this Court that Plaintiff Federal National Mortgage Association, a/k/a Fannie Mae, is entitled to and shall have judgment against Defendant Bobie Kenneth Townsend for all costs of Court and for post-judgment interest accruing thereon at the rate of 5.00% per annum from and after the date of final judgment herein until paid in full, for all of which let execution and such other writs as are necessary issue to enforce this judgment. __Bond is set at $4,500.00.__ This judgment disposes of all claims on file herein between the parties and is intended to be a final and appealable judgment.

__Signed: 1/30/2015 12:20 PM__

Laird
JUDGE PRESIDING

IT SHOCKS THE CONSCIENCE!!!!!

People witnessed Judge Laird failed to give the Defendants a Fair Trial—and the record proves it. Judge Laird should NOT be re-elected, as she has proven on the record she canNOT be unbiased, when confronted with *pro ses*. I filed a Petition For Writ of Mandamus with the Ninth Court of Appeals, whereby the 9th stated that they would ignore the petition. There was no need to Order Judge Laird to follow the rules when there is a fee to be had on appeal.

Since I believe Judge Laird's summary judgment was a void judgment, I did NOT appeal the decision. By the way, because the Justices of the Ninth Court of Appeals systematically and/or habitually rule against *pro ses*, there was little point to invest $4,500 to appeal—and stay in a Black Toxic Mold environment any longer than necessary. But, I refused to abandon the property and I wasn't leaving voluntarily.

CHAPTER 36
MY SEVENTH LAWSUIT
FANNIE MAE'S UNJUST ENRICHMENT

On or About August 6th, 2014, I made another effort within the injustice system. I filed suit against Fannie Mae, in the 284th District Court of Texas, Case No. 04-08-08592, The Honorable Judge Cara Wood presiding—in hopes to stop the forcible detainer while the Quiet Title action was winding down. The case was styled: *Bobie Kenneth Townsend v. Federal National Mortgage Association.*

It's break time, once more. Like Chapter 28, the following is more legalese that could give you a brain overload. I go into more detail than the average reader needs, but people that do not use attorneys or attorneys that get screwed over by the system need this detail. The readers that don't, I provide a book trailer, so they can skip ahead to Chapter 37.

Chapter 36 Book Trailer: The author files suit against an evil bank in State Court, where an evil law firm moves the author's case to Federal Court where Federal Judges hates pro ses and never reads the pleadings of pro ses. The evil law firm tells lies about the author, makes up quotes that don't exist in court cases. The evil law firm forgets to serve the author with an answer to his original complaint, but the judge determines that rules are just a guide line for attorneys. The case is passed from judge to judge. The Federal Judges, that hates pro ses, never grant requested discovery and ignores the evidence submitted by the author. The hanging judge then creates an Order dismissing the authors case based upon the defendant's first motion to dismissed that had nothing to do with the author's amended complaint. The author's amended complaint was allowed by the same judge to be filed by the author. But, the day **before** the defendant answered the author's amended complaint the hanging judge dismissed the case with prejudice based on defendant's first motion to dismiss that did NOT address author's newly cause of action "unjust enrichment". After the break, see details below or skip to Chapter 37.

If you are about to skip to the next Chapter, imagine the TV Jeopardy song as the audience waits for the question to the answer.

For those that did not skip, breaks over.

My pleading that was filed in State Court was entitled "Plaintiff's Original Petition & Application For Temporary Restraining Order." Judge Wood stated to me she would NOT Order a JP judge to stop a forcible detainer action. But later, Judge Spikes admitted he was ordered to stop all kinds of actions, since he had been elected—including forcible detainer actions by district court judges. Maybe Judge Wood was NOT one of the district court judges Judge Spikes was referring to, or maybe Judge Wood just doesn't do that for *pro ses*. I'll have to research the policy of Judge Wood, at a later time.

The sole cause of action against Fannie Mae was: "Townsend claims violation of wrongful non-judicial foreclosure by Fannie Mae." The elements I had to prove were: 1) a defect in the non-judicial foreclosure sale proceedings, 2) a grossly-inadequate selling price and 3) a causal connection between the defect and the grossly-inadequate selling price. See *Charter Nat'l Bank- Houston v. Stevens,* 781 S.W.2d 368, 371 (Tex.App.-Houston [14th Dist.] 1989, writ denied.) I objected to the elements the 14th Court of Appeals created out of thin air which had to be proven, by me, to establish a wrongful non-judicial foreclosure. The established elements by the 14th, does NOT abide by the mandates of the BCC or UCC. The BCC § 3.203 and the UCC § 3-203 contains the prerequisite which mandates only the "person entitled to enforce" (PETE) can authorize the commencement of a non-judicial foreclosure. The PETE must be able to prove it has obtained 100% of the rights, to the payments—and must be able to prove ownership of the original Note and original Deed of Trust. Any party that fails to produce the evidence mandated, by the BCC & UCC, obtains no right to initiate a non-judicial foreclosure and must be considered invalid by a court. There exist wide caverns of non-judicial foreclosure procedure defects, concerning Townsend's subject property being authorized to be sold, under the provisions of the original Deed of Trust. On or about March 8, 2012, I was sent notice by a foreclosure-mill law firm (BDFTE) giving me so-called notice Bank of America N.A. was the servicer and the Mortgagee; and allegedly had authorized the acceleration of the debt associated with the subject property.

The so-called Accelerated Debt Notice is flawed and fatally defective **(1)**; as it does NOT follow Section 22 of the Deed of Trust, which requires the Lender to give me a date to cure the default, and the date shall NOT be less than 30 days from the date of the notice.

Deed of Trust Section 22
*The notice shall specify: (c) a date, **not less than 30 days from the date the notice is given to Borrower**, by which the default must be cured;...*

The date of the notice was March 08, 2012, and the date of the substitute trustee sale was April 3, 2012, violating the "NOT less than 30 days" provisions set by the Deed of Trust. My property was allegedly sold on April 3, 2012, which is less than the thirty (30) day required notice, before the trustee's sale could commence.

The so-called Accelerated Debt Notice is flawed and fatally defective **(2)**, as it does NOT follow Section 22 of the Deed of Trust, which states there has to have been a default and what the action is needed to cure the default.

> *Deed of Trust Section 22*
> *The notice shall specify: (a) the default; (b) **the action required to cure the default**;...*

The so-called Accelerated Debt Notice is flawed and fails to state any balance owed by the borrower, or when the default occurred, or what I was required to do to cure the so-called default.

The so-called Accelerated Debt Notice is flawed and fatally defective **(3)**, as it does NOT follow Section 22 of the Deed of Trust, which states:

> *Deed of Trust Section 22*
> *The notice shall specify: (d) that **failure to cure the default on or before the date** specified in the notice will result in acceleration of the sums secured by this Security Instrument and sale of the Property.*

I obtained requested discovery, from the non-party BANA, and obtained 342 documents BANA indicated to be from a "Loan File" associated with Townsend's subject property. Townsend reviewed each and every one of the 342 documents produced by BANA, and NOT one of the documents produced could be considered any written direction from the PETE—as required by the Deed of Trust to authorize the acceleration of the debt, by any party that could claim to be the party entitled to enforce as mandated by the BCC or UCC. I obtained requested discovery from Vaughan, an employee of the foreclosure-mill law firm that claimed by affidavit to have care of **all** the "Foreclosure File" documents; and I obtained 74 documents from Vaughan. I reviewed each and every one of the 74 documents produced by Vaughan, and NOT one of the documents produced could be considered any written direction from the PETE—as required by the Deed of Trust to authorize the acceleration of the debt, by any party that could claim to be the party entitled to enforce as mandated by the BCC or UCC. On April 3rd, 2012, the alleged Substitute Trustee Jimenez (Jimenez) did NOT inform any potential buyer, in 2011 the Montgomery Central Appraisal District (MCAD) determined the aggregate market value of plaintiff's property was near $200,000. On April 3rd, 2012, Jimenez allegedly sold plaintiff's property for near-half of the market value determined by MCAD in 2011; and was the approximate cause of Townsend's harm—mainly due to the failure to follow the non-judicial foreclosure procedure, as mandated in the Deed of Trust. Because of the low-selling price accepted, Jimenez denied the equity due me, which also allowed Jimenez to obtain her fee; and such action enriched the client of BDFTE—for obtaining the property at such a low-selling price. Jimenez did NOT have in her possession, at the time of sale, the Note and Deed of Trust—as required under *WEST v. AXTELL et al*, 322 Mo. 401, 17 S.W.2d 328 (1929), or any other written direction by a person entitled to enforce the sale. Jimenez should have known Fannie Mae was NOT the Lender or its designee, and was NOT the current owner of the Note and Deed of Trust at the time of the sale; and Jimenez had no authority to auction off Townsend's property, to Fannie Mae.

There it was. I laid it out for Judge Wood a wrongful non-judicial foreclosure had occurred. Just like clockwork, the case was moved to Federal Court, about October 6th, 2014, Case No. 4:14-cv-02835. The case was assigned to United States Magistrate Judge Stephen Wm. Smith, with the United States District Court For The Southern District of Texas, Houston Division. The law firm that reached into the foreclosure bowl was McGuirewoods, LLP at 600 Travis Street, Suite 7500, Houston, Texas 77002. The attorney of record was Tamara D. Stiner Toomer, State Bar No, 24043940,

Southern District of Texas Bar No, 601672.

On or about November 10th, 2014, I sent Fannie Mae a request for discovery. I received a letter, dated December 9th, 2014.

Townsend v. Federal National Mortgage Association United States District Court, Southern District of Texas Case No. 4:14-cv-02835

Re: Discovery Propounded on Federal National Mortgage Association

Dear Mr. Townsend,
Our firm is in receipt of your discovery entitled First Request for Production, First Interrogatories, and First Set of Requests for Admission, served by regular mail on or about November 10, 2014, propounded on defendant Federal National Mortgage Association. **We will not respond to this discovery at this time, as it is premature under Federal Rule of Civil Procedure 26(d)(1).**
We appreciate your consideration of this matter.
Regards,
Seth P. Cox

I guess, I need to look up Rule 26(d)(1).

Federal Rules Of Civil Procedure
Rule 26. Duty to Disclose; General Provisions Governing Discovery
(d) TIMING AND SEQUENCE OF DISCOVERY.
*(1) Timing. A party may not seek discovery from any source **before the parties have conferred** as required by Rule 26(f), **except** in a proceeding exempted from initial disclosure under Rule 26(a)(1)(B), or when authorized by these rules, by stipulation, or by court order.*

This means, I now have to look up Rule 26(f).

Federal Rules Of Civil Procedure
Rule 26. Duty to Disclose; General Provisions Governing Discovery
(f) CONFERENCE OF THE PARTIES; PLANNING FOR DISCOVERY.
*(1) **Conference Timing**. Except in a proceeding exempted from initial*

disclosure under Rule 26(a)(1)(B) **or** when the court orders otherwise, the parties **must confer as soon as practicable**—
and in any event **at least 21 days before a scheduling conference is to be held or** a scheduling order is due under Rule 16(b).

(2) **Conference Content**; Parties' Responsibilities. In conferring, the parties **must consider** the nature and basis of their claims and defenses and the possibilities **for promptly settling or resolving the case; make or arrange** for the disclosures required by Rule 26(a)(1); **discuss any issues** about preserving discoverable information; and **develop a** proposed discovery plan. The attorneys of record and all unrepresented parties that have appeared in the case **are jointly responsible for arranging the conference**, for attempting **in good faith to agree** on the proposed discovery plan, and for submitting to the court **within 14 days after the conference** a written report outlining the plan. The court **may order** the parties or attorneys to attend the conference in person.

(3) **Discovery Plan**. A discovery plan **must state** the parties' views and proposals on:

(A) **what changes** should be made in the timing, form, or requirement for disclosures under Rule 26(a), including a statement of when initial disclosures were made or will be made;

(B) **the subjects on** which discovery may be needed, when discovery should be completed, and whether discovery should be conducted in phases or be limited to or focused on particular issues;

(C) **any issues about** disclosure or discovery of electronically stored information, including the form or forms in which it should be produced;

(D) **any issues about** claims of privilege or of protection as trial-preparation materials, including—if the parties agree on a procedure to assert these claims after production—
whether to ask the court to include their agreement in an order;

(E) **what changes** should be made in the limitations on discovery imposed under these rules or by local rule, and what other limitations should be imposed; and

(F) **any other orders** that the court should issue under Rule 26(c) or under Rule 16(b) and (c).

(4) **Expedited Schedule**. **If necessary** to comply with its expedited schedule for Rule 16(b) conferences, **a court may** by local rule:

(A) require the parties' conference to occur less than 21 days before the scheduling conference is held or a scheduling order is due under

Rule 16(b); and plan to be filed less than 14 days after the parties' conference, or excuse the parties from submitting a written report and permit them to report orally on their discovery plan at the Rule 16(b) conference.

Can anyone tell me the point, to all this BS? All this jumping through hoops is NOT necessary in Texas courts, and apparently cases still function to a conclusion. This is only a means for parties to have an excuse, for NOT providing discovery that may compromise their side of the case. The part I focused on, at the time was: "The court may order the parties or attorneys to attend the conference in person." I think, I will just wait for an Order.

I sent my own version, of the "Joint Discovery & Case Management Plan," to the attorney of record, and let her file what was necessary. What could go wrong?

On or about January 12th, 2015, I filed my Motion For Remand. Since I know by now, Federal Courts have no jurisdiction over Texas land; and the sole purpose for moving a case, to Federal Court, is to get the case dismissed. I tried multiple arguments, to move the case back to Texas court—a Snowball's chance in Hell.

On the same day of January 12th, 2015, I filed my, "Motion For Judicial Notice," to attempt to ward off the typical summary judgment—to which we have all become accustomed, in Federal Court.

My argument, to the court, consisted of:

"This Honorable United States District Court is to take judicial notice of the current, issued mandate, by the SUPREME COURT OF THE UNITED STATES (Supreme Court) concerning the *TOLAN v. COTTON* (*Tolan* Case), No. 13–551, Cite as: 572 U. S. ____ (2014), decided May 5, 2014, which is provided to the court, under Tab 39, showing the necessary information for the court to take judicial notice of the *Tolan* Case.

If a party makes a written request for the court to take judicial notice of *TOLAN v. COTTON* (*Tolan* Case), No. 13–551, Cite as: 572 U. S. ____ (2014), decided May 5, 2014, and supplies the court with sufficient information, which has been provided to the court; the court must take judicial notice of the court decision. Tex. R. Evid. 202; *see Daugherty v. Southern P.T. Co.,* 772 S.W.2d 81, 83 (Tex. 1989).

The decision found concerning the *Tolan* Case is relevant to Townsend's case, before the Honorable United States District Court, to find the summary judgment evidence in the light most favorable to Plaintiff—as mandated by the Supreme Court."

My intention is to focus the United States District Court, to consider "[t]he evidence of the nonmovant is to be believed, and all justifiable inferences are to be drawn in his favor." *Anderson* v. *Liberty Lobby, Inc.,* 477 U. S. 242, 255 (1986).

*Texas law is sensitive to the notion that summary judgment **should not allow a trial judge to infringe on the jury's role as fact-finder**. Huckabee v. Time Warner Entm't Co., 19 S.W.3d 413, 422 (Tex. 2000)*

*Summary judgment **does not allow for a litigant to be deprived of its right to trial by jury**. City of Houston v. Clear Creek Basin Auth., 589 S.W.2d 671, 678 n.5 (Tex. 1979)*

The Supreme Court focused upon Judge Dennis' (of the Fifth Circuit) dissent stating "that the panel opinion "fail[ed] to address evidence that, when viewed in the light most favorable to the plaintiff, creates genuine issues of material fact as to whether an objective officer in Cotton's position could have reasonably and objectively believed that [Tolan] posed an immediate, significant threat of substantial injury to him."

The Supreme Court recognized the claim of qualified immunity at summary judgment, courts should engage in a two-pronged inquiry; and the Supreme Court explained the differences of each prong, at length. But, the Supreme Court also held: "... under either prong, courts may NOT resolve genuine disputes of fact in favor of the party seeking summary judgment. See *Brosseau* v. *Haugen*, 543 U. S. 194, 195, n. 2 (2004) (*per curiam*); *Saucier, supra,* at 201; *Hope, supra,* at 733, n. 1. The Supreme Court held that such rule did NOT specifically apply to qualified immunity but as a general rule "that a "judge's function" at summary judgment is NOT "to weigh the evidence and determine the truth of the matter but to determine whether there is a genuine issue for trial." *Anderson*, 477 U. S., at 249. The Supreme Court reiterated: "In making that determination, a court must view the evidence "in the light most favorable to the opposing party." *Adickes* v. *S. H. Kress & Co.*, 398 U. S. 144, 157 (1970); see also *Anderson, supra,* at 255."

The Supreme Court mandates: "Accordingly, courts must take care NOT to define a case's "context" in a manner that imports genuinely disputed factual propositions. See *Brosseau, supra,* at 195, 198 (inquiring as to whether conduct violated clearly established law "'in light of the specific context of the case'" and construing "facts . . . in a light most favorable to" the nonmovant)."

I found it typical the Texas Ninth Court of Appeals cites its own case, "*Conquest Drilling Fluids, Inc.* v. *Tri-Flo Int'l, Inc.*, 137 S.W.3d 299, 309 (Tex. App.—Beaumont 2004, no pet.)," in various cases, where it is mandated summary judgments should be view in favor of the nonmovant.

In the *Tolan* Case, the Supreme Court shows where the Fifth Circuit failed in its deductions: "...the Fifth Circuit failed to view the evidence at summary judgment in the light most favorable to Tolan with respect to the central facts of this case. By failing to credit evidence that contradicted some of its key factual conclusions, the court improperly "weigh[ed] the evidence" and resolved disputed issues in favor of the moving party, *Anderson*, 477 U. S., at 249."

The Supreme Court indicates it is time to remind the inferior courts: "...while "this Court is <u>NOT equipped to correct **every perceived error** coming from the lower federal courts</u>," *Boag* v. *MacDougall* 454 U. S. 364, 366 (1982) (O'Connor, J., concurring), we intervene here because the opinion below reflects **<u>a clear misapprehension of summary judgment standards in light of our precedents</u>**. Cf. *Brosseau*, 543 U. S., at 197–198" (which was provided to the court under Tab 39, Page 10, Second Paragraph).

The Supreme Court vacated the decision from the Fifth Circuit, "so that the court can determine whether, when Tolan's evidence is properly credited and factual inferences are reasonably drawn in his favor, ..."

JUSTICE ALITO & JUSTICE SCALIA joined and concurred in the judgment, stating: "...the granting of review in this case sets a precedent that, **<u>if followed in other cases</u>**, will very substantially alter the Court's practice."

(Before the publishing of this book, I saw where the Defendant "Cotton" settled the case with "Tolan" since it was remained back to the trial court where a jury could hear the case.)

For the reasons stated in the *Tolan* case, I made a timely request for judicial notice. I was entitled to a hearing on the propriety of taking judicial notice and the tenor of the matter noticed. Tex. R. Evid. 202. Thus, I asked the court to hold a hearing, to consider the motion concerning the judicial notices given in the trial court, where "[t]he evidence of the nonmovant <u>is</u>

to be believed, and all justifiable inferences <u>are</u> to be drawn in his favor." *Anderson* v. *Liberty Lobby, Inc.*, 477 U. S. 242, 255 (1986), otherwise I would be irreparably harmed, their denying my entitlement to remedy.

But, since Federal Judges do NOT read pleadings from *pro ses*, I must be able to verbally direct the court, to my judicial notice in open court—but I was denied the opportunity.

On this same day, of January 12th, 2015, I had filed my, "Plaintiff's Motion For Default Judgment," and paid for service of process on Defendant, with the Montgomery County Clerk of Court. The Court Clerk served Defendant Federal National Mortgage Association (Fannie Mae), on or about September 18, 2014. Texas Rules of Civil Procedure (TRCP) Rule 99 informs the Defendant, service of Plaintiff's Original Petition was due to be answered, "on or before 10:00 a.m. on the Monday next after the expiration of twenty days after the date of service thereof." That being 10:00 a.m., on October 13th, 2014.

Defendant Fannie Mae moved the Texas case, no. 14-08-08592, to federal court, on or about October 6th, 2014—over my objection and without answering Plaintiff's Original Petition. Federal Rules of Civil Procedure (FRCP) Rule 12(a)(1)(A)(i) mandates Defendant, Fannie Mae, serve an answer on Plaintiff, within 21 days of service of complaint. That being October 9th, 2014.

FRCP Rule 36(a)(3) states: "A matter is admitted unless, within 30 days after being served, the party to whom the request is directed serves on the requesting party a written answer or objection addressed to the matter and signed by the party or its attorney." I had made claims in my Plaintiff's Original Petition that Defendant Fannie Mae has failed to answer, for over ninety (90) days, of which Defendant had admitted by default.

I claimed the right to a default judgment, under FRCP Rule 55(b)(2). The so-called Honorable Court should NOT rip the victory from my hands, merely because I am labeled as a *pro se*. I did NOT ask for the court to be burdened to hear this matter. The too-big-to-fail Fannie Mae will survive having one substitute trustee's deed ordered void, set aside and made of no effect. But, since Federal Judges don't read *pro se*'s pleadings, pissing into the wind comes to mind.

By coincidence, the attorney of record files a letter, to Judge Smith, dated January 12th, 2015.

> *Dear Judge Smith:*
> *My firm represents Defendant Federal National Mortgage Association ("Fannie Mae") in the above-referenced case. On October 9, 2014, **Fannie Mae filed a motion to dismiss** all of Plaintiffs claims. **Plaintiff contends that he did not receive a copy of Fannie Mae's motion. The parties have conferred** and today counsel for Fannie Mae **emailed a copy** of Defendant's motion to dismiss **to Bobie Kenneth Townsend, pro se** Plaintiff. **Accordingly,** Defendant **asks** that the Court set Fannie Mae's motion to dismiss for consideration 21 days from today on February 2, 2015 **to give Plaintiff an opportunity** to respond and allow Fannie Mae to file any reply in support of its motion.*
> *Very truly yours,*
> *Tamara D. Stiner Toomer*

What do you know? The attorney of record has to admit they forgot to serve me, with their Motion to Dismiss they had filed, on October 9th, 2014; but that's OK. Rules are meant to be just a guideline, Right? The attorney of record tells Judge Smith, by mail, we "conferred" and we worked everything out. (Like, I had a choice.) They emailed me a copy of their Motion To Dismiss, and we had agreed to allow little old me the consideration, of getting 21 more days to respond to their Motion to Dismiss— because they are gracious enough to give me more time.

I didn't know I could just write letters to the judge, in the middle of a case. I was told that was BAD behavior called *EX Parte* communications—and was NOT allowed. Where is my opportunity to object I was NOT properly served, and their Motion to Dismiss should be stricken from the record?

On January 13th, 2015, United States District Judge David Hittner denied my Motion for Default Judgment, filed the day before. All Judge Hittner needed to see was a letter, from the attorney of record to Judge Smith. No formal response was required. No hearing was needed. No due process was needed. Just nip it in the bud, before the attorney has to justify why I was NOT served, with the defendant's Motion to Dismiss.

Magistrate Smith sent an undated, "Order For Conference And Disclosure of Interested Parties," which scheduled a hearing, on January 22, 2015 at 02:00 PM, Courtroom 703, 7th Floor, 515 Rusk Avenue, Houston. Texas. But, because of the mess-up concerning the Motion To Dismiss, the hearing was rescheduled, to January 29th, 2015.

NOTICE OF SETTING
TAKE NOTICE THAT A PROCEEDING IN THIS CASE HAS BEEN SET FOR
THE PLACE, DATE AND TIME SET FORTH BELOW.
Before the Honorable   Stephen Smith
PLACE: **Courtroom 703**
United States District Court
515 Rusk Avenue
Houston, Texas 77002
DATE: **1/29/2015**
TIME: **10:00 AM**
TYPE OF PROCEEDING: **Initial Conference**
Date: January 12, 2015
David J. Bradley, Clerk

We had our hearing, on January 29ᵗʰ, 2015, where I never got the opportunity to object to anything. Judge Smith sets me straight. He is just a Magistrate; and a District Court Judge would have to hear my concerns. We were there, only to create a Scheduling Order.

RULE 16 SCHEDULING ORDER

*The following schedule **shall be followed**. All communications concerning the case **shall be directed in writing to** Ellen Alexander, Case Manager for United States District Judge David Hittner, P.O. Box 61010, Houston, TX 77208.*

1.   May 1, 2015

*NEW PARTIES shall be joined, **with leave of court**, by this date. The attorney causing such joinder shall provide copies of this ORDER to the new parties.*

2A.   July 1, 2015

*PLAINTIFF **shall designate** EXPERT WITNESSES. Designation shall be in writing to opponent. Expert reports shall be served within 60 days of the designation.*

B.   August 3, 2015

*DEFENDANT **shall designate** EXPERT WITNESSES. Designation shall be in writing to opponent. Expert reports shall be served within 60 days of the designation.*

3. July 1, 2015

*AMENDMENTS to pleadings, **with leave of court**, shall be made by this date.*

4. November 2, 2015

*DISCOVERY **shall be completed** by this date.*

5. December 1, 2015

*MOTION CUT-OFF. **No motion**, including motions to exclude or limit expert testimony under Fed. R. Evid. 702, **shall be filed after this date except for good cause shown**. See LR 7.*

6. February 26, 2016

*The JOINT PRETRIAL ORDER **shall be filed** on or before this date notwithstanding that a motion for continuance may be pending. Parties **shall exchange all** trial exhibits on or before this date notwithstanding that a motion for continuance may be pending. **NO LATE EXCHANGES OF EXHIBITS WILL BE PERMITTED. All** motions in limine **shall** be submitted with the pretrial order. **Failure to file** *timely a joint pretrial order, motions in limine, or exchange all trial exhibits **may result in this case being dismissed** or other sanctions imposed, in accordance with all applicable rules.*

7. March/April 2016

*TRIAL TERM. Cases will be set for trial at a docket call, conducted prior to the trial term or **by order of the Court**. Your position on the docket will be announced at that time.*

Jury/Non-Jury ETT: 2 days

***All documents filed must** be 14 point font, double spaced with not less than one inch margins.*

SIGNED on January 29, 2015.

Stephen Wm Smith

United States Magistrate Judge

The hearing is really just smoke and mirrors, to make a *pro se* or Plaintiff with an attorney believe due process could be had in a Federal Court. Nothing is further from the truth. Just look at the scheduling Order above. You see bias and restrictions that serve no purpose, other than to deny due process and hinder justice being done.

First, why is there a deadline to add parties, if it takes leave of the court to add new parties? Why is it only attorneys can join new parties? I had more than one attorney, and more than one employee of the court system, tell me you canNOT take the language, found in Judges' Orders, literally. Really? **IT SHOCKS THE CONSCIENCE!!!!**

Second, for what purpose do you allow one party a month longer, to designate an expert witness? Now, I understand the Plaintiff should have his/her ducks in a row, before filing suit, but discovery could change things a lot. Why does this Judge give the defendant a month longer, after the Plaintiff has to show his cards he/her plans to play? The Level Playing Field is tilted.

Third, I have a big problem with leave of the court, to amend pleadings. First, the Judge is never specific as to what is wrong with the original pleading he will allow you to amend. So you may amend the wrong part of the pleading. Everyone should know what happens in the public fool system. The teacher gives you back your paper with red marks all over it. The teacher had crossed out paragraphs and put a mark through an entire sentence the teachers did NOT like. The teacher then hands the paper back to you and tells you to do it over (amend) again. There is little to wonder what the teacher thinks is wrong with the paper. What would be so hard with that? Instead, the other party's attorney lies, and says evil things about your pleadings— Like, "the plaintiff's allegation is merely a conclusion and NOT a factual allegation." The judge says, "That's right, I'm going to allow you leave to amend your pleadings." I call up many attorneys and ask for an example, of a 'factual allegation compared to an allegation that is merely a conclusion,' and none of the attorneys have a clue. There is no example to be given by any attorney, but apparently my pleading has an example, in there somewhere. Due process means giving you an opportunity to correct something that canNOT be explained how to correct, but you do have the opportunity to do the impossible. Do you remember the opinion of the Fifth Circuit, in the previous Case No. 11-20319, *Bobie Townsend v. BAC Home Loans Servicing, L.P.* USDC No. 4:10-CV-3751?

Memorandum Opinion- Fifth Circuit, in the previous Case No. 11-20319
*"**Townsend failed to adequately brief** his contention **that the district court erred** by dismissing the claims in his original petition and **failed to explain** how the cases he cites entitle him to any relief on appeal. **The district court was not required to explain its reasons for dismissal**. See FED.R. CN. P. 52(a)(3)."*

IT SHOCKS THE CONSCIENCE!!!!

Fourth, in December there is a Motion Cut-Off Date, where no more motions are allowed to be filed, without good cause; then in February you are allowed to put in a motion *in limine*. A motion *in limine* is another BS rule. This is where each side gets to ask the court to restrict the other party from bringing things up, at trial. What is with that rule? I thought it was the purpose of making an objection. But, no, there is no reason to object to things forbidden, by the judge, to bring up. There is no level playing field. The fix is in. Due process, my ass.

Fifth, then there is a warning the case will be dismissed, if we fail to file a timely joint pretrial order. Since the attorneys want the case dismissed, why file a joint pretrial order, or exchange all trial exhibits?

Scheduling Order for February 26, 2016
__All motions__ in limine shall be submitted with the pretrial order.
__Failure to file timely__ a joint pretrial order, motions in limine, or exchange all trial exhibits may result in this case being dismissed or other sanctions imposed, in accordance with all applicable rules.

It Shocks the Conscience this Scheduling Order makes any sense to attorneys and judges.

The attorney of record and I are throwing paper at each other; and then, in April:

Notice of Reassignment
Pursuant to Special Order No. 2015-2, __this case is reassigned__ to the docket of United States District Judge __Alfred H. Bennett__. Deadlines in scheduling orders remain in effect. __All court settings are vacated.__
Date: April 24, 2015
David J. Bradley, Clerk

There ought to be a law against changing judges, in the middle of the stream. I have come to believe they do it on purpose, to give judges "justifiable deniability" of the violation of due process against parties of a case. Remember, Judge Hittner denied my Motion For Default Judgment and was replaced with Judge Bennett. Even if Judge Bennett does NOT agree with what Judge Hittner did before, the old attorney's oath, to his fellow attorney, does NOT allow him to strike any Orders previously done. I have no terminology for such loyalty, but Justice is NOT it.

Right after a new judge is in town, a new attorney—NOT the attorney of record—appears from nowhere. Attorney Randall B. Clark, State Bar No. 04294900, Federal Bar No. 3399, 600 Travis Street, Suite 7500 Houston, Texas 77002, files his, "Defendant Federal National Mortgage Association's Motion To Stay Pretrial Deadlines and Discovery" (Clark's Motion) on April 27th, 2015. Mr. Clark gives himself the title, of "Attorney-In-Charge For Defendant." I looked in the Federal Rules, for attorney in charge, but didn't find anything. I did find Rule 11:

> *Federal Rules of Civil Procedure*
> *Rule 11. Signing Pleadings, Motions, and Other Papers; Representations to the Court; Sanctions*
> *(a) SIGNATURE. Every pleading, written motion, and other paper must be signed by at least one __attorney of record__ in the attorney's name—or by a party personally if the party is unrepresented. The paper must state the signer's address, e-mail address, and telephone number. Unless a rule or statute specifically states otherwise, a pleading need not be verified or accompanied by an affidavit. The court must strike an unsigned paper unless the omission is promptly corrected after being called to the attorney's or party's attention.*

Mr. Clark doesn't want to burden his client, Fannie Mae, with Discovery, since we all know the judge is going to dismiss the action, anyway. As you might recall, in a previous action, Fannie

Mae stated it had no documents in its possession that concerned my discovery request—and Mr. Clark knows this.

Attorney in Charge-Clark's Motion
*Prior to filing this Motion for Stay, Defendant proposed Plaintiff **stipulate to a voluntary stay on discovery** pending a ruling on the Motion to Dismiss. **Plaintiff did not agree to so stipulate**. Thus, Defendant **now moves the Court** for an order staying discovery pending a ruling on Defendant's Motion to Dismiss Plaintiffs Complaint.*

I think we went over, basketball rules used in a baseball game does NOT work out, for everyone. Like using cheat-codes in a video game, where you place the power of God on your Player's Piece, and you claim you beat the game because of your great skill. Mr. Clark is claiming the "Power of Previous Judge Decision;" and Mr. Clark lays his Player's Piece on the board, and claims the "Shield of the Previous Judge" will hypnotize the "Current Judge," where he will have no other choice than to deny Plaintiff his requested discovery—since he is forced, by the magical term, "**the same core of operative fact**," to dismiss the case.

Clark's Motion
*The Court can and should stay all discovery in this matter. "A trial court **has broad discretion and inherent power** to stay discovery until preliminary questions that may dispose of the case are determined." Petrus v. Bowen, 833 F.2d 581, 583 (5th Cir. 1987) citing Landis v. North Am. Co., 299 U.S. 248, 254 (1936): Scroggins v. Air Cargo, Inc., 534 F.2d 1124, 1133 (5'h Cir.1976). Such "**preliminary questions**" include objections raised in a defendant's motion to dismiss under Fed. R. Civ. P. 12(b)(6). Petrus, supra, at 583. **The clearest case** for grant of a discovery stay is where a ruling on **a particular legal issue** before the court may dispose of the entire action, **thus mooting the need for all discovery**. See Harlow v. Fitzgerald, 457 U.S. 800, 818 (982). Here, Defendant moved to dismiss the entire Complaint, **chiefly alleging** that the action is barred outright and in full by res judicata. (See generally, Dkt. No.3).*

As in *Petrus*. **_nothing which Plaintiff may learn through discovery_** could affect Defendant's Motion to Dismiss, as it is based primarily upon **_a preliminary question of law_**; whether **_the current and previous actions_** are **_based on the same core of operative fact_**, **_involve the same parties_**, and whether the previous actions were decided on the merits in Defendant's favor. As the ruling on Defendant's Motion to Dismiss **_could resolve the entire action_** now at issue, the Court should therefore stay discovery in anticipation of such ruling.

I responded, with my own magical incognitions.

> *Texas Constitution, Article 1*
> *Sec. 15. RIGHT OF TRIAL BY JURY. The right of trial by jury **shall remain inviolate**.*
>
> *Sec. 29. PROVISIONS OF BILL OF RIGHTS EXCEPTED FROM POWERS OF GOVERNMENT; TO FOREVER REMAIN INVIOLATE. To guard against transgressions of the high powers herein delegated, we declare that **everything in this "Bill of Rights" is excepted out of the general powers of government**, and shall forever remain inviolate, and all laws contrary thereto, or to the following provisions, shall be void.*
>
> *Black's Law Dictionary Ninth Edition*
> *"**inviolate**" , ad;. (15c) **Free from violation; not broken, infringed, or impaired**.*
>
> *A judgment rendered **in violation of due process is void** in the rendering State and is not entitled to full faith and credit elsewhere. Pennoyer v. Neff, 95 U.S. 714, 732-733 (1878)."*
> *World-Wide Volkwagen Corp. v. Woodson, 444 U.S. 286 (1980)*
> *A judgment **may not be rendered in violation of constitutional protections**. The validity of a judgment may be affected by a failure to give the constitutionally required due process notice and an opportunity to be heard. Earle v. McVeigh, 91 US 503, 23 L Ed 398. See also Restatements, Judgments ' 4(b). Prather v Loyd, 86 Idaho 45, 382 P2d 910.*

*"The plaintiff may recover (1) by proving a regular chain of conveyances from the sovereign, (2) **by proving a superior title out of a common source**, (3) by proving title by limitations, or (4) by proving prior possession, and that the possession has not been abandoned. Turner, 377 S.W.2d at 183."*

*"... Rogers, as plaintiff, **need only demonstrate good title coming from that common source to meet its burden of proof**."*
See United States v. Denby, 522 F.2d 1358, 1362 (5th Cir.1975).
Rogers v. Ricane Enters., Inc., 884 S.W.2d 763, 768 (Tex. 1994)

*A trustee-removal action can also be analogized to a real-property action **to remove a cloud on title**. We have held that **as long as an injury clouding the title remains, so too does an equitable action to remove the cloud; therefore, a suit to remove the cloud is not time-barred**. (See Tex. Co. v. Davis, 113 Tex. 321, 254 S.W. 304, 309 (1923).)*
Ditta v. Conte, 298 SW 3d 187 - Tex: Supreme Court 2009

I then filed my Motion to Compel Discovery.

Rabbit Trail: While these pleadings are being considered by the new judge, and during one of those floods in the Conroe, Texas area, the system makes good on its threat—by finally kicking us out of the Black Toxic Mold Dream House, while we were at the store. We drive by the house, and some of the stuff that remained in the house was piled in the front yard area, as sheets of rain covered the items as we watched. We noticed many items were missing. We can only expect the Montgomery County Constable took what he wanted, and then left the rest for the people he contracted, to move our items outside. We expected as much. But, we knew about the thievery that takes place, when they think they are protected by a judge's Order; so we moved our most important possessions into storage, previously. The trespassing intruders had the advantage of armed thugs for security and enjoyed the air-conditioning (which they turned down so cold that allowed dew to collect on the outside of all of the windows) and turned on all the lights of our still working and paid for electricity as they threw our possessions outside in the rain.

(off the Rabbit Trail)

On or about the 24th of June, 2015, I filed my, "Plaintiff's Motion For Leave To Amend Complaint," to address the theft, of the Black Toxic Mold Dream House.

On or about the 25th of June, 2015, I filed my "Plaintiff's Notice Of Change Of Contact Information," since I was no longer domiciled in the Black Toxic Mold Dream House.

On or about the 17th of August, 2015, Judge Bennett was gracious to allow me thirty days, to amend my Complaint.

On or about the 9th of September, 2015, I filed my, "Plaintiff's First Amended Complaint." As a review, my original petition focused upon a temporary restraining order, against Fannie Mae. If the State judge would have signed my TRO it would have delayed attorneys from filing a forcible detainer and trying to get me out of the house—until this case was resolved. My only cause of action was, "wrongful foreclosure." There was no request for money damages. I wanted the State Court to determine procedurally the foreclosure was NOT done by law, and declare the previous actions were null and void. The proper party would then have to start over, if the proper party could be found. My amended Complaint was somewhat different.

In the amended complaint, my first cause of action was, "wrongful non-judicial foreclosure." I pointed to such irregularities, of the foreclosure procedure of the BDFTE law firm and in the behavior of the so-called Lender. A wrongful foreclosure claim shifts the burden of proof, to the party that claims a valid foreclosure occurred.

Legal acumen /liygal akyliwman/. The doctrine of legal acumen is that if a defect in, or invalidity of, a claim to land is such as to require legal acumen to discover it -1, whether it appears upon the face of the record or proceedings, or is to be proved aliunde -2, then the powers or jurisdiction of a court of equity may be invoked to remove the cloud created by such defect or invalidity -3.

My second cause of action was, "unjust enrichment of Fannie Mae." On or about July 1st, 2004, I gave a Lender a Note and took possession of the subject property. Fannie Mae claimed to be the current Lender associated with the original Note and subject property, on or about April 3, 2012. Fannie Mae forcibly took possession of my property; and I provided proof to the Court Fannie Mae claims possession of the subject property, as well as claiming to possess the original Note & the original Deed of Trust. I claimed Fannie Mae is unjustly enriched, by possessing the subject property and the Note, and the Note payments associated with the subject property—at the same time.

All I asked the judge to do was declare the non-judicial foreclosure invalid; or in the alternative, Order Fannie Mae to produce the Note, so it can be removed from commerce—or pay Townsend the value of the Note, being $99,900.00.

Fannie Mae had fourteen days to respond to my Amended Complaint, which gave counsel until September 23rd, 2015, to answer.

On or about the 23rd of September, 2015, the same attorney, Randall B. Clark, with State Bar No. 04294900 & Federal Bar No. 3399, filed an Answer to my Amended Complaint. The majority of responses to my Amended Complaint stated: "The allegations contained in Paragraph …. do NOT constitute factual allegations, but instead constitute legal conclusions to which no response is required." This is a typical "legalese" non-response. Kind of like saying, "Judge, Let's just ignore the statement by the Plaintiff, rather than admitting or denying what is said in the paragraph." But, there are court opinions that have concluded if you fail to deny a statement in a Petition or Complaint, then the paragraph will be considered admitted. Since Mr. Clark makes the same statement concerning many paragraphs found in my Amended Complaint; Judge Bennett should have concluded Fannie Mae has admitted to every allegation in my Amended Complaint. But, apparently, Judge Bennett understands the incognition stated by a fellow warlock, to mean, 'Ignore what the *pro se* says, as it will only confuse your obligation to your fellow warlock to dismiss the case—which is the sole purpose of moving the State case to Federal Court in the first place.'

Examples Found:

> ***Townsend's Amended Complaint:*** *"On or about June 11, 2015* ***Townsend and his family and their possessions were forcibly removed from the subject property by the direction of attorneys representing Fannie Mae.***"

> ***Mr. Clark's Response:*** *"Answering Defendant* ***has insufficient information*** *to admit or deny the allegations of Paragraph 13."*

This response, by Mr. Clerk, contends beyond ninety (90) days after the fact; Fannie Mae has no records (contract), giving its delegation of authority to any attorney—to have Townsend and his family forcibly removed from their home.

> ***Townsend's Amended Complaint:*** *"Townsend* ***is guaranteed*** *a Trial By Jury under Article 1, Section 15 of the Texas Constitution.*

> ***Mr. Clark's Response:*** *"The allegations contained in Paragraph 20* ***do not constitute factual allegations, but instead constitute legal conclusions*** *to which no response is required."*

This response, by Mr. Clerk, contends my Right to a Trial By Jury found under Article 1, Section 15 of the Texas Constitution, does NOT constitute a factual allegation. The apparent logic of Judge Bennett's opinion is if an attorney says it, it must be so.

> **Townsend's Amended Complaint:** *"Violating Townsend's right to a trial by jury **is a violation of due process**."*

> **Mr. Clark's Response:** *"The allegations contained in Paragraph 23 **do not constitute factual allegations, but instead constitute legal conclusions** to which no response is required."*

This response, by Mr. Clark, contends my so-called legal conclusion is correct, in that denying my right to trial by jury is a violation of my right to due process; but alas, I failed to say a magical term that would covert the legal conclusion into a factual allegation. Are you getting the picture? Attorneys should NOT hold office where laws are created.

Mr. Clark states, "no response is required," thirty-four different times, in his answer to my Amended Complaint. Mr. Clark admitted to sixteen different things, in my Amended Complaint. Mr. Clark denied Fifty-Three different things, in my Amended Complaint. But then, Mr. Clark claims he could NOT admit or deny, to Thirty-Three different things in my Amended Complaint.

Mr. Clark's cut and paste pleading does not mention the terms, "wrongful foreclosure," or "unjust enrichment." But, the day before (**NOT AFTER**) Mr. Clark filed his response, to my Amended Complaint, on the 22nd of September, 2015, "without" having an open hearing or allowing time, for the Defendant to answer my Amended Complaint with an additional cause of action; Judge Bennett dismissed my case, With Prejudice, based upon the defendant's first motion to dismiss that did not deny the unjust enrichment claim. The Great and Powerful OZ has spoken. **IT SHOCKS THE CONSCIENCE!!!!**

ORDER

Before the Court is Defendant Federal National Mortgage Association's ("Fannie Mae") Motion to Dismiss (Doc. #3), Plaintiff Bobbie Kenneth Townsend's Response and Objection to Defendant's Motion to Dismiss (Doc. # 14), and Plaintiff s First Amended Complaint (Doc. #31). After considering the arguments and evidence presented, __the Court GRANTS the Motion to Dismiss__.

This is Plaintiffs third attempt to challenge the foreclosure of his property at 1504 Memorial Lane in Conroe, Texas. See Townsend v. BAC Home Loans Servicing, LP, 783 F. Supp. 2d 968,969 (2011) aff'd, 461 F. App'x 367 (5th Cir. 2011) ("__Townsend 1__"); Townsend v. Bank of Am., NA., No. CIV.A. H-12-3568, 2013 WL 5755245, at *1 (S.D. Tex. Oct. 23,2013) aff'd, 572 F. App'x 266 (5th Cir. 2014) ("Townsend 11").1 __This action has no more merit than Plaintiff's last two filings__, and the Court finds it to be barred by res judicata. See __Townsend II__, 572 F. App'x 266, 267 ("we have __patiently reviewed__ the record on appeal .... [T]here is no merit in any of Townsend's contentions.").

A claim is barred by res judicata when: (1) the parties in the prior and present suit are identical; (2) a court of competent jurisdiction rendered the prior judgment; (3) the prior judgment was final __and on the merits__; and (4) __the plaintiff raises the same cause of action in both suits__. Maxwell v. Us. Bank Nat. Ass 'n, 544 F. App'x 470, 472 (5th Cir. 2013) (citation omitted). To determine whether two cases involve the same cause of action, __a court must engage in an analysis under the transactional test.__ Id. The transactional test extends the prior judgment's preclusive effect to all potential claims of the plaintiff concerning any part of the transaction, or series of connected transactions, out of which the original action arose. Id. __A subsequent claim is thus barred if it arises out of the "same nucleus of operative facts."__ Id. Res judicata extends beyond claims that were actually raised and bars all claims that could have been advanced in support of the cause of action on the occasion of its former adjudication. Id.

Here, Plaintiffs __claims for wrongful foreclosure and unjust enrichment__ against Fannie Mae are barred by res judicata based on

Townsend II First, the parties in both suits are identical. Fannie Mae was a named defendant in Townsend II and is the only defendant here. Second, the judgment in **Townsend II** was rendered by a court of competent jurisdiction, **namely this Court**. Third, the judgment in **Townsend II** was final and **on the merits** because it **was a dismissal with prejudice**. See Oreck Direct, LLC v. Dyson, Inc., 560 F.3d 398, 401 (5th Cir. 2009) ("A dismissal which is designated **with prejudice is normally an adjudication on the merits** for purposes of res judicata.") (citation and internal quotation marks omitted).

    Finally, **the claims arise out of the same nucleus of operative facts and could have been litigated in the prior action**. **Although** the cause of action in **Townsend II** was to quiet title and the causes of action here are for wrongful foreclosure and unjust enrichment, (Doc. #31 at 20, 25), **both claims arise out of the same operative facts**-the foreclosure of Plaintiffs property and its sale to Fannie Mae on April 3, 2012. See Maxwell at 472-73 (applying res judicata to bar claims related to foreclosure **where prior suit had already adjudicated party's standing to foreclose**). **Plaintiff could have** advanced his wrongful foreclosure and unjust enrichment claims **in the prior adjudication, but he did not**. Accordingly, Plaintiffs claims are barred by res judicata.

    For the reasons explained above, Defendant Fannie Mae's Motion to Dismiss is GRANTED. Plaintiff's claims are dismissed WITH PREJUDICE.

THE HONORABLE *ALFRED H. BENNETT*
UNITED STATES DISTRICT JUDGE

Don't you think, it is a slap in the face of justice, when the judges sign their signature over, "THE HONORABLE"? Understand, there is nothing in the Rules of Procedure that would inform you of anything concerning the fable that Judge Bennett is spinning in his so-called Order, shown above. You would have to obtain this garbage that Judge Bennett is selling, by osmosis, if you were not reading this book. But, this is the bait and switch game played to protect the system. Here, Judge Bennett jumps the gun, before Mr. Clark has time to respond to the new cause of action; but what's another cause of action, when the decision was already pre-determined?

Do you see how things have morphed into BAD case law, by the 5th Circuit? Before, the term "res judicata" only applied to the same parties and the same causes of action. Now, you have to be clairvoyant and know ALL the causes of action that could ever possibility apply to an incident where elements may or may not change in the future. Piece of cake.

Everything the judge's briefing attorney wrote, for Judge Bennett to sign, is BS. The Order does NOT follow summary judgment rules, found in the Federal Rules of Civil Procedure. Hopefully you have already deducted this—by reading the previous Orders, by the previous U.S. District Judges and the Appellate Judges, concerning this same matter. They, which control the outcome in a court case, canNOT go wrong, by parroting the defense attorney's pleadings, as nothing has to be proven. Merely making a statement, makes it so. "The Plaintiff has no evidence." The Plaintiff's claim is without merit." If we all had the ability to join a club, where you could be privileged to know the answer to a question, before the question is asked; just think how everything would be streamlined and efficient, like a well-oiled machine. Squeak, Squeak.

If logic had anything to do with justice, the judges should be intelligent enough to realize there could NOT be a claim, of "unjust enrichment;" until the property was physically taken from a Borrower, and keeping the Note (The Negotiable Instrument), as well. The taking of the subject property did NOT occur, until after the *Townsend II* case had finalized, but still, Judge Bennett parrots the attorney's pleading pointing to the *Townsend II* case—to justify their (The Judge's and the Attorney's) scam. See the above Order, where it states: "Plaintiff <u>could have</u> advanced his wrongful foreclosure and unjust enrichment claims in the prior adjudication, **but he did not**." This statement is obviously a lie, but the so-called Judge canNOT be unelected, as he is appointed by the President of the United States, and is unlikely to be removed because of his BAD behavior, lack of critical thinking—or how he treats *pro ses*, in his court.

This, by itself, is a good reason to believe Judge Bennett should be recalled from office, as he has shown to lack logic or critical thinking, when deciding at least one case before him. Lacking the ability to use critical thinking hinders the ability to reason, which causes BAD behavior, which causes BAD case law, in our country. This opinion, by Judge Bennett, will be in the law books—for centuries. People that read the opinion will have reason to believe the opinion given, by Judge Bennett, was correct, at the time it was given—but it is NOT, and could NOT be. From my experience, that which I am sharing with you, in these pages, has led me to question every judge's opinion I have ever read before, and will ever read in the future. Since the judges I have experienced use little, if any, logic or critical thinking in deciding what to write in their opinions, this by itself should make the reader question their previous faith and confidence, in the judiciary, to be unbiased in their decisions.

On or about the 22nd of October, 2015, I filed my Motion For A New Trial pointing out the errors of the trial court.

Rabbit Trail: I may have failed to mention a magical term appellate judges have to hear, in your appellant brief. The magical term, "The Trial Court Erred...." It will do you no good to just say the judge did NOT follow the rules of procedure, or the judge denied you discovery, or the judge told you he had the right to lie to you—because you had the right to appeal. Oh No, you have to say the magical term, "Erred," or your bitchin' will get you nowhere. But at least, the appellate judges will NOT be able to use that excuse, to get rid of your case.
(Jumping off that rabbit trail.)

I will try and just summarize what is found, in my Motion For a New Trial pleading, to Judge Bennett.

The Court Erred By Granting Defendant's Motion To Dismiss: The Order above granting Fannie Mae's Motion To Dismiss is fatally defective, as it is neither verified nor does it address my cause of action, of "unjust enrichment," I claimed in my, "Plaintiff's First Amended Complaint."

Fannie Mae's Motion To Dismiss does NOT contain an affidavit, by any employee of Fannie Mae, that could be used to support ANY allegation, by the alleged counsel of Fannie Mae. Pleadings of counsel, in their briefs or their arguments, are NOT sufficient for a motion to dismiss, or for summary judgment. See *Trinsey v. Pagliaro*, D.C. Pa. 1964, 229 F. Supp. 647. The Order granting the Defendant's Motion To Dismiss fails to indicate what magical term I failed to state in my pleadings, in a timely manner. **It Shocks The Conscience** it matters NOT to the court; there is no record of assignment, to Fannie Mae, concerning the subject property; and such claim I swore to is without merit, in the eyes of the presiding judge.

The Court Erred By Denying Townsend His Vested Right To A Trial By Jury: The presiding Judge is NOT the designated fact-finder, concerning case number 4:14-cv-02835. Article 1, Section 15, of the Texas Constitution, guarantees Townsend his vested right, to a trial by jury.

Texas Constitution
Article 1
Sec. 15. RIGHT OF TRIAL BY JURY. The right of trial by jury shall remain inviolate.

Article 1, Section 29 of the Texas Constitution forbids any rule making that would abridge Townsend's vested right to a trial by jury.

Texas Constitution
Article 1
*Sec. 29. PROVISIONS OF BILL OF RIGHTS EXCEPTED FROM POWERS OF GOVERNMENT; TO FOREVER REMAIN INVIOLATE. To guard against transgressions of the high powers herein delegated, we declare that **everything** in this "Bill of Rights" **is excepted out** of the general powers of government, and **shall forever** remain inviolate, and **all laws** contrary thereto, or to the following provisions, **shall be void**.*

I paid a fee, to secure my vested right to a trial by jury, even though such fee is unconstitutional, under Article 1, Section 29 of the Texas Constitution. In my Original Petition and in Plaintiff's First Amended Complaint, I gave notice of my demand, for a trial by jury. The Order (See Dkt #33) dismissing this case With Prejudice fails to address the authority, to deny me of my vested right to a trial by jury, after the court accepted the contract to adjudicate my causes of action, where the record shows I paid such required filing fee. **It Shocks The Conscience** a judge has found I am without remedy; to exercise my vested right—under Article 1, Section 15, to have a jury determine the facts of the case—I had paid for and am guaranteed to exercise— under Article 1, Section 29 of the Texas Constitution.

If the presiding judge did read Plaintiff's First Amended Complaint (See Dkt #31), the Order (See Dkt #33) dismissing this case should NOT have been signed. The presiding Judge's Order failed to address the court's personal jurisdiction over me, by the moving of my Texas case, to the United States District Court. I questioned the personal jurisdiction over me, since I am a natural born native of Texas; and it is NOT my belief or known to me of any privileged protection, by the Fourteenth Amendment of the Constitution for the United States of America.

I did NOT consent to moving my State case, to a Federal Court, as I lost the benefit of Texas Rules of Court—Like Rule 12, where I am allowed to challenge the authority of Fannie Mae's alleged counsel, of which I did challenge—but I lack any benefit, under Federal Rules, to have the challenge heard.

Evidence shows Federal Judges ignore the mandates, of the Texas Supreme Court, as in, *Ditta v. Conte* and *Rogers v. Ricane Enters., Inc.*—as well their own superior Supreme Court—mandates, as in *TOLAN v. COTTON* (*Tolan* Case), No. 13–551, Cite as: 572 U. S. ____ (2014), decided May 5, 2014 (See Dkt #5), of which I gave judicial notice to the court; and such notice was apparently ignored. *TOLAN v. COTTON* mandates summary judgment is NOT allowed, as long as one issue of fact is to be decided, by a jury. Such mandate was ignored, in *Townsend I*, *Townsend II*; and in this case before the court. *See Townsend* v. *BAC Home Loans Servicing, LP*, 783 F. Supp. 2d 968,969 (2011) *aff'd*, 461 F. App'x 367 (5th Cir. 2011) *("Townsend I"); Townsend* v. *Bank of Am., NA.*, No. CIV.A. H-12-3568, 2013 WL 5755245, at *1 (S.D. Tex. Oct. 23, 2013) *aff'd*, 572 F. App'x 266 (5th Cir. 2014) *("Townsend II").*

There is no assignment of the Note and Deed of Trust, to Fannie Mae, which is a substantive fact that supports my causes of action, which should be before the fact-finder— which is NOT the presiding judge.

It is my belief, and I have shown you just some of the evidence, all judges are prejudicial, against *pro ses*. The judges are charged, to follow the mandates—of their superior courts—and follow the rules that allow substantive justice to appear fair. The judicial opinions found, in *Townsend I* and *Townsend II*, contains lies, untruths and half truths. Pointing out such errors, to the court, and asking for reconsideration; Townsend received no explanation of such errors, but simply received the standard reply, "Motion Denied." If court rules can be ignored, for the benefit of attorneys; but held to strict standards, against *pro ses*, then there is no level playing field. Faith and confidence in the judiciary canNOT be maintained, under these circumstances. You canNOT use Basketball rules in a Baseball game.

Haines v. Kerner, 404 U.S. 519 (1972), another superior mandate, by the Supreme Court of the United States of America, **is** ignored by inferior courts concerning their obligation, of informing *pro ses*, of the defects in their pleadings, so they may be allowed to make such corrections. I now look at court opinions, in a totally different light; and I have no faith or confidence in the judiciary, to see justice is done—or opinions of courts reflect the evidence found in any other case.

The Federal Judge saw the light, and GRANTED me a New Trial.

OOPS, sorry, fell into an alternate universe, for a second. Nope, Motion For A New Trial is DENIED. Would you appeal the trial judge's decision, to the 5th Circuit? I decided NOT to waste the money. Mainly because, the trial judge's decision did NOT really change anything I was planning to do—in the future, anyway.

Right or Wrong, that's what I did. But, that is NOT the end of the story. Part 2 is being developed, as this goes to print.

Here is another one of my sayings: "It's Over When I Say It's Over." I will NOT say I originated that saying, but I will say I live by the saying; and nothing, yet, as of the publishing of this book, has convinced me to do otherwise. I strongly encourage you to believe likewise.

"Ours is a sick profession. [A profession marked by] incompetence, lack of training, misconduct, and bad manners. Ineptness, bungling, malpractice, and bad ethics can be observed in court houses all over this country every day."
— *JUSTICE WARREN BURGER*

CHAPTER 37
BOOK RECAP

How do I expect the reader will benefit, from getting through this book?

You have the ability to manage your fear. The only thing stopping you from managing your fear, is you—and nothing else.

Don't sweat the little stuff. Everything is little stuff. Major stuff is just little stuff that hasn't been broken down into its basic little-stuff parts to deal with.

Everyone you see in a uniform or a black nighty, is a neighbor, of someone just wearing a costume of a gang. Why so serious? Always ask for the supervisor. Remember, the supervisor has a supervisor. The Buck will stop, if it goes high enough. By what authority do you expect me to jump through your hoops? Where's the 'Contract' that obligates my performance? Where is the 'Known Legal Duty' that obligates my performance? I know you may have the ability to force me to perform, just like a thug with a gun could. But, I also know you lack the authority to require me to perform, if I am NOT charged with a common-law crime. For those who may NOT know: murder, theft, rape, battery and other such crimes, which physically damage people or property, are common-law crimes. There MUST be an injury. You canNOT harm a piece a paper, only the one that owns the piece of paper. The City Of..., The County Of..., The State Of..., is a piece of paper. The delegation of authority must come from the people, or the authority comes from a barrel of a gun. Sam Colt made everybody just about the same size.

Public Schools do NOT teach the children or the adults there is a first Thirteenth Amendment removed from the public eye, after the end of the War of the Northern Aggression Against

The Southern States; and after that War, it was replaced with a second Thirteenth Amendment. The original Thirteenth Amendment, of the U.S. Constitution, is found to be published in many State Archives, from 1819 through 1867. Stop electing attorneys, into the Legislative and Executive branches of government, as they are really NOT eligible to run for those offices. If they claim the privilege of esquire, they have no right to the judicial branch either. The original (first) Thirteenth Amendment was never repealed, but illegally removed from the Constitution, by 1867.

> First 13th Amendment to the U.S. Constitution
> "If any citizen of the United States shall Accept, claim, receive or retain **_any title of nobility or honour_, _or_** shall, without the consent of Congress, accept and retain any present, pension, office or emolument of any kind whatever, from any emperor, king, prince or foreign power, such person **shall cease to be a citizen of the United States, and shall be incapable of holding any office of trust or profit under them, or either of them**."
> (Virginia Civil Code: March 12, 1819 indicates the day of ratification of the first 13th Amendment of the U.S. Constitution and then illegally removed from the Constitution by 1867)

The Texas State Bar Association was created, in 1939, by unconstitutional means. The Texas Legislative Library has records that indicate the careers, of Twenty-Seven out of Thirty-One Texas State Senators in 1939, were lawyers. Texas State Senators are forbidden to vote, by the Texas Constitution, on any issue they may have an interest in. Creating a monopoly and private club, in which only attorneys can participate, clearly represented an interest to lawyers back in 1939—same as it does, today.

Article 1, Section 29 of the Texas Constitution forbids the Texas Legislature—from placing on a ballot—the means for people to restrict their rights, by voting their rights away. This is supposed to be a republican form of government, where 99.99% of the population canNOT vote to take a right away, from one individual man or individual woman. Only in a democracy can 51% of the population vote, to kill 49% of the population. Majority Rule is Mob Rule. People who started the Texas Constitution knew this, as it is apparent, when you look into the Appendix Notes of the Texas Constitution, which show: "**The amendment of any provision of this constitution <u>does NOT affect vested rights.</u>**" If you do NOT know what your rights are, you canNOT claim the rights you have.

Virtually all court cases resulted in a void judgment, due to the lack of due process concerning at least one of the parties. When I was in school, I was never taught to spell my name in all capital letters. I expect the rule was taught, that way, for a reason. I was taught a Noun was a person, place or thing. Back then in school, a "person" was a man, woman or child—or, at least, I was falsely led to believe this. My teachers taught me an all-capitalized name was considered a title of a thing. Evidence of seeing your name typed in all capital letters, in court documents, makes one believe courts can only deal with things—and NOT flesh and blood people.

Chief Executive Officer (CEO) is the walking, talking, breathing man or woman considered the responsible party, for the all-capitalized named firm, company or corporation he/she represents. The CEO, whether it be a he or a she, is the one placed in jail, for a violation of state or federal law, and NOT the non-living, the non-breathing, the non-moving "firm," "company" or "corporation." For verification, search what happened to the CEO for ENRON. A European manufacturing safety-standard, called the "CE Mark," specifically held CEOs or company presidents accountable—when their products damaged someone. It soon became very unpopular, with corporation bosses, and a lot of them stopped using that standard.

Of What "firm," "company" or "corporation" are you accused of being the CEO? There may be many of them you are NOT aware of. What is the title, of your "firm," "company" or "corporation" found on your Driver License? What is the title, of your "firm," "company" or "corporation" found on your utility statement, on your bank statement, on your credit cards, on your debt cards, on your social security card, on your social security check, on your doctor's statement, and on your blood test statement? I could go on, but that list should suffice—for you to realize you are assumed to be a CEO, of so many different "firms," "companies" and "corporations," you can go to jail for the all-caps name,—if you fail to claim your rights, and fail to claim your actual status.

Beware of patriot mythology. There are many out there that will sell their wares, in a way to try and convince you their way will make it all better; when in fact, their way will lead you straight into the "Gray Bar Hotel." As you hear the clink of the jail door slam, you will find the teacher of the scam, never did what he recommended you to do. He or she only was looking for a little more cash flow, to get him or her a few more cigarettes—or maybe he just needed a guinea pig, to try out something he just dreamed up. Either way, know this: experience has shown me it will take four (4) to five (5) years, before the powers-that-be will drop a hammer, upon a guinea pig. When you are a hammer, everything looks like a nail. So, research is vital, when contemplating to do something others are claiming is a silver bullet—against the gangs. You will NOT know for sure, until after four or five years, after you do it. Ask yourself if it is worth going to jail, to find out? If you can overcome "fear," then jail will be just another adventure; and an opportunity to learn from and educate your fellow man. Many great men and women have been placed in jail, in the attempt to set things right, while trying to be free. You will be in good company. Just don't subject yourself to be incarcerated by being a guinea pig for someone else to try something new. Verify everything, before depending upon others advice, especially attorneys.

It is my intention to place many supporting documents in an internet cloud, for those that find in their heart the desire to know and claim their rights, against overwhelming odds. I have reason to believe and do believe the pen is mightier than the sword, but also Sam Colt made everyone just about the same size.

It's OK to lie to the devil and to pretend you agree, under the law of necessity.

Be free or die trying.

"We can easily forgive a child who is afraid of the dark. The real tragedy of life is when men are afraid of the light."
— *Plato*

He Who Knows Not And Knows Not, Is A Fool – Shun Him
He Who Knows Not And Knows That He Knows Not, Is A Child – Teach Him
He Who Knows And Knows Not That He Knows, Is Asleep – Wake Him
He Who Knows And Knows That He Knows, Is A Wise Man – Follow Him

CHAPTER 38
RECOMMENDED READING

Congratulations, apparently, you made it through all, or most, of the rabbit trails. You should know quite a lot more, than when you first started reading this adventure, of mine. What you come away with will be up to you, and no one else. Hopefully, it will help lessen any anxiety or fear of being confronted, by a neighbor wearing a costume of a gang pretending to be a code, rule, ordinance, section, article, or I say so, enforcer. Learn to ask, "Why?," and always remember, "It's Over When You Say It's Over"—and NOT before. Make an affidavit, of any event that may affect you later (in life). Review the solutions found in this book, to combat the attacks, by the minions. "Eternal Vigilance" is a long time, but in a hundred years, who will be holding a grudge, for what you did in the past, what you do today; or for that matter, what you will do tomorrow? If you haven't already realized—and you will with a little practice—there is no reason for anxiety or fear when the system confronts you. It is just somebody's neighbor involved with the "Lucifer Effect", where he needs to be reminded who he really is; and you are just the guy or gal to do just that.

For further education, of the misgivings of the people working for the system, the following is recommended reading:

#1   "The State of Texas is a Liar!," by Daniel Schinzing, 1999
This is a fantastic book, well-researched, and it gives a lot of resources where Daniel found this information. Daniel was a friend of mine. I say, "was," only because Daniel is NOT around for me—or anyone else—to call him up any more; but he lives on, through me and those that were fortunate to have known him—and fortunate to find one of Daniel's writings. Daniel's fate is the best example, why you should NOT write your book with the

laptop in your lap, for hours at a time.

#2 "The Constitution of No Authority," by Lysander Spooner, back in 1869

This was written, back in the 1800's. It puts the light on who is subject to a document created by a few people. Here is a spoiler reference. "If a couple of people sign a contract to pay for a house and they both die, are any of the children obligated to make the house payments that their parents were paying?" If you say "Yes, they do have the obligation to make the payments," you really need to read, "The Constitution of No Authority."

#3 "Atlas Shrugged," by Ayn Rand, 1957

I cheated and listened to the audio book, from a library. If you just look around your environment, you will see the reflections of characters, found in the book "Atlas Shrugged," when dealing with public servants. I do NOT know if you will realize how elegant Ayn Rand writes, but I did realized how elegant the writing is, by listening to others reading the pros, from the book.

Reading my book is associated with watching the movie, "Deliverance." My youngest calls my writing, "Southernism." Ya'll know what I mean. Don't ya? Must be my rabbit trails leading in the Southern direction.

#4 "The Creature From Jekyll Island" by G. Edward Griffin

Another must have book, showing the history of banksters. This should convince you that you must convert the funny money you work for into tangible things that hold value, like gold and silver, 1st edition "Spiderman", a good woman (I've always been a male chauvinist pig. Tried to be better, can't help it, but I am fully vested in a good woman), classic cars, baseball cards, coin collections, art, guns and ammo. People are a good investment. Give to your fellow man that is down on his luck, you'll know which one when you see him or her. First Rule of the pursuit of happiness; invest in what you like to be around. It is a win, win.

#5   "The Law" by Frederic Bastiat
This has been called an essay that was created way back in 1850, but could easily have been written today. When States subject their might upon society, international law throughout the centuries directly gives labels to certain acts by such people as tyrants. Learn if the people that claim to represent you, act as tyrants by international law standards.

#6   "Sundown At Coffin Rock," by Raymond K. Paden (LINK: 1994, [http://rkpaden.com/])
It is just a few pages you may be able to download, off the web. I usually send this out to my internet list, of about 200 people, at the beginning of each year. It is a wake up call for those that believe Blood has some kind of connection, when it comes to wanting to be free. The connection is in the heart and soul, and NOT in the Blood. I have an old saying, "You Can't Pick Your Relatives."   As you will find out, in "Sundown At Coffin Rock."

#7   "Fighting the Foreclosure Machine" by Robert M. James B.B.A., M.P.A., J.D..
Mr. James has done most of the research that I reference about MERS of which I verified to be correct and used in my court cases. Mr. James also has a research paper called "Shellgame-MERS" that you can acquire that goes into MERS in more detail. A must have book, if you intend to know anything about foreclosures.

#8   The Most Dangerous Superstition – by Larken Rose
Larken Rose is well known in the tax protester arena where he spent some time in the Gray Bar Hotel for "tax evasion". The judge refused to allow Larken to present a defense or enter his evidence. The prosecution always objected to Larken's questions to the prosecutor's witnesses stating Larken's questions

were "Beyond the Scope of Questioning". This is why you always subpoena the same witnesses the prosecutor uses, but then call them as a hostel defense witnesses, then ask them anything you want. It drives the Judge and prosecutor nuts. While in jail Larken wrote books and developed ideas for videos of which he created later. I have much respect for Larken Rose as he has dedicated his life in the pursuit of happiness of being free. Freedom is a state of mind, but unfortunately there is normally more than one of your neighbors that objects to that direction of the pursuit of happiness.

#9   Miracle On Main Street – by Tupper Saussy

Mr. Saussy was a rebel at heart and had plenty opportunities to converse with the Great and Powerful Oz. 'Miracle On Main Street' shows that change can occur when focus is concentrated on local government duties. When local governments follow the constitutions, the higher governments will fall in line if they wish to keep their job.

#10   Trance Formation of America – by Cathy O'Bren

Ms. O'Brien's story is one of tragedy and sorrow and to many, unbelievable. Go with Ms. O'Brien down the rabbit hole into the pit of Hell where government officials take privilege with the very young. Take note in the back of her book of the hundreds of government officials that were given a copy of this horror story that turned a blind eye and refused to call for an investigation into Ms. O'Brien's claims. Be for warned of the adult content of vivid accounts of her abuse by well known public figures.

For further education, of the misgivings of the people working for the system, the following is recommended viewing on YouTube and other places:

1. The Story of Your Enslavement – by Stefan Molyneux
2. The Jones Plantation – by Larken Rose
3. The Tiny Dot – by Larken Rose
4. The Collapse of the American Dream Explained
5. The Philosophy of Liberty – by Ken Schoolland

"The average man doesn't want to be free. He wants to be safe."
H.L. Mencken

The United States is the greatest law factory the world has ever known. - Charles Evans Hughes

When there's a single thief, it's robbery. When there are a thousand thieves, it's taxation. - Vanya Cohen

CHAPTER 39
SOLUTIONS

1. For every Traffic Ticket.
   A.) I Plead, "NOT Guilty, I want a Trial By Jury"
   B.) I will usually get the opportunity to plea bargain before having the actual trial.
   C.) I ask the court clerk for a form the court uses to get discovery, and use it to gather the evidence they have against you.
   D.) If they actually charge me with a Code and Section, file the form mentioned in Section 402.010 (a-1), in the Texas Government Code. I claim the Code Section is unconstitutional, as it violates Article 1, Section 27 of the Texas Constitution. The Texas Legislature is forbidden, to create a law that would abridge your right to assemble, as confirmed by Article 1, Section 29 of the Texas Constitution.
   E.) I usually plan on a trial by jury and I always file a document I want the judge to inform the jury about the law. It is sometimes called a 'jury charge' or 'jury instructions.'
   F.) I know of one fellow who subpoenas the cop, to bring the radar unit and calibration records, and Section 201.904 of the Transportation Code that shows the only definition of the term "Speed Signs."
   G.) It is my understanding, a subpoena can be served by anyone, 18 years or older, and has no interest in the case. Its fun to watch the cop get the subpoena, from my friend.

2. Public Information Request.
   A.) I learned about the public information request act, found in the Texas Government Code, Chapter 552.

Texas Government Code
CHAPTER 552. PUBLIC INFORMATION
SUBCHAPTER A. GENERAL PROVISIONS
Sec. 552.001. POLICY; CONSTRUCTION. (a) Under the fundamental philosophy of the American constitutional form of representative government that adheres to the principle __that government is the servant and not the master of the people,__ it is the policy of this state that each person is entitled, unless otherwise expressly provided by law, at all times to complete information about the affairs of government and the official acts of public officials and employees. __The people, in delegating authority, do not give their public servants the right to decide what is good for the people to know and what is not good for them to know.__ The people insist on remaining informed so that they may retain control over the instruments they have created. The provisions of this chapter shall be liberally construed to implement this policy.

B.) I believe it is our responsibility to keep the government in check. People that work for the government do NOT want the government to be restricted, as it slows down the pay raises.

C.) This solution is essentially the same function, as a Freedom of Information Request (FOIA), I send to Federal Agencies, but instead I send it to State Agencies. I found the FOIA procedure in Title 5, United States Code, Section 552. Notice the association with the section numbers of the State and Fed statutes? It is no coincidence.

D.) I can only ask for documents that are in the agencies' possession, as the agency employee is NOT required to create documents I desire to have.

E.) I always state at the beginning, or at the end, of my request for information: "If a search is done and no records were found, please state so in your response."

F.) Having a response stating a search was done, and no document was found, is sometimes more important than receiving the document requested—like me asking for a copy of an Oath of Office.

G.) The Texas Legislature has made it easier for us to obtain documents, by email, rather than sending a snail mail request. I always use the easiest method, to get to the end result I am striving for.

H.) I get a copy of the Comprehensive Annual Financial Report (CAFR) for each municipality and taxing unit that claim interest in my property, and learn where the money comes from and is going. (See also, Item J, just below.)

I.) I find out how much of the municipality's Budget is based upon crime; and why any part of the budget is based upon how many traffic tickets are written, each year. I go to the City and County Council Meeting; and ask why their courts have no incentive to find anyone NOT Guilty, because it would cost the municipality money.

J.) I found "Walter Buren," on the great wide web. Walter is the foremost expert on the CAFR.

3. I am a court watcher, whenever I can. When the Bailiff asks why I am there, I don't say I am a witness, but instead, I say I am a court watcher. They are more nervous of me, than I ever will be of them. If the Bailiff says I have to leave, if I do NOT have a ticket, or there is too many people in the court room for me to sit; I go outside and call the fire marshal that I am concerned there are too many people in the building, under the fire code—and have the Bailiff investigated. They will find me a seat, for me to watch the court activities, usually up front. Also, Article 1, Section 13 of the Texas Constitution says, All courts are open, to the public. That is another one of my rights I must claim, or I will lose it.

4. I find retirees I can pick up, to be court watchers with me. They will love getting out of the house.

5. I always write an affidavit, within a week of any event. It may come in handy later down the road. I don't need a Notary in Texas anymore. I always look up Tex. Civ. Prac. & Rem. Code, Section 132.001, and add the part that doesn't require a Notary.

6. I know my rights enumerated in Article 1 of the Texas Constitution, especially Article 1, Section 27 and Section 29.

7. I suggest starting a Study Group and meet, at least once a month. Place a small notice at local restaurants, of the time and location of the meeting. Many community centers, libraries and restaurants will accommodate your meeting, at little or no cost. If you have at least two people at the meeting, you are at an assembly that is guaranteed under Article 1, Section 27 of the Texas Constitution, of which the Texas Legislature canNOT make a law to abridge your right to assemble—as enumerated under Article 1, Section 29 of the Texas Constitution.

8. I study Chapter 11, in the Texas Code of Criminal Procedure that tells me about a Writ of Habeas Corpus. I made a Note, in my phone about Chapter 11, as it may come in handy, when I least expect it. Writs originated way back in time. It was commonly used to get people out of jail, who were unjustly put there, in the first place. It still works today, for some unknown reason. I can actually take an Application, for a Writ of *Habeas Corpus*, to every judge that gets a paycheck—until I find one that plays golf with the judge that put the fellow or lady in jail. I hand the application to a

judge. He recognizes the name of the judge that did the awful act, picks up the phone and asks what's going on with Mr. So-in-So. The judge says to me, your friend will be out in a couple of hours. My incarcerated friend has to sign a promise to appear but, he is released very shortly after he signs the promise to appear. I have seen a fellow write a letter telling what had happened to a certain guy that wound up in jail. Hands the letter to a judge. The judge says: "I could take this as an application for a Writ of Habeas Corpus." A few hours later his friend walks out of jail. Go figure. Study Chapter 11.

9. When I have a question about a law, a good source is the Texas Legislative Library. The librarians are the ones that located those documents I have recorded in the Montgomery County Clerk's Office, concerning property tax. Good people will help you find what you are looking for.

Help me, NOT to elect attorneys for positions of governmental functions, which do NOT concern the judicial branch of government, then watch things change.

I would like to un-elect and un-appoint all the judges every eight (8) years or sooner and watch things change. Judges do NOT become intelligent simply by putting on a black nighty.

Support a Bill that would mandate that an audio recording be made of ever utterance a judge makes while sitting on a bench in a court room and make it available to the public. Allow a party to record the hearing. Every Judge; every judge needs monitoring for violation of due process. This will stop bad behavior of judges or at least slow it down to a crawl.

CHAPTER 40
YOU HAVE THE RIGHT

This list, by no means exhausts the rights you have. Each Right expands and evolves, as would a flowchart that tracks conditions of change in your environment. The Bill of Rights, found in various Constitutions supports your vested rights which have already been paid for, by blood, sweat and tears. Eternal vigilance may cause necessity to rear its ugly head to defend and protect these vested rights, as life goes on. I have reason to believe and do believe:

1. You have the right to self-defense. The force initiated by you, is determined by the extent of the potential harm that may occur by the threat to you or your fellowman's well-being.
2. You have the right to water. Life can only be sustained by water. Those who withhold from you, or take from you such life-sustaining water, may cause the initiation of the right to self-defense.
3. You have the right to gather food. Life can only be sustained by food. 'Hunting' and 'Fishing' are commercial terms, and such are not associated with gathering food. Those who restrict you from gathering food, or take from you such life-sustaining food you have gathered, may cause the initiation of the right to self-defense.
4. You have the right of liberty, to be left alone. Unless your activity has the potential threat to harm, or has harmed, people or property, you have the right to be left alone—and enjoy your pursuit of Happiness.
5. You have the right to travel, from point A, to point B. Unless your activity has the potential threat to harm, or has harmed, people or property, you have the right to get there, and return with minimal delay.
6. You have the right to use the mode of travel you can afford, but obligated to obtain the ability to control it, in a safe

manner. As a neighbor, I expect my neighbor will be responsible during his travels; and I have granted my power of self-preservation, to people certified as peace officers, to incarcerate you, if you attempt to fly a F-15 fighter jet, without the proper training and certification to be considered proficient, in flying this plane in a safe manner. As certification is different than a license, I do NOT desire my neighbor to be licensed to do an illegal act; but rather, fully-certified to do a potentially-dangerous activity, well.

7. You have the right to assemble. You have the right to go to church, to a restaurant, to a store, to gather food—and with loved ones, friends, and enemies. This means, you have the right to get there, by whatever conveyance you can use—in a safe manner.

8. You have the right to be involved with any religion, and believe whatever you want to believe—as long as your beliefs do not threaten my pursuit of Happiness. If your religion threatens my pursuit of Happiness, where practicing such religion may cause harm to people or property; I have the right to invoke my right to self-defense—and act accordingly.

9. You have the right to resist anyone's attempt to search or seize people or property, whether it concerns yourself, your family, friends or neighbors or such property belonging to you or other people; unless a witness will swear, or has sworn, under the penalty of perjury, a common-law crime has occurred—and such evidence of such crime is located in such place, as described by such witness.

10. You have the right to see and receive a copy of the warrant signed by a judge, and the affidavit sworn under the penalty of perjury, if a common-law crime was alleged, which would allow a peace officer to search or seize someone or such property—as described in such documents.

11. You have the right to know what specific law you are being accused of violating, and where you can physically view such specific law and have the opportunity to question its authority.

12. You have the right NOT to be a witness against yourself.
13. You have the right to be appointed standby counsel, if you have been charged with a crime. You have no obligation to spend your money and hire an attorney. If the State elects to prosecute, then it should absorb all cost until which time a conviction is upheld in appeals. People of means, accused of a crime, should not be discriminated against for not being indigent.
14. You have the right to be confronted with any witness that has a claim against you and obtain such witnesses that can testify in your behalf.
15. You have the right to a public trial.
16. You have the right to a have a trial, in a timely manner.
17. You have the right to a jury that will NOT believe the testimony of a peace officer, simply because he has a police uniform on, while testifying. I consider costumes in a court room a distraction to a judge and jury and should NOT be allowed. Would a judge allow me to dress as Superman while I testify on the stand?
18. You have the right to jury nullification. This is where a jury determines a law is unreasonable under the circumstances, and finds the accused NOT Guilty—no matter the amount of evidence presented, by prosecutor, the accused actually committed the crime alleged. Unless your neighbor has the authority to regulate your activity, then the neighbors elected to create laws have no more authority to create a law, than they have as a private Citizen. People elected to create laws do so, for those entities created by the State, which have asked for the privileges to operate a business—with limited liability. Laws that regulate corporations do NOT apply to the people, except by consent of the people.
19. You have the right to know what your government is doing. The National Security claim only applies while the operation is ongoing; and when the operation is concluded, the people have a right to know what their government has been doing.

20. You have the right to say what you want, where you are—as long as the statements are true, and it does NOT encroach upon the pursuit of Happiness, of another.
21. You have the right to write and publish what you want, as long it is the truth, or have a disclaimer warning of possible exaggerations.
22. A reporter has the right to publish the truth as they know it and NOT give up the sources of such information, but it must be the truth as they knew it at the time of publishing.
23. You have the right to a reasonable amount of Bail—to be let out of jail, while the legal process is ongoing, except where there is a sworn affidavit indicating that there is evidence in the record alleging the accused is a danger to a particular someone or to the public, if allowed to be released. If the evidence proves to be false, the affiant serves the same amount of time as the accused.
24. You have the right of common law process, the writ of *habeas corpus*. This is like a second opinion from a doctor; but in this case a judge gives the second opinion, whether there is probable cause the accused should be held in jail for the alleged offense, while the trial is set for a later date.
25. You have a right to a reasonable sentence, if convicted of an alleged offense. A jury should be impaneled, if the sentence is deemed unreasonable by the Defendant, but then the jury may determine that the sentence was too lenient and give the defendant more time and increase the fine. It is wrong that juries are not told the amount of time and fine that a defendant may get, if found guilty.
26. The jury has a common law right to be confronted with all the facts and law of the case before a verdict is considered. A judge as well as the jury must be provided notice of the law and substance to support such notice. There is no judge on the planet that knows all the laws on the books. The custom and policy of the courts to require the judge to tell the jury what the law is BS when the record does not reflect the evidence of law that the judge alleges to know. Creating law

from the bench is nowhere to be found in any constitution. Don't let them blow wind up your skirt. Ask for the known legal duty.

27. You have a right to have court watchers observe the proceedings of any court, to see what occurred in any court, and to be able to hear everything being said, in any court. Open courts are not allowed to whisper. The judge must speak up for the hearing impaired.

28. In Texas, you have the right to record any conversation that you are part of.

29. In Texas, the Open Meetings Act allows you to record court hearings, as long as you give the court prior notice you will be videoing (taping, etc.) the hearing. The court has the right to tell you where to set up the recorder, in the courtroom.

30. You have the right to due process. That being: To be informed of your rights. Like the right to shut the hell up. The right to stand-by counsel. The right to be noticed, of every court proceeding. The right to Bail, if put in jail. The right to a trial by jury. The right to have discovery and be provided with the evidence, against you. The right to have an impartial judge. The right to be in a court with jurisdiction. The right to be confronted with the two or more witnesses to be used against you. The right to witnesses in your favor. The right to be treated fairly. The right of respect. The right to be heard. The right to appeal. The right to have the case dismissed, if the prosecution fails to prosecute.

31. You have a right to be made whole, from an injury caused by someone or something, whether by compensation or replacement, in kind—or both. You have the right to remedy.

32. You have the right NOT to be required to again defend oneself, against the same charge one was accused of doing, before—and was found NOT Guilty, of the alleged offense.

33. You have the right, in all civil matters, to have a trial by jury. All summary judgments are unconstitutional, if a trial by jury was demanded by one of the parties. A court rule cannot

lawfully deny your right, of a trial by jury. No statute or rule can overturn the constitution.

34. You have the right to contract.

35. If you had the right to do something, before; no law can be created, to forbid you doing that same something, in the future. This grandfather clause pertains to newborns as well.

36. You have the right to be fairly compensated for any property you may own, where the government wants to use it for public use. As you have learned before in this book, you can only own property the jury will let you own, or you may die trying to keep it from a gang.

37. You have the right NOT to be placed in jail, for simply not paying a debt. Even if you can afford to pay the debt. Civilly, politically and lawfully, there are many ways other than jail time to discharge a debt. You must claim your right NOT to be jailed, for a debt.

38. You have the right to be let alone, no matter if a family member has committed a crime.

39. You have the right to be incarcerated, in the same State of which you have been found guilty, of committing the offense. You must make it known—by notice—you demand your right, to be incarcerated in the State of which the crime was committed—and you object to being transferred to another State.

40. You have the right to the same property, to which you claim to be an heir—whether the owner of the property is a convicted criminal, or NOT.

41. You have the right to question the minimum of two witnesses that have accused you of treason. The witnesses must claim you had levied war against the State, or adhered to the State's enemies, giving them aid and comfort.

42. In Texas, you have the right to carry anything you have determined necessary, to defend your life; or to defend the State on which you depend for protection. The lawmakers can only regulate the wearing of the equalizer, to prevent a crime.

I would demand to know what crime they were preventing, by such regulation.

43. You have the right to know who the local, civil somebody is, the military must answers to.

44. You have the right to tell the military to leave your home. If they do NOT, they have levied war upon you and yours by violation of their Oath to the Constitutions.

45. You have the right to demand perpetuities and monopolies are unconstitutional, in Texas and attorneys canNOT sustain a closed shop (guild/union) in Texas Courts.

46. You have the right to demand the courts and police go by the law of the land, and NOT their custom and policy.

47. You have the right to see laws, created to challenge the rights of the people, are found unconstitutional and void—under Article 1, Section 29 of the Texas Constitution.

48. You have the right to be treated with fairness.

49. You have the right to be treated with respect.

50. You have the right to notification of court proceedings.

51. You have the right to restitution, if you are a victim.

52. You have the right to access and use a public beach.

53. You have the right to access and use a public restroom.

54. You have the right to be homeless and gather food and water.

55. You have the right to shelter, if the environment is life threatening.

56. You have the right to stop a war, by way of any means possible. Haven't we heard anything goes, in love and war?

57. You have the right to yell, "Hay!!," when you see Hay lying in a farmer's field, of Hay. Pay attention to your surroundings, and you will not get surprised to find out what is in plain view.

58. YOU HAVE THE RIGHT TO BE CONSIDERED INNOCENT, UNTIL PROVEN GUILTY.

CHAPTER 41
YOU HAVE NO RIGHT

I have reason to believe and do believe:

1. You have no right to kill me by simply saying: "I was in fear of my life." Attorneys appear to be the cause of people being killed instead of being wounded by Police. Police have an obligation to be proficient with a firearm and be held accountable where they shoot someone.

2. You have no right to be judge, jury and executioner. Just showing that you are armed has stopped millions of potential crimes from occurring.

3. You have no right to put a gun to my head and take my life or my property.

4. You have no right to violate the right of another when you or others are not being threatened with harm.

5. You have no right to lie to harm another, and should be held accountable when caught. Lying to harm is just another form of fraud. Some Attorneys do this on a regular basis, because their brethren turn a blind eye and allow the harm to continue.

6. You Judges have no right to lie to either party of a court case, simply because they have a right to appeal. Judges are public servants. You must earn the title of "Your Honor". You deserve the respect you project.

7. You public servants have no right to qualified immunity, when you are noticed of being wrong—and fail to correct the situation.

8. You have no right of discretion, to do that which is wrong.

9. You have no right to yell, "fire," when there is no fire.

10. You have no right to yell, "wolf," when there is no wolf.

11. You have no right to start a war, but rather the right to finish that which has been started.

12. You have no right to be happy. You have the right to pursue Happiness, but such right does NOT guarantee happiness.

13. You have no right to harm people or property, except under the common law of self-preservation. Following Orders is no excuse, to harm the innocent.

14. You have no right to health care you cannot afford. Moral obligation of compassion should be sufficient to comfort the suffering. Those that except donations, to help the poor and sick, are in breach of contract if they turn away the poor and sick requesting their help. Those that except taxes are under contract, to perform their duty of which they pledged their support.

15. You have no right to welfare. No one has the right to stick a gun to my head and reach into my pocket, take my property and give it to another, more deserving; unless I have breached a contract, pledge or other such obligated duty to perform. Theft is theft. It matters NOT, whether the thief has good intentions and does good or better, with the money he steals.

16. You have no right to a home you do not pay for, in some way or another. Then again, there is no right to take property from another when the perpetrators can neither prove their interest in the property they wish to take.

17. You have no right to print money, out of thin air. Counterfeit is counterfeit, no matter if it is authorized by employees working for an entity, or another acting upon his own behalf. Counterfeiting is a crime, per the Constitution. Those that authorized the counterfeiting are criminals and have created an unconstitutional act. Inflation steals your savings, everyday. Research—Link: [https://adask.wordpress.com] and find articles in the "Inflation/Deflation" subject line.

18. You have no right to tax my labor. I have sold an hour of my life under contract for an agreed amount of compensation. There is no gain, but an equal exchange. My right to contract cannot be legislated away, as my hour of life cannot be returned to me that which I have sold.

19. You have no right to a running mate, when running for President. Nowhere in the Constitution allows someone, running for President, to pick a running mate. The office of

Vice-President is a separate office as is a Justice of the Peace. People that want to run for Vice-President should be grouped together, on the ballot, and NOT attached with another office. Lincoln was Republican and his Vice-President Johnson was a Democrat. I don't think Lincoln picked Johnson as a running mate. Look up the twelfth amendment in the U.S. Constitution, ratified on June 15, 1804.

20. You have no right to base a municipality's, public subdivision's, or other such corporation's budget on crime. Arresting people and issuing traffic citations should NOT create a profit for the municipality. Victims of crimes should be compensated—and NOT the State. Stop the incarceration for victimless crimes.

21. You have no right to national security, if you can NOT keep a secret and the truth gets out. You made your bed, so lay in it.

The author reserves the right, to amend the material found in this publication—to correct any information within, found to be incorrect in anyway.

DISCLAIMER

Bobie Kenneth Townsend

"Now remember, when things look bad and it looks like you're not gonna make it, then you gotta get mean. I mean plumb, mad-dog mean. 'Cause if you lose your head and you give up then you neither live nor win.
That's just the way it is."

Clint Eastwood in Outlaw Josey Wales

ABOUT THE AUTHOR

I, Bobie Kenneth Townsend, at no fault of my on, became a native born Texan in 1951. I was raised in Hobbs, New Mexico. I was declared Ping Pong Champion in Heizer Junior High School in 1966. I attained the position of Master Counselor of the Order of DeMolay. I declined to become a Mason due to certain accepted members of that organization, that I believed were of the unsavory type. I graduated Hobbs High in 1969. I graduated New Mexico Junior College in 1972 with an applied science degree in computer programming. I became an Instrument & Analyzer Technician, which led to my independence and financed my pursuit of Happiness. I married my partner, Carolyn, in 1975 on Halloween, since I thought it to be a scary event. I was audited by the IRS in 1989. During a Tax Court hearing, I questioned the Tax Court Judge's declaration that he stated during a court hearing. When I found the Tax Court Judge's information was false, I asked the Court Clerk to see the Judge. The Tax Court Judge told my wife and I, in the court building hall way, "You see son, I have a right to lie to you because you have the right to appeal." The Judge smiled, turned and walked away. This was the day, I started asking "Why?". I was taught the meaning of the Texas and U.S. Constitution by Dr. Norris Austin in the late 1990's. I became the Director of the San Jacinto Constitutional Study Group in the Houston Texas area shortly thereafter and am considered such today. I acquired a patent for a special air mattress that will move a coma patient in bed onto his either complete side and return him to his back without a nurse having to touch the patient, no matter the size of the patient. I found a manufacture to construct the device, but the manufacture was threaten by a Medical Supplier that it would keep the device off the market, by whatever means possible. I am still trying to find a manufacture for the devise. I then became a pro se, looking for a remedy. I now claim to be a published author and an expert witness concerning the material found in this book.

If the Montgomery Central Appraisal District would have Granted me the same Variance, in 2005, that was Granted to the previous owners of my wife's Black Toxic Mold Dream House in Conroe, Texas, this book would never have been written. Funny how things work out.

www.ingramcontent.com/pod-product-compliance
Lightning Source LLC
Chambersburg PA
CBHW070758280326
41934CB00012B/2965